PRAISE FOR PERSPECTIVE AGENTS

"This may be the definitive book of the decade on how to make sense of the changing world around us and practically prepare for what comes next."

—**TRACEY FOLLOWS,** author of *The Future of You*

"To navigate the fast-changing media terrain, *Perspective Agents* will undoubtedly be our North Star. Much like Jung did for our unconscious, Perry deconstructs, diagnoses, and delivers a step-by-step map to make sense of what is hidden in plain sight: platforms, channels, networks, surfaces—the stuff of our social infrastructure, the air we breathe. Perry skillfully weaves accessible stories, engaging personalities, and powerful tools and frameworks. For executives, thought leaders, and lay people alike, the book is a valuable companion to understand where we've come from and where we are going."

—**SUDHIR VENKATESH,** William B. Ransford Professor of Sociology at Columbia University and best-selling author of *Gang Leader for a Day*

"Chris Perry first sees and understands the patterns underlying social change and determines how to act on them best. If you're in a business where knowing what's going on around you is of value to your decision-making, then you owe it to yourself to engage with his ideas."

—**DOUGLAS RUSHKOFF,** best-selling author of *Team Human*

"Many authors are trying to help us understand the revolutionary impacts of new technology on our information ecosystem, but none so effectively strike the balance between sounding necessary alarms and recognizing the real opportunities these technologies provide. The focus on the perspectives we can take flipped the way I approach these questions. A really important book."

—**CLAIRE WARDLE,** cofounder of Information Futures Lab, Brown School of Public Health

"*Perspective Agents* introduces us to the new era, in which AI and associated technologies will radically transform the business and social landscape, as the internet did. Perry argues that we live in a liminal moment—understanding these technologies and their uses is as important as ever. *Perspective Agents* is a robust guide to the intimidating labyrinth of technology, social change, and professional decision-making. Buy it. Read it (before an AI tries to summarize it)."

—**JOHN BORTHWICK,** founder and CEO of Betaworks

"This is an essential book for leaders trying to make sense of the new world order. Perry brilliantly distills the dislocation and angst of the modern era and helps us find meaning and opportunity in chaos."

—**VIVIAN SCHILLER,** executive director of digital at the Aspen Institute

"Chris's distinguished mind for change makes him our needed guide in navigating strategies for human flourishing in the coming age of machines. In this moment of acceleration, automation, and required sense-making, Chris's words are worthy of our strained attention."

—**MATT KLEIN,** head of global foresight at Reddit

"If you're like me, you're looking to the future with part wonderment and part horror. You sense that, harnessing new technologies, we are on the cusp of almost unimaginable change. Chris Perry bravely plunges headlong into that future, providing not only new perspectives but new and practical ways to both cope with and harness it all. If you want to lead in this new era, you'll want to read this book."

—JACK LESLIE, former chairman of Weber Shandwick

A HUMAN GUIDE TO THE AUTONOMOUS AGE
PERSPECTIVE AGENTS

A HUMAN GUIDE TO THE AUTONOMOUS AGE

PERSPECTIVE AGENTS

CHRIS PERRY

FAST
COMPANY
Press

Fast Company Press
New York, New York
www.fastcompanypress.com

Copyright © 2024 Chris Perry

All rights reserved.

Thank you for purchasing an authorized edition of this book and for complying with copyright law. No part of this book may be reproduced, stored in a retrieval system, or transmitted by any means, electronic, mechanical, photocopying, recording, or otherwise, without written permission from the copyright holder.

This work is being published under the Fast Company Press imprint by an exclusive arrangement with *Fast Company*. *Fast Company* and the *Fast Company* logo are registered trademarks of Mansueto Ventures, LLC. The Fast Company Press logo is a wholly owned trademark of Mansueto Ventures, LLC.

Distributed by River Grove Books

Design and composition by Greenleaf Book Group
Cover design by Jen Brower

Publisher's Cataloging-in-Publication data is available.

Paperback ISBN: 978-1-63908-082-3

Hardcover ISBN: 978-1-63908-084-7

eBook ISBN: 978-1-63908-083-0

First Edition

To Missy, Isabelle, Audrey, and Nick. You are my bright lights.

CONTENTS

Foreword: Understanding Is Not a Point
of View by Andrew McLuhan xiii
Author's Note xvii
Introduction: Where Has the Gravity Gone? 1

PART I: Perspectives in Transition 9
1 Technology: Decode the Environment 11
2 Social Change: See the Future through History 23
3 Media: Recognize the Changing Currents 37
4 Cultural Fractures: Adjust Your Lens 55
5 Networks: Make New Connections 67

PART II: Beliefs in Transition 81
6 Identity: Peer into Inner Worlds 83
7 Work: Redefine Value 99
8 Relationships: Look into the Void 117
9 Spirituality: Rethink Faith 131

PART III: Leading in Transition 145
10 Mindset: Build Cognitive Stamina 147
11 Models: Frame a Path Forward 161
12 Instruments: Illuminate the Invisible 179
13 Design: Build New Worlds 193

Conclusion: Agents of Well-Being 207
Acknowledgments 211
Notes 213
Selected Bibliography 257
About the Author 261

FOREWORD

UNDERSTANDING IS NOT A POINT OF VIEW

There's a sometimes-subtle distinction between *perspective* and *opinion*, but it's a world of difference.

Among the many things my grandfather Marshall McLuhan said is "understanding is not a point of view." Though he said it many places, I discovered it in one of his copies of his book *Understanding Media: The Extensions of Man*. I refer to it from time to time when teaching my class about that 1964 gift to perception and perspective. He wrote it then in pencil, and it's something I treasure.

Understanding is not a point of view, and it's no longer a resting point. Not something you can achieve and rely on. When every time you wake, you wake into a changed world, where is the luxury of rest? When you look out to the world or into a metaphorical or literal mirror and see someone new looking back at you, where's the comfort of an understanding that no longer fits? It is quite the opposite of comfort.

A single perspective can be valuable but can only give one a partial picture.

Marshall McLuhan had a rare grasp of the limitations of specialism, especially for his time and situation. The first half of the twentieth century did not welcome a generalist approach. In the academic world, knowledge was (and still very much is) significantly and conservatively siloed. An expert in modernist poetry—Pound, Eliot, Yeats, and the like—he was expected to stay there.

In the early 1950s, with colleagues at the University of Toronto, Marshall McLuhan won a grant. He began the Culture and Communication seminar, an interdisciplinary group assembled to try and make sense of communication and technological change. English literature shared a round table with anthropology, psychology, history, economics, and more. The group intended to be as wide-ranging in experience as possible because none of the conventional, linear approaches seemed to be making much headway in gaining new insight and understanding.

One of this group's products was a journal (1953–1959) called *Explorations*, which was highly influential at the time. Its editorial statement read:

> *Explorations* is designed not as a permanent reference journal that embalms truth for posterity but as a publication that explores and searches and questions. We envisage a series that will cut across the humanities and social sciences by treating them as a continuum. Anthropology and communication are approaches, not bodies of data. Within each, the four winds of humanities, the physical, the biological, and the social sciences, intermingle to form a science of man.[1]

This then became McLuhan's modus operandi: to cultivate perspective. He had many methods for doing so, but one he used regularly, achieving several objectives at once, was reading his bible every morning.

That, in itself, is not too unusual. Many Christians do, and McLuhan was a devout Catholic. But he read more than one bible. He would pick up the bible from his hotel room when he traveled, amassing a collection of bibles in various languages. The great thing about the bible is that its translators are very particular about language. It's a great control because exquisite care is taken to get the translations right, making it an ideal text for studying a language. And if you know your bible front to back, so much the better.

McLuhan understood that our most powerful medium, which shapes our self and our experience (and our perspective) of the inner and outer world from a very young age, is our mother tongue. Each language, each culture, is a perspective with insights and limitations. Rarely can we grapple with, much less grasp, things for which we don't have words.

McLuhan raided the storehouses of knowledge and perspective available from any source. If there is a secret to his success in being able to see and understand more than a lowly English professor probably should, this is a large part of it.

Marshall McLuhan's most enduring message is that the message of any medium or technology is in the changes of scale or pace or pattern that it introduces into human affairs. He reminded us that the effects of technology do not occur at the level of opinions or concepts but alter sense ratios or patterns of perception steadily and without any resistance.

Limited perspective is a distinct liability in an age when change happens so quickly. The wider your field of vision, the more you're likely to see and take advantage of or avoid.

In the following pages, you'll find a font of anecdotes and flips on conventional wisdom that can expand your frames of reference. Chris Perry maps changing terrain that reflects enduring truths of our humanity and fluid currents of culture reshaping life as we know it.

—**ANDREW MCLUHAN**
The McLuhan Institute

AUTHOR'S NOTE

In the 1960s, Marshall McLuhan emerged as an oracle of media culture. His seminal book *Understanding Media* examined how technology molds the human psyche, culture, and society. Riding the swell of this groundbreaking meditation, which would be one of many, McLuhan became one of his era's most debated and influential cultural critics.

McLuhan spent decades understanding technology-induced transitions, studying their causative factors and effects. His exploratory methods and poetic insight made him a leading figure on perspective-building, the topic extensively examined here in *Perspective Agents*.

A "McLuhan revival" formed in the late 1990s, when *Wired* magazine crowned him their "patron saint" of the publication.[1] Now, as we traverse twenty-first-century digital life, analysts and scholars again revert to McLuhan's perspectives for clues on what the future holds.

According to McLuhan, the medium is the message. He suggests that the message of media is subliminal and total in its effects on our sensibilities and on our social and political lives. If we're to accurately assess changing affairs, we need to study technological effects in a methodical and objective manner—meaning, we can't just investigate AI in terms of automating human thought; we need to study subliminal and social impacts of handing agency over to machines. As we explore throughout the book, maintaining a sense of control in the age of autonomy requires that we recognize the effects of media and technology and the impact they have on us.

McLuhan said, "In today's rapidly changing environment, people have two major concerns: to discover the new problems this environment poses, and to develop ways of coping with these problems."[2] This point reverberates today, characterized by intense polarization, conflict, and bewilderment.

McLuhan's insights continue to spark profound contemplation of our relationship with technology. McLuhan and his son Eric greatly influenced how I interpret transitions we face and the book's direction. I'm honored to have Marshall's grandson, Andrew McLuhan, write the foreword for this book.

INTRODUCTION

WHERE HAS THE GRAVITY GONE?

▼

Despite the enormous potential of the new technologies we explore in the following pages, I begin the book on a cautionary note. For over three decades, I've worked at the intersection of new technology, media, and culture. Transitions move rapidly at this nexus; from the beginning of my career, it became clear that the big ones are not theoretical or academic. They reorder power, beliefs, and paths to well-being. In extreme cases, they're about survival.

I felt the personal repercussions of automation thirty years ago. In 1992, I landed out of college in my dad's business, a graphic art studio at the center of the Detroit advertising scene. My father was a genuine article, a one-of-a-kind, life-of-the-party, go-for-broke type. It was fitting, then, that he built an artistic madhouse. Set in the shadows of the famed GM Design Center, his studio employed a band of rough-and-tumble artists, illustrators, typesetters, and camera technicians. It was a craft business. Their handmade creations made cars and the advertising campaigns that sold them famous.

Back then, Take Your Child to Work Day wasn't a yearly event. I often went to his studio. Looking back, I picture a kid in a creative candy store, a curious type at play with acetate paper, brushes, paints, stencils, and markers.

Years later I experienced a different, darker side of working there. Out of the blue, the studio production model broke. Remember the sledgehammer from Apple's 1984 campaign introducing the Macintosh? Steve Jobs's bicycle for the mind was an automation machine. It smashed the commercial art world and my dad's business into pieces.

The laser printer, Adobe PostScript's font and graphic system, and Aldus PageMaker helped Apple pioneer a new field called *desktop publishing*. It took roughly five years from the inception of these new technical wonders to destroy our business model. You could see it coming if you happened to look.

Creative labor was displaced, like typesetting by hand, painting illustrations, and manually assembling page layouts. The desktop publishing revolution streamlined design and production, making it quicker, more efficient, and more accessible for advertising creatives to produce work. Most relevant to the period we've entered today, human methods were built into the software. This democratization upended media production and paved the way for a new era for content creators.

That we didn't see this development coming is still seared into my memory. It remains a formative lesson. Being on the wrong side of big technology shifts is economically and emotionally painful. My dad's stance stood in stark contrast to McLuhan's seeing-eye ethos. He didn't see the shift until it was too late.

For me the break wasn't an end; it was a nudge into the future. I later found myself immersed in the inception of a new technological era. Following time working with my dad, I joined a start-up on the cutting edge of mobile computing, followed by a decade working with emerging e-commerce and social computing companies. I later worked with the world's largest corporations, architecting new ways of communicating and using social media, digital video, blogs, wikis, and apps. Embracing social technologies helped us build Weber Shandwick into one of the largest integrated-communications consultancies in the world.

I still work in the same field where my career began, though with a vastly different vantage point. I lead innovation and futures research at Weber Shandwick. Our Futures team helps clients worldwide discern cultural and societal changes triggered by new technologies like AI. Our insights help them define business strategies, elevate human factors in planning, and effectively communicate using cutting-edge tools.

My formative lesson and subsequent career mission endure. I'm driven to help leaders stay on the right side of technology-fueled transitions. This book is a way of carrying the mission forward. It has lessons from formidable thinkers, transformation stories, and research affecting future planning. It's been shaped, critiqued, and refined through interviews, ideas, and suggestions from contacts and friends with deep intellectual, technological, and social understanding.

The Autonomous Age

Our research points to an inescapable conclusion: The human mind and experience are changing. The last gasps of an industrial, mass-market, command-and-control paradigm rattle around us. The coming Autonomous Age will thrust us into a realm of the surreal—what analysts refer to as a changing paradigm, "a new beginning," or a "five-hundred-year event." The coming epoch currently lacks coherent visions and narratives.

This book crafts a way to see a revolutionary period that confronts us. It's one where supercomputing combined with artificial intelligence will operate independently of human intervention. Like desktop publishing software that codified creative methods thirty years ago, repositories of human knowledge will transfer into autonomous agents. Unprecedented efficiency and productivity through automation will reshape entire industries and precedents.

The rise of automated machines is just one side of the coin. Simultaneously, a less analyzed but equally consequential revolution is well underway. Human autonomy and coordination are also on the ascent. Personal autonomy will rise as traditional structures crumble and fade into memory. The continued move toward decentralized communities and peer-to-peer networks will lead to new belief systems, working models, and paths to well-being. We've seen the impact of autonomous thinking as it reshapes politics, finance, media, and healthcare in the last decade. Phenomena like Make America Great Again (MAGA), high-speed trading, the Black Lives Matter movement, and accelerated mRNA experiments powered by AI are just the beginning.

Autonomous machines, individuals, and networks will radically change how we interpret and act in the future. The two sides of the Autonomous Age, technological and human, are not in opposition but are intricately linked. As AI and automation become more ubiquitous, they will evolve from productivity tools to instruments for personal growth and exploration. What we discover will surprise us, throwing conventions, habitual life, and established social norms into chaos.

How will we find a semblance of order? We'll need new grammar and language to interpret new realities in play. The term *perspective agents* will enter the vocabulary. These new, trusted agents will span human experts, AI mash-ups, simulated environments, and networked collectives. The most influential will become "super nodes," centers of gravity affecting what we see, believe, and act.

To make sense of what's happening around us, it's essential to understand the fundamental elements of the Autonomous Age. These include

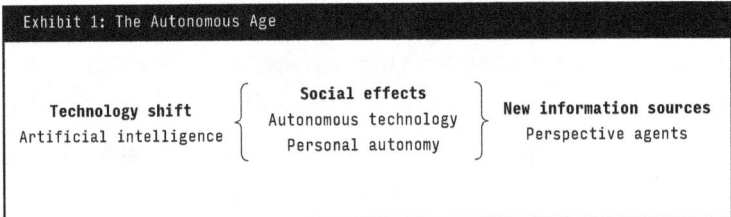

the societal effects of new AIs, how autonomy takes shape in humans and machines, and new sources we'll rely on.

A new paradigm, driven by AI, will create autonomy within tech platforms, individuals, and groups. This autonomous revolution will spawn new agents to help us interpret changes we face. The elements are reflected in exhibit 1.

We're not always aware of the ways our perspective is steered. This recognition will dim further as new agents shape how we see the world. The concept of the attention economy was first theorized by Herbert A. Simon, an American economist and political scientist in the 1970s. Like oil or gold, human attention could be extracted as a highly valued resource. Simon's idea that attention would become an economic asset brought us information-age behemoths like Google, Apple, and Facebook. Sensemaking is now in short supply. We'll need new ways of seeing, thinking, and acting as strange new technologies and unthinkable events infiltrate and alter our lives.

We have some experience in how new perspective agents filling the sensemaking gap work. Think platforms like ChatGPT and AI-enhanced Google search; subreddits, hashtag movements, and interest-based communities; social influencers with mass reach and trust; and new AIs that assemble, package, and propagate information. No one will be immune to revolutionary change and new sources of influence.

A Historic Turning Point

Those I interviewed for the book reference the Autonomous Age in a historical context. They retrieve stories of discord caused by the wheel, the printing press, and electricity. They cite how these facilitated revolutions like the Renaissance, the Enlightenment, and industrialization. Some go next level, saying the Autonomous Age is more consequential than these previous revolutions.

Intellectual breakthroughs that accompany great transitions displace us psychologically. Using new mathematical calculations and astronomical tables, Copernicus found that Earth wasn't the center of the universe, only to be contradicted by Einstein's relativity of motion. Darwin upended human exceptionalism by compiling and interpreting evolution in a new light. Freud found that the ego surpassed rationality. These intellectual breakthroughs tore apart the seams of conventional wisdom and sensible life.

The Autonomous Age represents another major displacement of the human psyche. For the first time, a creation of our own will rule the intelligence kingdom. With AI, we're no longer the only species shaping the world and our place in it. How lives will be reshaped in the Autonomous Age is yet to be determined; what is clear is that we must cultivate radically different perspectives to adapt and thrive in it.

This book provides you with an understanding of the underlying factors shaping the Autonomous Age, its implications, and how to grow with them. As you will discover in the following pages, beyond existing sightlines, it's possible to find an order behind the disorder. You'll see transitions taking form through a cascading series of stages and how to orient yourself to them. Along these lines, the book's trajectory follows a cyclical path.

Part I outlines perspectives in transition. The starting point of change is an alteration of sensibilities. History shows that during disruptive eras, hardwired worldviews and beliefs begin to break down. Making sense of changing events through old frames clouds confidence and judgment. Questions of self-preservation arise, and conflict escalates. The faster we alter our perspectives and see new realities, the more agency and potential we gain. Chapters 1–5 outline problems with conventional wisdom and how we overcome them.

Part II covers beliefs in transition. Predominant technologies of an era shape new values, norms, and behaviors. Changes in sensibility lead to changes in belief. Many of us exhibit the adage "I'll see it when I believe it." In this part, you'll find examples of change en masse that may seem unfathomable to you. Here we explore how people redefine sense of self, seek meaning, find love, and deal with disruptions to their daily lives. Chapters 6–9 explore how beliefs and values change as alterations in identity, relationships, spirituality, and work occur.

Part III explores leading in transition. As new norms and behaviors take hold, they lead to structural change, altering specter of risk and new opportunity. In chapters 10–13, we probe forward-leaning leadership paths and new case studies to learn from. This section is about action, including pioneering mindsets, models, resources, and strategies vital to future success.

The Autonomous Age will be disruptive, scary, awe-inspiring, and empowering. To face it with optimism, perspective becomes a vital, profoundly creative pursuit worth building.

As you read on, reflect on your own point of view. What phase of transition are you in? Do you feel something's not quite right? Are you doubling down on what you know or leaning into the unfamiliar? Are you filled with a sense of dread about what the future holds? If so, you may be feeling a perspective transition.

Are you wrestling with new ideas of identity, religion, work, and relationships? Exploring new ways to understand yourself and others? Taking action to change your view? If so, you're navigating a transition of belief.

Are you facing the future directly and calmly? Excited by this generational moment? Collaborating on breakthrough ideas? If so, you're leading. You're defining the new rules for the future by altering how you see and shape them.

The ideas and stories that follow are intended to be provocations. Each on its own could be a complete book. Think of the chapters as kaleidoscopic trailheads, starter depictions of new, alternative realities and influences behind them. The territories will stimulate more expansive questioning in you. While much feels strange and new in the following pages, the book focuses on what endures.

The meta-story is how we can elevate understanding, meaning, and contribution as we transition into a radically different future. How we speak to human needs and address new challenges with clear eyes requires that we intentionally widen our lens.

PART I

PERSPECTIVES IN TRANSITION

On an overseas flight, a *Financial Times* article caught my eye. A few days before the World Economic Forum, the story warned of a generational crisis.[1] Heading into the 2023 event, elites were consumed by a *polycrisis*, a set of interconnected risks spanning climate change, a looming recession, and geopolitical conflict. The prevailing mood was one of impending doom.

There was a different, less visible crisis embedded in the *Financial Times* story. It said, "The C-suite is contending with a baffling world that most are ill-equipped to analyze." Gillian Tett, the gifted writer and business anthropologist who penned it, added, "The issues facing business leaders can't be understood by the concepts usually taught in business schools, such as economic models or financial statements."[2]

I read this while traveling to Davos for the first time, to hear from elites shaping the year's agenda. I wondered, if the masters of the universe were ill-equipped to guide us, who would?

In this context, I watched how people interpreted events over speakers' remarks projected from the podiums. Waning belief in institutions and elites was center stage. Throughout the week, the Davos glitterati got hammered by critics and activists. These antagonists cited how often leaders missed or misinterpreted consequential events, using the 2008 financial crisis, Brexit, Trumpism, and COVID-19 as reference.

From afar, Elon Musk threw shade on them for trying to "boss the Earth."[3] An op-ed in the *Guardian* called Davos an exercise in mutual self-affirmation.[4] As a famed investor once said on CNBC, "The Davos consensus is always wrong. One hundred percent of the time. The challenge is to determine why it's wrong, how it's wrong, and what can be done to rectify it."[5]

The critics' underlying beef was credibility. The criteria for leadership had changed, while the attendees and agenda had not. The dissonance led one to ask a semi-serious question: Does Joe Rogan, who attracts tens of millions of people to his podcast, set the global agenda more than Klaus Schwab, head of the World Economic Forum?[6]

Around the world, new power gained through networked forces changed the game. In this context, the tongue-in-cheek question about Rogan is a legitimate consideration.

How we perceive the world, the issues we take seriously, and who we turn to in times of need are no longer shaped in ivory towers. To gain a better sense of why, we need to deepen our understanding of the environment we find ourselves in.

CHAPTER 1

TECHNOLOGY: DECODE THE ENVIRONMENT

Any sufficiently advanced technology is indistinguishable from magic.

—ARTHUR C. CLARKE[1]

This book's creative challenge was different from staring at a blank page or facing writer's block. I often see new technologies well before mainstream use. This project would be a race against the machine.

What if writing a book—this book—was a fool's errand? Seeing demos from various start-ups in late 2020, it became clear to me that AI-powered agents would soon transform how knowledge is constructed and interpreted. Instead of people holding the pen, machines would soon generate thoughts, ideas, and language that seemed human.

Stunned best describes how I felt using a GPT-powered agent for the first time. In 2021, I tested generative AI tools to create sample story ideas, ad headlines, and social media posts in seconds. Subsequent platforms wrote songs, stories, essays, and technical briefs. At the time, bots writing college essays or news articles was still on the fringe.

By the time Open AI released its GTP-4 model, in April 2023, more than one hundred million people had used the platform in two months.[2] By the time this book goes to print, generative AI will augment hundreds of millions more human minds as autopilots get embedded in Google, Microsoft, Alibaba, Badu, and Meta platforms, to name just a few.

Nothing in history compares to the power and pace of AI's deployment. Open AI's CEO, Sam Altman, predicted that compounding power would revolutionize everything, a modern equivalent to fire or electricity. Moore's Law said computing power and speed would double every two years. Altman claimed artificial intelligence would double every eighteen months.[3]

NVIDIA's CEO took scaling of AI's powers beyond what we can realistically contemplate. Speaking to investors in early 2023, Jensen Huang said, "Over the course of the next ten years, through new chips, new interconnects, new systems, new operating systems, new distributed computing algorithms, and new AI algorithms and working with developers coming up with new models, I believe we're going to accelerate AI *by another million times.*"[4]

A friend tried to put the coming intelligence leap into context for me. Consider that the average IQ is somewhere between 85 and 115. It's been said that Einstein's was around 160. Einstein is, on average, 1.6 times more intelligent than the norm. A 1.6-times advantage led to his theory of relativity, among other intellectual breakthroughs. It transported human understanding and new recognition of space and time. His theories shaped modern electronics, nuclear power, and GPS navigation.

This world-altering impact came from one incrementally smarter mind. How can we imagine where infinitely more powerful, ubiquitous intelligence may take us?

Soon we'll experience the fusion of lifelike interfaces, greatly advanced learning models, and virtual worlds. Our social system, not to mention our cognitive makeup, is not ready to deal with these technological wonders. Imagine millions of AI agents becoming part of the public sphere. These agents, capable of continuous interaction without fatigue or emotions, tailor knowledge and information to individual preferences through near-perfect prediction. With their advancing abilities to craft stories and ideas, their omnipresence changes our relationship and reliance on technological assistance. Soon, these agents won't be solely accessible by phones or wearable devices. Through brain-computer interfaces, agents are embedded in us, altering our biology from the inside out. In the wrong hands, they're used to manipulate our actions, undermine human interaction, and destroy trust among people.

Such "advances" in AI and biotech require great leaps of imagination on potential effects. A deductive, rationalist perspective is no match for tech-induced mind benders we face. The AI challenge is one of many quakes to shake us. How will we blunt the impact of climate change? Be influenced by geopolitical struggles? Rethink society when normal lifespans extend beyond a hundred years old?

Seeing a Composite Picture

These questions point to different scenarios than we're accustomed to contemplating. Personal acts like writing a book, finding love, or pondering life's meaning are mediated by technology. With newfound powers delivered by increasingly powerful agents, human–machine collaborations will uncover new truths, throw shade on old ones, and transcend the current limits of our understanding. We'll need to expand our intelligence, and perspective, to shape a future we want to live in.

Understanding how technological elements shape us is where we start. Marvin Minsky, remembered as the "father of AI,"[5] envisioned natural intelligence as a "society of mind."⁶ His analogy likened intelligent agents to Lego blocks that when combined lead to infinitely greater intelligence. Other philosophers framed agents as notes that, when accentuated by skilled conductors, create scores that shape how we perceive happenings around us.

Intelligence mash-ups that Minsky envisioned decades ago will guide us into mysterious new worlds. They will also help us make sense of them.

While ChatGPT is praised for handling individual tasks, the convergence of multiple AIs collaborating and problem-solving takes AI's potential to a new level.

The potential is realized through large language models (or LLMs). These are AIs that train on vast amounts of text to understand and generate additional data and original content.

Inventive agent combinations that utilize them will function as sounding boards, information synthesizers, and simulated societies. For instance, Opinionate.io uses LLMs to debate any topic.⁷ It's designed to analyze opposing positions and determine the best arguments among them. Another platform, Consensus, aggregates research papers on any subject.⁸ Like Google Search, it provides the best peer-reviewed studies to offer evidence-based summaries instantly. Other apps like ChatPDF unlock knowledge in academic papers, ebooks, and research reports.⁹ It extracts and summarizes key points, allowing for an interactive dialogue with the content. It's like conversing with a PhD or analyst team behind published research.

BloombergGPT, a purpose-built generative AI, exemplifies a super-synthesizer. Inspired by ChatGPT, it trains on financial documents and business coverage collected over four decades.¹⁰ Accessing an immense dataset, it can accelerate analysts' understanding of the nuances of finance and investing. BloombergGPT's early-use cases span analyzing SEC filing development, uncovering missed signals in financial data, and automating market reports.

Things get even more interesting when agents come together in "simulated societies." For instance, Smallville's creators at Google and Stanford built twenty-five "generative agents" that exhibit realistic human behavior.[11] Resembling a fusion of *The Sims*, *Westworld*, and MTV's *Real World*, Smallville's virtual agents, powered by LLMs, populate a metaverse where they interact and form cliques. Researchers watch simulated interactions like a human field study. Like in MTV's *Real World*, these include personal meltdowns, infighting, and clique-building. According to the research team, generative agents in Smallville "wake up, cook breakfast, and head to work; artists paint, while authors write; they form opinions, notice each other, and initiate conversations; they remember and reflect on days past as they plan the next day."[12]

Smallville and derivatives like it will be proxies to understand social dynamics and decision-making better. As agents come together into novel configurations, new guides will emerge. They will become vital perspective agents, critical to understanding new phenomena and maintaining social cohesion.

Perspective will also be embedded and elevated in commonly used tools. Google Search, for instance, now features a Perspectives tab that changes how information is organized and ranked.[13] The filter displays videos, images, and written posts. Individuals on discussion platforms, Q&A websites, and social media networks also contribute to the results. Supplementary details about sources, including identity, profile image, and content popularity metrics, are also made known.

We need new sources like these as sensemaking becomes scarce. Gaps in understanding critical issues—like the lack of coherent COVID-19 guidance—require better filters. We've seen them in social communities like Reddit and Substacks that democratize expertise. We'll find better signals in the noise through AIs such as BloombergGPT and Smallville. We will soon wade into new virtual worlds, in large part built through generative AI tools. Some, like philosopher David Chalmers, believe these worlds will be every bit as real as real life. He notes that in centuries past, families questioned if they should immigrate to a new country to start a new life. In the future, we'll ask if we should immigrate to a virtual world to live a different life.[14]

Adapting to Unthinkables

As part of research for this book, I used a mix of agent tools to generate and catalog a growing list of "unthinkables," like Chalmers poses. Largely automated, this research platform aggregates real-life phenomena that span escalating weather devastation, new digital currencies and economic models, metastasizing culture wars, and pervasive disinformation.

Given the accumulation of evidence that has built up over the past five years, it's clear that we need to consider the unimaginable thinkable. The problem is, as media critic Neil Postman said, that we'd rather "amuse ourselves to death" than contemplate future scenarios.[15] The bias against cognitively challenging investigations is a distinct liability for leaders and laypeople, given the technological and social turbulence we face.

A study published in the *Psychological Review* found that only 1 percent of those polled wanted to know their future.[16] A separate study by the Institute for the Future (IFTF) revealed that most Americans couldn't envision life ten years from now. Fifty-three percent of participants rarely entertained such thoughts, while 32 percent admitted it never crossed their minds.[17] According to Marina Gorbis, executive director of the IFTF, we've entered the "decisive decade," a period that will determine everything from the health of our planet to the stability of our societies. She says, "The future is where people can abandon their immediate turf interests and think about new possibilities, new constituencies, things that may be unthinkable today."[18]

Lack of foresight around disruptive developments is a form of deliberate ignorance. Jane McGonigal, a game designer and futures researcher, warned against it and the dangers of another change-blocker: normalcy bias. It's the belief that, despite evidence to the contrary, life will continue as it always has. In her book *Imaginable*, McGonigal says the business world is particularly susceptible to it.[19] Normalcy bias accounts for approximately a quarter of CEO dismissals. Those fired denied reality or refused to acknowledge the necessity for change.[20]

How do we overcome hardwired, protective biases? Who can we turn to for a sense of control when facing unknowns? Where do we gain confidence that we grasp the essence of new situations?

We return to the foundational piece of perspective-building: technological environment.

Depicting the composition of the technosphere requires analogical thinking. A way in is using McLuhan's figure-ground metaphor. In visual perception, *figure* refers to the object that focuses attention, while the *ground* is the background or context within which the figure exists.

When analyzing the *environment*, the *figure* (the specific medium or technology) is often the focus of our attention, like a new book, smartphone, or AI agent. The *ground* refers to the psychological and societal changes these technologies facilitate. While we tend to focus on the figure (the specific technology), it's equally important, if not more so, to understand the ground (the larger societal context). In other words, while we might be aware of the content or the specific use of new technology, we are often less aware of the broader societal and cultural changes it brings to us.

Change as a Cascade of Transitions

To build perspective, it is essential to understand the context of a situation more than the objects shaping it. Exhibit 2 shows the cascading sequence of human and social change caused by pervasive new technologies.

Exhibit 2: A Generational Phase Change

	OVERVIEW	PHASE	MINDSET
G	Great transition	Generational change from industrial to intelligent society	Unaware
1	Sensibility transition	Inner sensibilities change because of predominant technologies	Denial
2	Behavior transition	Shifting norms breed contention between old and new values	Contention
3	Society transition	Invention, adaptation change and improve society	Innovation

This model shows how technology serves as a driving force in shaping society, culture, and human response. It borrows from notable thinkers, including Thomas Kuhn, Carlota Perez, and Joseph Schumpeter. It's informed by some of McLuhan's studies, particularly how new technologies first alter our senses.

History shows that major paradigmatic change occurs in cycles. Carlota Perez is an economist and expert in technology and socioeconomic development. Her most notable work, the book *Technological Revolutions and Financial Capital*, investigated five tech-induced paradigm shifts over two centuries. They spanned the industrial revolution (1771); the age of steam and railways (1829); the age of steel, electricity, and heavy engineering (1875); the age of oil, the automobile, and mass production (1908); and the age of information and telecommunications (1971).[21]

Her analysis found that each socioeconomic turn happens through two phases. During the *installation phase*, new technologies emerge, fueled by an influx of capital investment. User growth escalates through peaks and valleys until the speculation bubble bursts. We're witness to this in the current AI boom.

In the *deployment phase*, validated technologies with proven business models become widely commercialized. Once installed, they drive productivity gains and socioeconomic recalibration. She noted that in both phases, societies are profoundly shaken and reshaped.

Societal change comes from Thomas Kuhn's enduring idea: the paradigm shift. A philosopher of science, Kuhn popularized the term *paradigm* in his book *The Structure of Scientific Revolutions*, where he described a paradigm as a break in dominant worldviews or operating philosophies. Paradigms shift when new sensibilities and discoveries replace dated conventions. The great transition underway may be among the most jarring of all paradigm shifts humanity has faced.[22]

Social discord is a common outcome of that "creative destruction" that occurs with such a shift. Austrian economist Joseph Schumpeter argued that capitalism incentivizes entrepreneurs to innovate and improve productivity. By doing so, new ideas disrupt existing markets and displace older, less efficient businesses.[23]

As new technologies embed into society, they send psychological, economic, and physical shocks through the system. In the end, the fittest ideas in the system survive.

With these cyclical patterns, paradigm shifts, and innovation tendencies fused, we find a cascading pattern, as seen in exhibit 2.

The Environment Alters Our View

We're too often blind to this transitional change's influence on us. We focus on the thing, not the effect.

The parable "This Is Water," popularized by David Foster Wallace, is another way to think about environmental blindness.[24] Two young fish are swimming along when they meet an older fish. The older fish nods at them and says, "Morning boys, how's the water?" The two young fish swim for a bit, and then eventually one of them looks over at the other and asks, "What the hell is water?" In the parable, the water is the environment. We can only see it if we are attuned to it.

Consider that studies show Americans spend more than thirteen hours a day interacting digitally through gaming, social media, virtual work, and streaming media.[25] Through AI and spatial computing, the "water" will run in new directions.

Now let's get literal about it. Think of the cascade in exhibit 2 as if we're a writer displaced by ChatGPT. It's a cursory example of cascading effects represented in the framework.

Technology transition. The creative environment is forever changed through this generative AI. It eliminates the "blank page" by prompting AI to write a story's outline or first draft. The technologies become exponentially more powerful and ubiquitous. Chat-based AI assistants integrate new platforms, apps, and plug-ins into existing software suites such as Microsoft Office or Google Search.

Sensibility transition. We feel something has changed when we first hear of or use generative AI like ChatGPT. We sense that the craft of writing and authoring (and future income reliant on it) will be altered. That a machine delivers written content in seconds instead of hours is a paradigm break. We may not be able to articulate the unease felt, but subconsciously we know the craft of writing is altered forever.

Belief transition. We begin experimenting. We join millions of others using ChatGPT to solicit ideas, write first drafts, and edit copy. The best writers master prompts, interacting with generative AIs to develop compelling, factually accurate, and informative copy. Instead of laboriously generating and editing copy, effort moves to creative exploration and editorial oversight of AIs. The act of writing, historically a human domain, is irreversibly changed.

Leadership transition. Those who employ writers and knowledge workers—universities, law firms, media companies, and creative agencies—are forced to change. They must rethink business models, reorder their staff mix, and invest in reskilling to use new platforms effectively.

To add to this, they face operating adjustments and ethical quandaries. Educators reconsider how we learn, who teaches us, and what cheating looks like. Lawyers take on new questions concerning copyright and fair use. Economists question productivity gains, the trajectory of job loss, and ideas like universal basic income. The most adept business leaders design new business models that put generative AI at the center.

New leadership and power are built from intimate knowledge of new systems and adaptation to how they're best leveraged. Practically speaking, leadership and power warrant understanding our present and future environments. In this case, the cascading effects can be a way to see it and determine where we sit in a cycle of change.

Eleanor Roosevelt famously said, "Great minds discuss ideas, average minds discuss events, and small minds discuss people."[26] An alternative interpretation might read: "Great minds create the future, average minds fight the future, and small minds ignore the future."

Revisit this truth as you move through the pages that follow. You'll see yourself, and social changes afoot, differently by the end.

CHAPTER 2

SOCIAL CHANGE: SEE THE FUTURE THROUGH HISTORY

```
The longer you can look back, the farther you can
look forward.
```
                              —WINSTON CHURCHILL[1]

While researching this book, I began to grasp the magnitude of the shift in our shared consciousness. Emblematic of this feeling were the social networks trafficking eerie depictions of "liminality." Metaphorically speaking, liminality is like a doorway where we traverse from one place to the next.

When we can't see to the other side, ambiguity and fear seep in. It's no wonder that images of abandoned buildings, empty gyms, and isolated objects became a pervasive aesthetic and vibe. Visions blurred, darkened, or veiled in ambiguity mirrored a collective mood.

On Twitter, the account @SpaceLiminalBot, dedicated to liminal imagery, grew to 1.3 million followers.[2] Reddit's r/LiminalSpace engaged a community of 655,000 members.[3] On TikTok, content tagged #LiminalSpaces amassed over 4.3 billion views.[4] It was all a cultural response to the feeling that something's not quite right.

The term "liminal" captures the feeling of disorientation accompanying transitions. It's a state of in-betweenness, symbolized by a gas station on a long road trip. No more than a rest stop, it sits between a departure and a destination. This emotional limbo, characterized by a seeming lack of end, clarity, or sense of control, was punctuated by COVID. While disorienting, it also created space for reflection, discovery, and reinvention.

To see liminality positively, we need a sense of where we stand. Here we take the abstract call to action to understand changing environments and make it quite literal.

Life in Transition

A starting point is found in a report from the US National Intelligence Council (NIC). Established in 1979, the NIC is a bridge between intelligence analysts and policymakers in the US government. As part of its remit, the NIC publishes a strategic view of the future every four years. In its latest assessment, the NIC warned of security risks caused by a converging set of global challenges. Their forecast said that pandemics, climate change, and technology disruptions will test the resilience and adaptability of all leaders.[5]

The report said responding to change will exceed the capacity of current frameworks, strategies, and operating modes. No organization will be immune to risk. The NIC added that unprecedented events and structural change across all sectors of society will sweep away resistance and inertia.

On the flip side, massive opportunity accompanies these concerns. Ark Investments' "Big Ideas, 2023" forecast suggests five emerging sectors that could generate an investment potential of over $50 trillion by 2035; they span genomics, automation and robotics, energy storage, next-generation internet technologies, and advanced materials.[6]

Collectively, presenting a $50 trillion figure distorts what is clear: Building the future is a massive, paradigm-breaking undertaking. To see it that way, we must alter our perspective to realize the benefits of its construction.

While new technologies and economic promise can scale, humans and systems lag far behind potential. Given the breathtaking opportunities that await, how can we realize the scope of such dramatic change? Will we break under the pressure of too much change hitting us too soon?

The autonomous transition will feature extreme volatility and creativity. It will be a renaissance period, igniting a rebirth of culture, intellect, and artistry. In this light, liminality can be a liberator.

Rather than viewing liminality like the dystopian portrayals pervasive on the internet, anthropologist Victor Turner wrote about liminality as an "anti-structure" that catalyzes personal growth and creativity. He said liminality harbored tremendous transformative potential, a "realm of pure possibility."[7]

Another scholar in the field, Timothy Carson, noted that we traverse three transitional stages: pre-liminal, the known and assumed structure of life; liminal, the ambiguous transitional period; and post-liminal, a newly adjusted, transformed state of being. Crossing these thresholds can leave an indelible mark on our psyche.[8]

For some, what appears on the horizon is thrilling and opportunistic. Others feel trapped in a weird, dreadful purgatory. Every day we hear of unprecedented incidents, the unthinkable, and another "one-thousand-year event." Newfound perspectives, and lessons from history, can help us better discern and act on new forces swirling around us.

History Informs the Future

Marc Andreessen looks to the past to find what lies ahead. He cofounded the venture capital firm Andreessen Horowitz and cocreated the first commercial web browser. He says, "The further I read back, the more universal themes I find. The more things that I think are remarkable and unique to our era turn out to be universal. I don't know; at least for me, that's a calming experience. It makes me feel less like the world is spinning."[9]

Historical lessons, particularly for pioneers like Andreessen, are grounding agents. A century ago, electricity, telephones, and internal combustion engines transformed society. Industrial progression caused periods of disorganization and strife before ultimately instilling order. Industrialization caused leadership voids, class conflict, and emotional chaos. Its progression mirrors what we've experienced since the internet upended the world.

The past helps us see how previous generations capitalized on new, mysterious innovations. Inventions from the twentieth century (electricity, telephones, and internal combustion engines) led to social innovation and changed lives (timekeeping, media, suburbs).

History proves that hysteria and fear accompany new cultural phenomena. When novels first gained popularity, they were met with skepticism and fear. In the eighteenth and nineteenth centuries, some believed reading fiction, particularly for women, would lead to moral decay, emotional instability, and physical ailments. Critics argued that novels were a dangerous form of escapism that could corrupt the minds of impressionable readers.

The introduction of bicycles in the late nineteenth century sparked widespread anxiety and criticism. Medical professionals claimed they would lead to various health problems, including "bicycle face," a supposed condition in which riders developed a strained, anxious facial expression. Even dance was scorned. The tango was considered scandalous in the early twentieth century because of its close embrace and sensual movement. Similarly, the waltz faced criticism when introduced to European society in the eighteenth century as the close contact between partners was deemed inappropriate and immoral.

History suggests that the convergence of media and politics is the fastest, most influential territory for social change. Radio sparked Hitler's rise and World War II catastrophes in Europe. TV fueled Kennedy's presidential run, reactions to the Cuban missile crisis, and national mourning following his assassination. Social networks brought Obama to the world stage while reigniting populism. Twitter was instrumental in Trump's rise to power and his ability to propagate false narratives. In each case, cascading effects of political innovation amplified cultural discord and conflict.

Depicting a Paradigm Change

Beyond a litany of provocations and industry estimates, how do we determine what paradigm change looks like in real life? How does it manifest in form? How does it influence our day-to-day existence?

Another framework puts generational change into context. Exhibit 3 depicts how dominant communication technologies and media shape social change. Though rooted in the United States, the examples have resonance globally.

In the industrial complex of the twentieth century, mass media, embodied by television, was the dominant means of communication.

Exhibit 3: Paradigm Influence: From Industrialism to Intelligence

	1950-2000	2000-2020	2020 →
DOMINANT TECHNOLOGY	Broadcast media	Social computing	Intelligence
PREDOMINANT STRUCTURE	Hierarchical	Transitionary	Distributed
ECONOMIC PARADIGM	Industrial production	Information access	Experience
MEDIA FORMS	Evening news Print media Prime-time TV	Mobile computing Content sharing Social networking	Metaverse Video networking Encrypted chat Generative AIs
DEMAND DRIVER	Advertising	Adtech	Virtual commerce Influencers Skill builds
RETAIL PARADIGM	Shopping malls	Online commerce	Blockchain/Web3
CONTROL SYSTEMS	Government Higher ed Journalism	Algorithms Apps Data ownership	LLMs Private networks Digital states Surveillance

Branches of government, the US military, and corporations used it to communicate and exert centralized control of their messages. Broadcast advertising created the demand for industrial output like cars, appliances, and consumer packaged goods. Higher wages and the ensuing rise in demand led to the growth of the middle class.

Media forms were finite and familiar. Papers, magazines, and TV networks delivered world news to our homes. With the growth of consumer goods, shopping malls, grocery stores, and catalogs became commonplace. Iconic tropes such as the Marlboro Man, *Star Wars*, Sears, *M*A*S*H*, and Ronald Reagan's "Morning in America" reflected and shaped our values.

Digital computing broke this paradigm. Unlike broadcast-based projection, computing technology facilitates memory. It integrates the storage, synthesis, investigation, and leverage of data. Social computing added a new dimension that decentralized influence. Access to vast information stored in databases, and limitless connection to each other, upended the status quo.

It introduced an era of transitory and conflicting modes of thinking. Capturing and optimizing public attention depended on massive ingestion and parsing of data. AOL emails, Google searches, YouTube videos, Facebook posts, and Amazon purchases changed communication, information access, cultural production, and retail.

Social platforms then displaced TV networks and the province of newspapers as information gatekeepers. While advertising remained the dominant form of demand-creation, methods changed. Marketing became more focused on peer influence and personalization, best mastered by Amazon. Systems of control became the domain of algorithms. Internet titans kept them under lock and key.

We will transition again into the Autonomous Age. "Old wine poured into new bottles" is not an option. AOL failed when it attempted to bridge TV and print brands into digital platforms. Facebook's social graph failed to translate into the algorithmic world of TikTok. Organizations relying on mass media to combat networked disinformation will be undone.

A Vastly Different World Awaits

So what might an intelligence-powered future look like? While foolish to predict in absolutes, present trends bolstered by history indicate where we're headed.

For starters, think the digitization of everything. It will accelerate through continuing chip evolution, powerful graphics processing units (GPUs), new materials, and quantum computing. A vast technical architecture will feature decentralized computing, massive data repositories, Internet of Things (IoT), and networks of billions of intelligent connections.

Application of genetic information and technological advances will limit disease, reframe how we age, offer defense against pandemics, and introduce the emergence of human variants.

AI will help fight climate change and associated crises. Breakthroughs may reduce carbon and water footprints, halt deforestation and depletion/pollution of ocean resources, and enable coastal defense against storms and ocean rise. Post-carbon energy production will expand through nuclear fission and renewables.

Structures will change. We are witnesses today to the breakdown of hierarchical nation-states (highlighted by fractures in US democracy) and cultural and business institutions. New and old factions compete and continue attacks on multiculturalism and globalism. Free trade competes with protectionism versus multinationalism. The idea of a unified globalist vision is no longer viable.

To sustain life, we'll move to post-agricultural food production in vitro. This will coincide with planetwide curtailing of land farming and extensive freshwater demand. Food production will port to space-based communities, enabling human migration off planet.

Aging populations will create markets for androids and robotic workers. In the meantime, economists will address whether enough jobs for humans exist after robots take over many workloads. Some efforts to build a welfare state will gain momentum as we gain productivity from human beings training machines.

These innovations will create new languages, values, and use cases. In the process, innovators will redistribute power and influence.

A Combustion of the Old and New

The depiction of such a revolutionary transition brings us back to the human psyche. A depiction of the future came at the end of 2019, when *New York Magazine* announced, "The weirdness is coming":

> Today, the world has the uncanny shimmer of future weirdness; every week is stuffed with new events that seem to open up strange new realities only to be forgotten as the next wave of strangeness hits. The future is present in these moments—epic, like the battle for Hong Kong; eerie, like virtual makeup; and personal, like contemplating gender-confirmation surgery.[10]

Weirdness persists. In 2022, *New York Magazine* again reflected cultural disequilibrium, warning that a "vibe shift is coming."[11] Hipsters veered off in varied directions, absent "any coherent, singular vision for music or fashion." A sense of doom shaped aesthetics and behavior. The article read, "There's a nihilism to how people dress and party; our heels get higher the closer we inch to death."

Brands responded to the vibe shift with a parade of bizarre mashups. To solve the problem of "meat sweats," Arby's and Old Spice teamed up to create a $60 Meat Sweats Defense Kit.[12] For Mother's Day, KFC and ProFlowers partnered on the perfect gift: a dozen roses, a KFC glass vase, and eight skewers to hold a fried chicken.[13] Oscar Mayer joined forces with Seoul Mamas to put out hydrating face sheet masks resembling bologna.[14]

These strange ways are just the beginning. Consider another plausible scenario, this one a future for digital twins.

Consider that each of us already exists as an avatar of data. It depicts our actions, passions, relationships, and psychology. It continually updates. The feedback loops from our digital fidgeting continually cycle in new intelligence about us. Each credit card swipe, phone screen tap, and mouse click refine our digital record. Navigation maps, video posts, comments, and likes continually add to our profiles. The keepers of the data know more about us than anyone, including us. Like a scene out of *Westworld*, overlords can program our emotions in ways we can't see.

In another part of the engineering sphere, product managers will master the digital look-alike. These computational agents will become picture-perfect avatars of us. To refine them, deepfake engines scrape photos from the internet to clone our look. From TikTok videos, our mannerisms. From YouTube, our voice. They're cartoonish today. But soon, our avatars will be rendered in 8K quality.

Now recall the makeup of Smallville's generative agents in the introduction. They combine AI learning models (the avatar's intelligence) and computational agents (the avatar's depiction). An experiment like Smallville has a pixelated, Atari-like feel today, but with virtual reality (VR) coming, these simulated worlds will eventually get hyperrealistic, powered by spatial computing technologies.

You can see where this is going. Imagine we're reborn in digital forms that inhabit virtual worlds.

We will envision and shape this future for our benefit. We will avoid the autocratic *Westworld* scenario by harvesting our own data. We will create our digital twin in the image we aspire to be. We will shape norms and laws of digital societies that our "second selves" inhabit.

So what will this digital twin do in these other worlds? For starters, multiply into derivatives of us. There can be as many versions of our digital selves as we'd like. Being generative, we can become anyone or anything we can imagine. Think Pixar-quality depictions of us. Digitally adorned or transformed presentations of us. Invisible, encrypted profiles of us. A constantly regenerated identity of us.

Our physical body may no longer be the center of our existence. Maybe there is no center. Like McDonald's or Starbucks, our replicating avatars will have an omnipresence throughout virtual communities.

Virtual society may mirror IRL reality. We'll extend and transcend how we think about relationships. We will create new forms of government and policing. We will deal with digital misdemeanors, psychological trolls, and street corner shakedowns. The stressors accompanying a new social life will be reduced through rituals, digital drugs, and emotional balancers.

Our jobs today will be gone or changed drastically by 2050—it won't matter. Building mirror worlds of the real thing requires massive infrastructure builds, city planning, virtual-based commerce, and entertainment. A new economic sector will form to build, operate, and maintain these virtual worlds. Jobs will be plentiful but work on a different timescale. The five-day workweek, a relic of industry, will be cut by half. Immense productivity gains from AI will give us life back. Leisure, not work, will become the bedrock of culture.

Paradoxically, a world with less work ends the idea of retirement. With bioengineering advances, people will live longer lives, some well past one hundred. But it won't matter. Our digital twins will work and last for an eternity.

The Value of Depicting the Future

Futures thinkers help us imagine preposterous yet plausible scenarios like this. My first encounter with the practice came from a *Fortune* cover story, circa 1967. The cover image features a dimly discernible image of 1977, still indistinct but beginning to assume a definitive shape. The title reads straight as an arrow: "How to Think about the Future."[15]

The issue is a time capsule. Legal-size pages feature explanatory, text-based ads from early computing pioneers, adding heft to the coffee-table-ready, two-hundred-page issue. Advertisements featured Remington (typewriters), NCR (data processing), UNIVAC (networks), Scientific Data Systems (software), Xerox (copiers), Texas Instruments (components), and AT&T (communications).

The development of these technologies led *Fortune* to contemplate a scenario facing high school and college students ten years forward, depicting life in 1977. They would inhabit a world of "more," meaning more automobiles, televisions, sirloin steaks, medicines, art museums, mobility, opportunity, and variety. College-aged kids would benefit from new forms of private and public planning, problem-solving, and choosing. The orchestration of innovation promised to add a missing ingredient to the quality of American life.

The provocateurs featured included Henry S. Rowen (president of RAND Corporation); Bertrand de Jouvenel (Ford Foundation); Stephen R. Graubard (Brown University); and Daniel Bell (Columbia University). Max Ways, who authored the piece, noted their forecasts came from synthesis.

These futures thinkers distilled a Cambrian explosion of haphazardness into an aggregate picture coming into view. Ways called the environment in development an "archipelago of successes glittering in the swap of unintended consequences."[16]

Alvin Toffler made one such consequence a business meme (though it wasn't called that at the time) that projected over a longer period than a typical ten-year futures scenario. Distinct from *Fortune*'s futures board working in academia and think tanks, Toffler achieved mainstream prominence by coining the term *future shock* through his book of the same name.[17] In that 1970s best seller, Toffler said a modern state of tension and disorientation would emerge, caused by too much change in too short a time. He likened it to PTSD felt by soldiers and disaster survivors, wholly disoriented and shaken by their experiences.

Half a century later, future shock is real. The poet Arthur Symons said at the start of the twentieth century, "The visible world is no longer a reality, and the unseen world no longer a dream."[18] A modern adaptation might be, "We're so wired, we can't see."

Future shock aptly applies to corporate life and longevity. Consider *Fortune*'s annual list of the five hundred largest companies. What was originally conceived as a list of the most powerful corporations is now a barometer of change. Only 10 percent of companies from the original 1955 list remain on the current roster.

The executive suite is going the way of the *Fortune* 500s. To illustrate, Russell Reynolds, an executive recruiting and leadership advisory firm, maintains a CEO turnover index. The firm found that COVID-19 significantly affected CEO turnover trends. Throughout 2020, facing unprecedented risks, there was a noticeable decline in CEO departure. The trendline persisted into 2021, with the global annual turnover rate dropping from 10 percent in 2020 to 8.9 percent in 2021. However, as countries began to recover in 2022, organizations' risk tolerance rebounded, leading to a five-year peak in global CEO turnover at 11.2 percent. In the first half of 2023, this elevated rate continued, with more than one hundred CEOs stepping down.[19]

Even more telling is the cycling out of chief marketing officers (CMOs), those in charge of aligning company offers with market sentiment and behavior. Spencer Stuart found that CMO tenure fell to its lowest level in over a decade. The leadership advisory firm reported that, on average, CMOs working at the top hundred US advertisers had been in the role for just thirty-nine months.[20]

The C-suite faces a double bind: How do you simultaneously navigate a complex period while future-proofing business models? In another 2023 survey, the consulting firm PwC polled more than four thousand chief executives on how they planned to address this dilemma. When asked if their organization would be viable in another ten years by staying on its current path, remarkably, 40 percent said no.[21]

If their projections are accurate, continued rearrangement in the upper ranks is assured. According to the *MIT Sloan Management Review*, most firms have material leadership gaps to realize new opportunities. For their report, "New Leadership Playbook for the Digital Age," they surveyed 4,394 global leaders from more than 120 countries. The findings were sobering. Just 12 percent of respondents strongly agreed that their leaders have the right mindsets to lead them forward.[22] Even more, the report cited that leaders maintain behaviors that stymie the talents of their employees. It's a warning sign on the path to exploring and creating new value.

The temporary nature of our liminal state is a transitional phase, a rite of passage requiring adaptation and evolution. Adjusting our lens to recognize new patterns doesn't solely apply to C-suite leadership; it's relevant to all of us.

A different world is coming to life. It's apparent to those watching the signs. Arundhati Roy, the best-selling author and activist, captured the emergence from liminality, voicing, "Another world is not only possible, she is on her way. . . . On a quiet day, I can hear her breathing."[23]

CHAPTER 3

MEDIA: RECOGNIZE THE CHANGING CURRENTS

Whoever controls the media controls the mind.

—JIM MORRISON[1]

Peter Thiel is said to ask a question of everyone he meets: What widely disbelieved truth do you hold as true?[2] Thiel is one of Silicon Valley's most preeminent investors and cofounder of PayPal and Palantir. I haven't met Thiel, but I have one: Social media companies are not solely to blame for media and cultural turmoil. We need to look at the long-term effects of digital media pioneers who took advantage of them. Blaming social media for societal tumult spans the gamut, from the end of democracy[3] to mental health crises to the end of truth.[4] Critics blame the big platforms for the erosion of institutions, culture wars, and media addiction.[5] Some suggest social media is destroying the world.[6]

Technology doesn't change the world; the changes come from how early users shape its use for the rest of us. It's instructive, then, to revisit the rise of early digital media minds, their founding ideologies, and inventions. While intentions varied, the goal behind building new media businesses was uniform: Ignite a firestorm of interest and keep it burning as long as possible. To do so, these figures focused on the algorithms that automated information distribution as much as the humans on the receiving end.

There is an underlying logic to the strategy. The more attention gained via autonomous means, the richer, more famous, and more influential one could be. The more influential, algorithmically driven digital media became, the more operatives saw it as an avenue for power. The more competition for power, the more brazen the tactics.

In this cycle, information integrity was cast aside. Data showed that outrage drove clicks. Fake news traveled up to six times faster through social networks than real news.[7] Ideologically driven media created billionaires, elected politicians, and shaped, in some cases, devastatingly destructive factions.

New media practices led to severe distortion of reality. Twenty-five years later, attention engineering blurred truth, celebrity, and influence into one. When we trace the intricate web of attention-hoarding connections that brought us here, the picture of distortion and what we can learn from it going forward becomes clear.

The Double Meaning of the Long Boom

The sentiment wasn't always so pessimistic. In 1997, a *Wired* magazine story predicted a technologically induced period of unrelenting growth. Editors titled it "The Long Boom." The cover showed a happy face, depicting a carefree vibe. With a blissful grin, a daisy hung from its mouth. The message asserted, "We're facing twenty-five years of prosperity, freedom, and a better environment for the whole world. You got a problem with that?"[8]

The early promise, advanced by scenario-planning guru Peter Schwartz, banked on two seismic forces: new participatory technology and an open ethos to take advantage of it. Together, the forces would create unprecedented wealth and autonomy for all. In an enduring sense, the "long boom" foretold the information boom-and-bust we've experienced.

Wired's point of view reflected strong libertarian values popularized and sustained in Silicon Valley. These principles were ingrained in the magazine and passionately championed by its founder, Louis Rossetto. In framing *Wired* as the totem of a transformational epoch, Rossetto said, "This is the mainstream culture of the twenty-first century. It's a new economy, a new counterculture, and beyond politics. In ten or twenty years, the world will be completely transformed. Everything we know will be different. Not just a change from LBJ to Nixon, but whether there will be a President at all. We're in a phase change of civilizations here."[9]

The movement had other evangelical voices. John Perry Barlow's "A Declaration of the Independence of Cyberspace" was likened to Thomas Paine's *The American Crisis*, which preceded the American Revolution. In 844 powerful words, Barlow, the former Grateful Dead lyricist, called for governments to keep their hands off the internet. With Jeffersonian vigor, he said, "Our virtual selves are immune to your sovereignty, even as we continue to consent to your rule over our bodies. We will spread ourselves across the Planet so no one can arrest our thoughts."[10]

Wired masterfully shaped the early digital vanguard, transmitting the Silicon Valley ideology of change worldwide. Readers felt what it was like to live in the future. Attention-grabbing, dayglow hues projected vivid, forward-leaning optimism. Before *Wired*, the digital age was imperceptible. John Plunkett, the magazine's early design chief, said, "Since we couldn't be the new medium we were reporting on, what could we do to signify it? What does that invisible future look like? Perhaps more importantly, what does it feel like?" He added, "Is the future good or bad, scary or friendly?"[11]

This question remains unanswered today.

The Autonomous Media Mind

By 2006, *Wired*'s predictions on personal autonomy took hold. *Time* magazine unveiled "You" as its Person of the Year.[12] It was "us" who, together, changed the world. Anyone could "self-IPO"[13] as the internet morphed into a fractured, money-making attention market. It paid out social capital to anyone making clicks rain. Those cashing in the fastest stumbled into newfound celebrity and influence. An artisan media craft would morph into an industrialized social science.

The "self-IPO" is best embodied by Kim Kardashian. Few figures, if any, monetized instincts for social reach combined with celebrity attraction like her. In one masterfully conceived campaign, a *Paper* magazine cover featured Kardashian balancing a champagne glass on her behind while spraying a bottle of champagne into the glass.[14] While triggered by print, the project was an intended assault on the internet.

The idea had all the ingredients for virality.[15] The article, titled "Break the Internet: Kim Kardashian," featured a polarizing celebrity, high/low culture, an active social network, and a call to action. At press time, Kardashian had twenty-five million Twitter followers, equal to Oprah Winfrey and more than CNN.

When Kardashian's cover hit newsstands in 2014, more than fifty million hits overwhelmed *Paper*'s website.[16] It captured 1 percent of all US web traffic. The balancing butt image became a news story and late-night comedian talking point. Kim Kardashian's behind became a piñata, a Thanksgiving turkey by Ellen DeGeneres, and Portia de Rossi's Christmas card.

Other micro-celebrities would follow her lead. They used new media forms like blogs, vlogs, and live streams to make their mark. In the world of blogging, influential voices emerged, such as Heather Armstrong, who wrote a blog under the pseudonym Dooce; Cory Doctorow of blog *Boing Boing*; and Robert Scoble of blog *Scobleizer*.

Pioneer Ze Frank built an influential following with his video blog, *The Show with Ze Frank*. Meanwhile, Casey Neistat redefined storytelling and filmmaking through YouTube, with notable works such as his "Make It Count" video for Nike and his daily vlog series that offered an authentic, behind-the-scenes look into his life. Live streamers like iJustine, Chris Pirillo, and Justin Kan, cofounder of Justin.tv (which later became Twitch), offered unprecedented levels of intimacy and connection to their fans, drawing voyeurs into their daily lives.

News Becomes Content

Unattracted to the niche of celebrity-building, Arianna Huffington envisioned a content platform that would aggregate individual voices. As web publishing emerged, Huffington built a vast and influential network through her roles as an intellectual, gubernatorial candidate, and activist.

Her travels and instincts built her reputation as a super-connector, heralded by the press as the world's greatest networker.[17] Huffington brought together A-list celebrities and new media masterminds, including Jonah Peretti, Andrew Breitbart, and Matt Drudge, to create the internet's most influential newspaper.[18]

Huffington's network of nineteen thousand contacts shaped the *Huffington Post* into a first-of-its-kind, celebrity-studded opinion page.[19] It went live on May 9, 2005, turning heads with posts from celebrities like Larry David, John Cusack, and Ellen DeGeneres.[20] *HuffPo* became a "paper of record" without actual paper or editorial boundaries. It aggregated news from news sources on everything from Federal Reserve policy to Islamic State atrocities.

HuffPo slanted left of center, presenting content from thousands of unpaid bloggers alongside news aggregated from competing sites. Attention-capture tactics conflicted with standards for responsible journalism and maintaining public trust. Thorough research, verification of facts, unbiased reporting, transparency, and accountability didn't sync with fast publishing and optimizing page views.

Blending blog-like celebrity opinion with reporting turned news into "content." By 2012, HuffPo's aggregation colossus featured sixty-eight sections, three international editions, 1.2 billion monthly page views, and 54 million comments in that year alone. The site was so vast, the Columbia Journalism Review likened it to a trip to a mall where the exits were impossible to locate.[21]

Aside from occasional scoops, it did little in the way of breaking stories, journalism's traditional ground of credibility. The emphasis on high-volume social distribution over top-notch reporting was a seminal moment. The Huffington Post fed a media distribution machine that ruptured the news business. HuffPo published almost two thousand stories per day. It outperformed leading newspapers like the New York Times in terms of traffic, simply by aggregating and repackaging the New York Times and other outlets' journalism.[22] The ascent made Arianna Huffington one of Time's most influential people in 2011.[23]

The New York Times "Innovation Report," a groundbreaking internal document leaked in 2014, provided an unflinching analysis of the challenges faced by newspapers in the digital age. The report became a touchstone for the entire industry, sparking a broader conversation about the future of journalism and the need for legacy media to embrace traffic-building techniques embodied by HuffPo to remain relevant. Insiders described it as "transformative, incredibly important, and a big moment for the future of news."[24]

Like many of their counterparts, the *Times* didn't recognize social factors upending the media economy. They failed to realize the endgame: Maximize readership at any price.

A War for Attention

With the tagline "Today's gossip is tomorrow's news," Gawker Media became another attention-generating maximalist. Working from his SoHo apartment, founder Nick Denton built Gawker into a digital media giant, attracting mass internet readership through a blog network that included *Jezebel, Lifehacker, Kotaku, Deadspin,* and *Gizmodo*. It began with two websites and two freelancers who were paid $12 per post.[25]

The namesake site, *Gawker*, was the centerpiece brand. Its tabloid-style, conversation-rich mix was a messy, destructive, engaging way to win the war for attention. Denton was the perfect man to direct it. He spent years crafting a reputation predicated on frankness and fearlessness. Writing earlier for the *Financial Times*, he learned the best stories took readers deep behind the scenes. He said the real ones were those you hear at the bar with colleagues after deadlines. That meant gossip.

His hearsay read differently from *Page Six*, the *Daily Mail*, or TMZ. At *Gawker*, he demanded posts read like real talk. His guidelines said it was okay to be weird but fast. Lists are useful, as are FAQ or Q&A formats. Readers forget Friday's big story by Monday morning. Hit publish first, and beg forgiveness later.[26]

Denton's newsroom published at an extraordinary pace. At *Gawker*, you didn't take nights and weekends off. Denton said, "Whatever information we have, whatever insight we have, whatever knowledge we have, our impulse is to share it as quickly as possible, and sometimes with little thought. Before you can think about it too much, just put it out there, just share it out there."²⁷

Attention mining became so competitive that they assigned staff writers "traffic-whoring duty."²⁸ Writers each produced as many as fifteen daily posts when called on. Traffic whoring was embedded into the newsroom's sensibilities. Clickbait leads became a distinct style. They read like "How the Internet Beat Up an 11-Year-Old Girl," "Clueless Secretary Prompts Hilarious Office Email Thread," and "Glenn Beck Is Going Blind."

Exemplified by *Gawker*'s unapologetic reporting and tone, online civility began to wane. Weber Shandwick's "Civility in America" survey, conducted annually from 2010 to 2019, found toxic conversation to be a rising challenge. In 2010, 95 percent of Americans said that civility was necessary for a healthy democracy and that citizens should be able to "disagree without being disagreeable." By 2017, 75 percent of Americans believed that online incivility had risen to crisis levels, and 69 percent believed that it would lead to violence. Concluding the annual survey in 2019, Weber Shandwick found nearly two-thirds of the American public believed that social media was undermining civility in America.²⁹

With all the experimentation, growth, and controversy, Denton admitted that *Gawker* eventually overextended itself. "We were internet exceptionalists, believing that a new world of unlimited freedom to associate and express would emerge from blogs, forums, and messaging. We still believed we could, like the early bloggers, say everything."³⁰

The end of *Gawker* proved to be its most enduring story. Terry Gene Bollea (Hulk Hogan) sued Denton for posting portions of a sex tape. Peter Thiel, a longtime foe of Denton, bankrolled the suit. The fight became a sordid tale of celebrity, sex, infidelity, deceit, and First Amendment protections. The saga culminated in poetic retribution. *Gawker* had previously revealed Thiel's sexual orientation, the lead reading, "Peter Thiel is totally gay, people."³¹

By way of a professional wrestler, Thiel got his revenge. Hogan won the $140 million judgment against Denton. It forced *Gawker* into bankruptcy and, later, the sale of Gawker Media's other publications to Univision. Gawker.com, the center of the Hulk Hogan lawsuit, was shut down. Denton settled with Hogan for $31 million.[32]

Viral Culture Becomes the Culture

A rule of attention extractors is the smaller the act required of a user, the more they participate. It's how blogs became tweets. Comments became likes. Likes become swipes, and so on. Design for micro-actions was baked into participation and virality, which, in turn, fueled meme culture.

Few understood this culture and how to shape it like Jonah Peretti, founder of BuzzFeed. His master's thesis was unexpectedly deep for a site that would later gain fame for exploding watermelons, dress debates, and listicles. His academic paper "Capitalism and Schizophrenia" investigated the psychological motivations of media consumption. He wrote, "The process of forming one's identity is inseparably connected to the impulse to consume; thus, the acceleration of capitalism requires an increase in the speed at which individuals adopt and discard identities."[33]

Like a logo on a shirt, he found that what we share online projects how we wish to be seen. Like fashion, online identity can be fleeting.

Peretti would gain early fame for the viral takedown. Responding to a Nike campaign to create custom sneakers, Peretti selected "sweatshop" as his design. When Nike refused, an exchange of emails followed, ending with Peretti asking for a photo of "the ten-year-old girl from Vietnam making his shoes."[34] Peretti shared the email exchange with twelve friends, and it took off. The email exchange went viral, eventually landing coverage in *Time*, the *Guardian*, the *Independent*, and the *Wall Street Journal*. He later appeared on the *Today* show to debate labor policy with Nike's

PR head. Peretti said, "Without really trying, I had released what biologist Richard Dawkins calls a meme, a 'unit of cultural transmission.'"[35]

The thing about memes, Peretti said, is that they replicate themselves, spreading from brain to brain.[36] Peretti codified his experimental lessons into nineteen principles of media virality. The first one broke convention. He observed that global capitalism produced hundreds of millions of bored office workers who spend the day forwarding emails and surfing the web. These alienated white-collar professionals spent half their day sharing media with their friends. He called it the "bored at work" network (BWN).[37]

Peretti considered it the largest invisible alternative to visible media audiences. Activists, artists, and hackers could reach millions through the BWN. Traditional media speak didn't fly; the BWN trafficked jokes, games, stupid videos, and political memes.

BuzzFeed's editors homed in on things people liked but couldn't say why. One example is "basset hounds running." No one searches for it, but everyone clicks when they see it.[38] Peretti said, "The intellectual challenge of understanding why ideas spread, how they spread, human psychology, those kinds of things, is infinitely rich. I don't feel like you ever figure that out. The more BuzzFeed focuses on understanding people, the better the business will be."[39]

Typical newsrooms orient around content. At BuzzFeed, behavioral insight was king. The company conducted thousands of experiments to optimize and refine its output. All published content is fed back to BuzzFeed's data science team for analysis and further distribution of high potential stories.

Remember "the dress"? In 2015, the image divided the internet, sparking a worldwide debate over perception. It featured a photograph of a dress that some saw as blue and black, others as white and gold. In a style known to BuzzFeed readers, the headline of a story about said dress pleaded for participation: "What Colors Are This Dress?" The story's subhead read "There's a lot of debate on Tumblr about this right now, and we need to settle it. This is important because *I think I'm going insane.*"[40]

Cates Holderness, then–community growth manager at BuzzFeed, initially dismissed its big bang potential. She then found that the post generated five thousand notes, indicating it could be "insanely viral." Holderness doubled down, following the post with a poll about the color. It broke BuzzFeed's record for the most concurrent visitors to the site, totaling 673,000 simultaneous views at its peak and 28 million views in a day. It became an international meme, spawning hashtags, celebrity debates, and conspiracy theories.[41]

Triggers like "the dress" became calculated bets on virality. In another case, BuzzFeed staff methodically wrapped rubber bands around "the watermelon." Social paydirt came as an invitation: "Watch us explode this watermelon one rubber band at a time." The live-streamed stunt on Facebook drew millions of viewers anticipating the watermelon's destruction.[42] On an ordinary Friday, over eight hundred thousand in the "bored at work" network simultaneously viewed two BuzzFeed employees demolishing a piece of fruit.

The stunt made media executives question how journalism could stay competitive in an industry fixated on page views. Would reporting crumble as outlets re-formed as entertainment venues in pursuit of watermelon-sized numbers? In BuzzFeed's case, the answer was yes. In 2023, BuzzFeed News shut down its Pulitzer Prize–winning site to focus on its more profitable and viral content businesses.[43]

To Enrage Is to Engage

Keeping readers engaged has long been part and parcel of the news business. In the 1960s, critics lamented a new era of "pseudo-events," happenings presented as news by media operatives and the press. The 1970s took the critique one step further. Celebrated journalist Tom Wolfe coined "Knockoff Pseud" to describe life-forms that existed only in the press but were acted out by people who believed they were real.[44]

A digital interpretation of knockoff pseud is pseudo-rage. In the previous era, print editors followed the rule "if it bleeds, it leads." The digital translation is "to enrage is to engage." The potential to amass attention through sensation is based on human nature and algorithmic priming.

A peer-reviewed study published in *Nature* showed how negative headlines drive engagement. It found each additional negative word in an online story increased the click-through rate by 2.3 percent for a headline of average length.[45]

That percentage pales in comparison to engagement on Twitter. Another research team from New York University analyzed over five hundred thousand messages on hot-button political issues, including climate change, gun control, and LGBTQIA+ rights and legislation. Each moral, emotional word people added to a tweet translated into a 15 to 20 percent increase in the likelihood that others would retweet it.[46] Separately, Princeton-backed research found that each word of moral outrage added to a tweet increases the rate of retweets by 17 percent. The research team noted, "It takes very little effort to tip the emotional balance within social media spaces, catalyzing and accelerating further polarization."[47]

For Andrew Breitbart, deliberate, manufactured pseudo-rage was a path to enduring political influence. His founding ideology continues to rattle the foundation of democracy in America.

Without a counter from the right, Breitbart believed left-leaning elites had eaten away Americans' values from the inside out. He called the cultural machine propagating liberal values the "Democrat Media Complex" and took up arms to fight it. Breitbart waged an explicit act of war on the media, saying, "It's not Nancy Pelosi, and it's not Barack Obama. It's Katie

Couric, Brian Williams.... It's CBS, NBC, ABC, Paramount, Sony, and the people in Hollywood who hide their message in art."[48]

Breitbart fashioned himself as a reluctant cultural freedom fighter, uniquely suited to shoot the messengers. He earned his digital-news chops as a long-serving lieutenant to the news-aggregation king Matt Drudge and content-as-news queen Arianna Huffington.

Breitbart rebuilt the *HuffPo* model into a distinct, explicitly combative voice for conservatives. Breitbart fused performance art, cultural crusading, and outrage baiting into a distinct art form. His entire business model hinged on offense. He said, "They want to portray me as crazy, unhinged, and unbalanced. OK, good, fine. Fuck you. Fuck you. Fuck you."[49]

Beyond refining his reputation for red-faced, pseudo-comedic rants, Breitbart knew dull, bureaucratic policy debates were a media showstopper. He said, "I'm trying to shift the focus of conservative movement from the narrow—the policy—to a much higher elevation, granting them a greater perspective."[50] He successfully tapped into wells of frustration among conservatives who felt their point of view wasn't adequately represented in the mainstream media.

Breitbart's crusaders fed off hard-hitting exposés and takedowns of the libs. From exposing Anthony Weiner's dick pics to amplifying "Pizzagate" conspiracy theories, he was unapologetic in confronting liberals, their agendas, and integrity.[51] Breitbart's early hits included releasing videos implicating ACORN and USDA official Shirley Sherrod and targeting Obama administration appointee Kevin Jennings.

His personal crusade ended on March 1, 2012, when Breitbart died of heart failure at age forty-three.[52] The media offensive was just starting. A few days after his death, Breitbart.com was relaunched.

Under Steve Bannon, Breitbart expanded its influence, becoming a shaper and voice of the alt-right movement. Bannon's vision, prominently featured in his rhetoric, was informed by *The Fourth Turning*, a book by William Strauss and Neil Howe.

In their book, Strauss and Howe asserted that a profound sociological transformation occurs every eighty to one hundred years, known as a "turning."[53] Their theory said the United States was on the cusp of such a moment. Bannon often referenced it as he trafficked his prophecy of a forthcoming revolution, envisioning freedom fighters on the right as the catalysts for a generational turning of history.

The Fourth Turning posited that a new society would emerge after a great unraveling, shaped by a new generation of visionaries. In Bannon's interpretation, these individuals would be akin to "artists," imbuing the new society with profound meaning and purpose.

Backed by billionaire funders Robert and Rebekah Mercer, Bannon fueled a populist insurgency, waging information warfare to shape a new form of conservatism. Breitbart News would play a central role, organized across cultural battle lines with sites focused on big Hollywood, big government, and big journalism.[54]

Discrediting became the standard. Breitbart.com's newsfeed propagated lib fails, elites cheating the system, media cover-ups, and the collapse of journalistic objectivity. Bannon coined the now-infamous phrase "Honey badger don't give a shit," the motto of *Breitbart News*.[55]

On the surface, the strategy was deceptively simple: Win by highlighting real and perceived flaws in mainstream media coverage. Do the same with liberal ideology. Below the waterline, a more complex orchestration was at work.

Breitbart.com became a central source in a burgeoning, networked conservative media sphere. A network of conservative news brands proliferated, including the *Federalist*, the *Daily Caller*, *Gateway Pundit*, and *Rebel News*. Content published through them flowed in and out of 4Chan, Reddit, Facebook, and Twitter.

First views of this coordinated ecosystem materialized at Harvard's Berkman Klein Center (BKC), led by law professor Yochai Benkler. In the book *Networked Propaganda*, Benkler and his coauthors described it as an "attention backbone" propelling a cohesive conservative ideology.[56]

Benkler's research team visualized it through social network graphs, sourcing four million political articles housed in the Media Cloud, an analytics platform developed by BKC and the MIT Media Lab. The team saw how articles were connected, tweeted, and shared over three years. The picture revealed no similarity or symmetry with the center and left-leaning press.[57]

Roughly a third of network activity flowed through this conservative chamber. Robert Faris, research director at the BKC, said, "There are clearly two sides, and those two sides are not the same. The right is more insular; it's more extreme; it's more partisan. That's not a subjective opinion; that's an empirical observation."[58]

Rather than control the legacy media, Bannon's war plan was to destroy it and build a new one. The insurgency ran by different rules and messages about what's best for America. Bannon's influence shaped the editorial agenda and flow of storylines shared through right-wing media. Conservative media orchestration actively played off, and often into, coverage from figures higher up the media chain like Matt Drudge, Sean Hannity, Laura Ingraham, Tucker Carlson, and Rush Limbaugh.

BKC network graphs revealed American media breaking into two distinct, structurally different camps. On the one side, it illuminated an insurgent, digitally sophisticated media network anchored by Fox News and Breitbart. Conversely, tradition-bound outlets like CNN and the *New York Times* propagated liberal values. As the 2016 election and Trump's entire presidency proved, precedent fell out of favor along with traditional media influence.

Beyond building this new networked ecosystem, Bannon's directive to "flood the zone with shit" was a potent weapon of the right's media strategy.[59] Known as "active measures" in covert operations, the deliberate weaponization of information is a fundamental element in fighting shadow wars. Inundating the public with exaggerated, poor-quality, or deceptive content overshadowed objective reporting. Gaslighting, trolling, using dog whistles, and other dark arts changed media norms. The flood of bullshit made it impossible for people to understand what was happening, which was the whole idea.

"Flooding the zone with shit" distorted public perspective by design. Perception casualties were part of the fight. Bannon said, "We call ourselves 'the Fight Club.' You don't come to us warm and fuzzy. We consider ourselves virulently anti-establishment, particularly 'anti-' the permanent political class."[60]

The media crusade persists, with culture wars as the front line. Left- and right-wing proponents at both extremes fight for radical, even destructive, endgames using similar divisive tactics. Media figures and politicos advocated scorched-earth strategies accelerated on the right and co-opted by the left.

"Woke freedom fighters"—denoting advocates fervently championing social and racial justice—adopted similar media tactics to amplify their causes. Using the tactics of the far right, they use social media platforms' power, create hashtag movements that grow into global phenomena, and craft compelling narratives, personal stories, and digital art that resonate with millions. Platforms like Twitter, Instagram, and TikTok are battlegrounds for these activists as they navigate the delicate dance of advocacy in the digital age.

Yet this drive for social change is not without its critics. Detractors argue that a darker side of these movements emerges through "cancel culture"—by which individuals (often high-profile) face public backlash and sometimes professional consequences for perceived transgressions, even if they occurred years ago.

Critics contend that this culture enforces censorship, silencing voices and stifling debate. One notable instance involved comedian Kevin Hart, who stepped down from hosting the Oscars after old tweets—deemed homophobic—resurfaced.[61] Other figures like Dave Chappelle and Lizzo, champions of free speech and social activism, faced the wrath of cancel culture. While some view the oustings as a necessary consequence for past mistakes, others see it as a symbol of an unforgiving online tribunal that permits little room for growth or redemption.

McLuhan warned about politicized media Armageddon more than half a century ago. In 1970 he wrote, "World War III will be a guerrilla information war with no division between military and civilian participation."[62] While prophetic, McLuhan could not anticipate how information weaponry would evolve and multiply. In the bowels of the internet, digital street fighters employ dark ads, hacks, bots, fake news, and trolls to attack the enemy. They're battle-tested, informed by attention sciences pioneered by figures we've just met.

It's no wonder we sense that the truth is unknowable. What started as a commercial fight for attention morphed into an all-out information conflict.[63] We each face our own battle to find a signal in a combative fog of war. While internet pioneers prophesied an era of prosperity and participation, in the end, we paid way too much for a new whistle.

The repercussions of manufactured media noise, and a resulting coherence crash, came as a result.

CHAPTER 4

CULTURAL FRACTURES: ADJUST YOUR LENS

To the blind, all things are sudden.

—MARSHALL MCLUHAN[1]

On March 26, 2020, the US Securities and Exchange Commission (SEC) halted trading shares of Zoom Technologies.[2] Volume in ZOOM transactions soared. Its valuation increased seven-fold monthly, from around $3 a share to over $20. The company had no meaningful operations and hadn't reported financial results in five years. And yet shares of a defunct company shot through the roof.

What's wrong with this picture? Stay-at-home orders shot Zoom's stock through the roof. With workers grounded, its valuation topped the six airlines' major stocks combined. The platform was a default virtual meeting app, helping global companies continue operating as people worked from home. Why did regulators act?

The SEC stepped in to protect traders from themselves. It's true, Zoom was high-flying pandemic stock. But a growing number of investors bought shares of the wrong stock. They traded the ticker symbol ZOOM (the dead company) versus ZM (the pandemic-era highflier). Herd mentality was so extreme that the herd didn't know what it was buying.

Around the same time, the Department of Homeland Security was working on a different issue. It warned wireless telecom operators and law enforcement agencies about pending assaults on cell towers and telecommunications employees.

Across Europe, arsonists took to the streets to burn down 5G towers.[3] In the bowels of Twitter, YouTube, and Facebook, a cornucopia of conspiracy theories about COVID-19 ran amok. A growing cohort believed that 5G technology caused the pandemic, including a range of celebrities like Woody Harrelson, John Cusack, and Keri Hilson.[4] Attackers eventually torched more than one hundred towers. There was no scientific evidence linking the pandemic to 5G.

As the COVID-19 virus rapidly propagated, the public found it challenging to grasp the nature of its transmission and impact. Desperate for explanations, scapegoating proliferated. Bill Gates found himself at the center of the storm. In 2015, Gates had warned that the greatest risk to humanity was not nuclear war but an infectious virus that could threaten millions of lives.[5] However, anti-vax advocates, QAnon, and right-wing freedom fighters saw his warning as evidence. They believed one of the world's wealthiest men planned to control the global health system. Digital mobs accused him of being responsible for the pandemic and claimed vaccines were a ploy to implant microchips in billions of people.

Disinformation about Gates prompted over sixteen thousand different Facebook posts, along with nine hundred thousand likes and comments.[6] The ten most popular YouTube videos spreading lies about Gates amassed millions of views. A weave of fear and uncertainty provided fertile ground for the defamation of public figures like him. A Pew

Research Center survey found that 25 percent of Americans believed in a conspiracy theory alleging that powerful people intentionally planned the coronavirus outbreak.[7]

As the surge of COVID conspiracies continued, one unexpected pragmatist emerged. Founded in the 1970s as a way to monetize low-quality cuts of meat, Steak-umm became an authoritative "random-as-hell" COVID information source.[8] Its Twitter account took an unlikely detour, pivoting toward becoming a voice of reason. It addressed the dangers of COVID misinformation and the need for critical thinking surrounding it. The surprising position struck a chord.

Steak-umm's social media manager, Nathan Allebach, struck internet gold with a public seeking straightforward, no-nonsense guidance. One tweet read, "Friendly reminder in times of uncertainty and misinformation: anecdotes are not data. (Good) data is carefully measured and collected information based on a range of subject-dependent factors, including, but not limited to, controlled variables, meta-analysis, and randomization."[9]

Allebach's fans included the scientific community, some of whom endorsed Steak-umm as a clearheaded voice for the masses. As unlikely as a scientific endorsement as the company is, the media showed appreciation as well. The *Wall Street Journal*, the *Atlantic*, the *Washington Post*, and Vox drew attention to Steak-umm's clear-eyed advice.[10] Allebach said, "What kind of a world are we living in where frozen beef is making this much sense?"[11]

Fact-Finding as a Game of Clue

In 2020, making sense of major events became a game of Clue. As access to information radically expanded, our capacity to make sense of or prepare for pending dangers rapidly diminished.

That the public was ill-prepared for COVID's catastrophic effects will be studied for generations. Security analysts and forecasters warned about pending dangers for years. Nonprofits like the Gates Foundation prepared for the eventuality through vaccine development. You could see the COVID-19 crisis coming months before it landed in the United States. And still, here in America, we weren't prepared for the moment.

A personal reflection on the timeline of events is instructive. Like those with business operations in China, I had an early read on what might come. In January 2020, the novel coronavirus brought Chinese cities to a standstill, leading our firm to close offices in Beijing, Shanghai, and Shenzhen. The crisis naturally led to speculation on its origin and the likelihood of it spreading to the United States and Europe.

Seeing the crisis unfold overseas and feeling a sense of panic, I went to Costco. We loaded up on a strange mix of rice, potatoes, bulk frozen items, flats of water, and, of course, toilet paper. I warned friends, families, and neighbors that a big one might be coming. They thought I was being overly alarmist. In January, even with a line of sight into China, I was the crazy one.

By early February, the World Health Organization had classified the virus as COVID-19.[12] When Italy became a global COVID-19 hotspot, the government issued Decree-Law No. 6., which locked down the country.[13] Two weeks later, the CDC's Dr. Nancy Messonnier held a telebriefing to warn the American public about the eventual spread of the virus. She said that the "disruption to everyday life may be severe."[14]

The World Health Organization classified COVID-19 as a pandemic on March 11, the same day Tom Hanks announced that he had contracted the virus.[15] NBA players walked off the floor mid-game.[16] Through popular culture—not medical guidance—it became the day of recognition (or so I thought).

NBC News polled US citizens about preparation for what was to come. Despite guidance and mounting evidence, remarkably, 56 percent of Americans believed that their lives would not change, or only very slightly. A glaring partisan divide shaped sentiment. Seventy-nine percent of Democrats felt that the worst was yet to come. Forty percent of Republicans held the same opinion.[17]

The lack of recognition that life would change was a remarkable oversight. Within days states began the lockdowns. People hoarded, panicked, and bought and sold stocks based on insider information. The enduring image of response became shoppers fighting over bulk packages of toilet paper.

The pandemic morphed from public health to an information crisis. By June, it was a political event. Egged on by President Trump to "save your great Second Amendment," anti-lockdown protesters took to the streets with signs saying COVID-19 was a lie.[18] Over six million people died from the virus. In 2021, it was the third leading cause of death in the United States.[19] The virus persists around the world. Understanding its health, economic, and social toll will take years to fully understand.

A Coherence Crash

Forecasters gravitate to things that don't fit, that defy common categorization or language. In consulting parlance, they're called "outliers." I've led a forecasting team at Weber Shandwick to monitor and classify them for the last five years. To inform our thinking, we systematically evaluate ideas on the fringe that, at first look, seem irrelevant. Given the data we aggregate, forecasting moved from nice-to-have to necessary and urgent.

In his book *Bots against Us*, cybersecurity analyst Alan Silberberg said, "The cyber world has taught me many lessons, but number one is when a pattern is not right it is almost always indicative of something more serious going on."[20] This includes media patterns.

By 2020, media outliers we tracked became so common, vast, and frequent they broke our models like a hammer to glass. We had to create something different. We needed networks of diverse experts to make sense of an anomalous pileup of pattern-breakers. It materialized through an open-access platform and a communal learning lab at Weber Shandwick. Media Genius, as it became known, included new cultural and media study guides, summer schools, and a thousand-person student-led community. It became a platform for us to document new, weird, and alarming effects of digital media proliferation.

The team tracked thousands of outliers dating back to 2018 to inform our thinking. We studied the human effects of technological innovations. New everyday media behaviors, genres, and roles emerged. Terms like *algorithmic bias, meme stocks, troll fighters, social credit scores,* and *NFTs* entered the vernacular. Our team worried about how darker media arts had become common, exemplified by pervasive mis- and disinformation campaigns.[21] As mediated life became all-consuming, we observed the rise of digital detoxes and media diets framed in the context of mental nutrition.

Weird went mainstream. Slime videos racked up billions of views. Dronestegrams, metaverse shows, and hearables altered how we experienced digital surroundings. All this, in turn, created new roles. A media metamorphosis created karma whores, meme debunkers, cyborg journalists, and computer-rendered influencers.

Digital life resembled a simulated experience to be gamed. People pretended to be dead on Instagram to get likes.[22] Teens racked up thousands of followers by posting the same photo every day.[23] Led by Peloton, people joined "stationary-biker gangs."[24]

There was a lot to take in. The velocity of the new created more noise than signal. To get a clearer read, we focused on a singular existential challenge: *How will people make sense of a world that doesn't make sense anymore?*

The question led to a research project conducted with the Institute for the Future and media theorist Douglas Rushkoff. It asked: What comes after a coherence rash? We found a singular commonality through field studies conducted in thirteen global markets.[25] We collectively got, as Rushkoff frames it, "present shocked."[26]

We simultaneously joined a sobering, painful process of adjusting to a new normal as COVID took hold. We rethought the meaning of career, family priorities, and life choices. We reconsidered who and what was essential. With familiar contexts collapsing, we did what humans do when facing a void: We improvised, adapted, and experimented to understand a changed world and our place in it.

The public hacked sensemaking. It happened without the aid of and in opposition to authorities. QAnon attracted millions to build a depiction of reality collaboratively.[27] Membership multiplied, prompting the creation of QAnon Facebook pages in over seventy countries worldwide. While there weren't definitive beliefs, all shared a core tenet—that a deplorable, corrupt cabal of insiders controlled the government. It was less important that people agreed on the details or overarching truth; what mattered was that a cause unified them.

Divisiveness and uncertainty led to new spiritual practices and forking of old ones. Spirit-seekers connected digitally to modernize witchcraft, tarot reading, mystical art, and divination meetups. DIY spiritualists sought new avenues for artistic expression, political activism, and safe spaces to have a voice, particularly among marginalized communities.

Meaning-making became ritualized. New genres of spirituality aided by how-to guides helped people build rituals to navigate uncertainty. Spirituality and politics blended. A group of over thirteen thousand witches and mystic enthusiasts called the #MagicResistance held monthly online gatherings. They cast "binding" spells on the president.[28]

A breakout outlier was WitchTok, a vibrant witchcraft community sparked on TikTok. Tarot readings and spells, tutorials, and educational videos about crystals, candles, and plants were live streamed via the platform. #Witch, #BabyWitch, and #WitchTok hashtags encouraged explorations of "magick" to be shared. Over 21 billion views and counting have been generated by videos labeled #WitchTok.[29]

As digital monitoring became more common, circumvention became another form of sensemaking and expression. On the subreddit r/UnethicalLifeProTips, users shared tips on how to avoid being monitored by proctoring software.[30] Students felt their privacy was being violated and were actively fighting back.

Lacking human touch, people turned to robots for social and emotional support. They used bots for playful encounters, companionship, advice, and mental health relief. They interacted with digital beings through texting, voice-activated commands, and role-playing. These bots included Gatebox, a virtual home robot designed as a voice-powered companion that cares for its "master." It lives in a glass shell that texts reminders (e.g., "Don't forget your umbrella") and sends girlfriend-like messages (e.g., "Can't wait to see you").[31] Another like it called Replika became a "digital friend" to over ten million people.

Life events took on a different form. People hosted funerals on Zoom. Mourners created virtual memorials inside the game *Animal Crossing*. Collectives created guides to help people design their services, complete with templates for service design, slideshows, and tips to help people create meaningful experiences.

Ceremonial innovations altered who could take part in them and how. One couple in Hangzhou, China, streamed their wedding on Bilibili, allowing viewers to leave likes, comments, and virtual gifts. In the end, they had more than one hundred thousand remote well-wishers.[32] Facing graduation cancellations, students at more than twenty schools and universities rebuilt their campuses in *Minecraft*. At the University of California, Berkeley, students built Blockley, a scale replica of the campus, a virtual college graduation, and a music festival, all in *Minecraft*.[33]

Bigger than each of these instances of change was a deeper pattern of behavior that the field study codified. Tens of millions of small autonomous acts amounted to revolutionary cultural change. The pandemic forced a mass adaptation aided by new apps, social networks, metaverses, and, most importantly, common human interests.

While some cases were isolated to the lockdown, the events of 2020 permanently broke conventions that indelibly changed our perspective.

The pandemic fast-tracked outliers we studied that otherwise would have taken years to take hold. The behaviors showed what life looks like after a coherence crash. We live in a fundamentally altered public sphere and a new collective sensibility.[34]

Fit Ideas Trump the Facts

Is it possible to find coherence as millions operate through their own convictions or versions of truth? Can polarization sweeping the globe be reversed? Are these even relevant questions to ask?

A controversial science category suggests there's more to these questions than meets the eye. Donald D. Hoffman, a professor of cognitive science at the University of California, Irvine, spent three decades studying perception, artificial intelligence, and evolutionary game theory.

Hoffman works in an academic and scientific community codifying the science of perspective. In the field of psychophysics, scientists unravel the mysteries between physical stimuli and perceptual response. They've found our perceptions are like masks, hiding reality's true face.

Hoffman uses computer speech to explain his ideas. He introduced a groundbreaking idea, the "interface theory of perception" (ITP), grounded in evolutionary psychology. His papers argue that perceptions direct behavior toward survival and reproduction, not truth.[35]

He tested the theory through simulations, based on a mathematical theorem that takes a quantitative measure of the extent to which the fitness-only strategy dominates the truth strategy, and of how it increases with the size of the perceptual space.[36] Hoffman's research confirmed that winning genes don't code for perceiving truth. Hoffman tested the theory through thousands of evolutionary computer simulations. Backing Darwin's case, his simulations said we're wired for survival, not fact-finding.[37]

Hoffman's computing metaphors run even deeper as he explains his theories. ITP posits that each of us is a conscious agent, acting with a unique perceptual interface. According to Hoffman, we unconsciously assess clues in each personal encounter. What we find influences our perceptions and decisions.[38] In social networks, conscious agents that shape us multiply and recombine to form new ones, creating an infinitely expanding intelligence network.

If Hoffman is right, we now inhabit a vast network of conscious agents that perceive, decide, and act together. While media narratives would lead us to believe otherwise, he's found that networks exhibit a degree of stability and order. The direction of network energy shapes what's deemed to be most fit as opposed to what's commonly viewed as correct. The ITP thesis suggests the pursuit of a unified understanding of "the truth" distracts from how we seek and find meaning.

Our cognition protects us from underlying complexities that shape it. Hoffman uses the blue rectangle metaphor to land this point.[39] The blue rectangular icon on a computer's desktop may be blue, rectangular, and situated in the bottom right corner. But it doesn't contain actual file processors, voltages, and software layers at work. By design, the blue rectangle hides the complex truth through simple icons so we can function.

Our perceptions are like the blue rectangle. They're an interface to navigate the intricacies of our environment. The metaphor also applies in more human terms. He notes that when you look in a mirror, you see skin, hair, eyes, lips, and the expression on your face. Beneath one's face lies a profound universe. Dreams, fears, interests, and experiences that shape our consciousness aren't apparent from our appearance. Much like a simple blue rectangle, our face serves as a facade, concealing the intricate world within and around us.[40]

Now consider Hoffman's theories in the context of ideas. We don't see the underworld of biases and machinations that mold collective actions. Through the Interface Theory of Perception, analogous to the natural world, depictions of reality vie for survival. A dominant idea today might face abrupt obsolescence tomorrow.

Hoffman says pursuing the fittest ideas rather than the absolute truth is based on scientific pragmatism. Just as Darwin's survival of the fittest theory focused on the adaptation of species, the same notion applies to beliefs.[41]

As forces of change alter depictions of reality, seeking "fitness" over "truth" allows us to better interpret and respond to change. How we've adjusted to the coherence crash of 2020 proves how adaptive and different our views can be.

CHAPTER 5

NETWORKS: MAKE NEW CONNECTIONS

Knowing how to look is a way of inventing.

—ATTRIBUTED TO SALVADOR DALÍ

In the 1980s, Alan Kay delivered a lecture emphasizing perspective as an essential problem-solving strategy. Kay was a giant in computing, known for his groundbreaking contributions to object-oriented programming and the graphical user interface (GUI). His visionary work at Xerox PARC laid the foundation for modern personal computing. Reaching such heights requires a special genius. He is believed to have stated in the lecture, "Perspective is worth eighty IQ points."

Over the last two decades, financial crises, Brexit, US elections, COVID-19, and climate impact left leaders surprised and unprepared. The sluggish reaction of leaders altered the economy, politics, and healthcare worldwide. There was much miscalculation in the system; a lack of perspective might be to blame.

For centuries people have struggled with mistaken perspectives. In the seventeenth century English painter William Hogarth created *Satire on*

False Perspective to remind us how deeply our views can be distorted. He used an array of optical illusions to present his case. One illusion displays a man lighting his pipe from a far-off candle.[1] Another features a group of sheep, which looks larger as it turns a corner. As you look deeper, you find a flag in the foreground that appears to vanish in the backdrop behind a distant tree, and many more.

Altogether, the painting includes twenty-two optical illusions. Hogarth included a warning: "Whoever makes a Design without the Knowledge of Perspective will be liable to such. Absurdities as are shown in this Frontispiece."[2]

Signs Hiding in Plain Sight

The 2016 US election night illuminated expert delusion. Nate Silver, the founder of FiveThirtyEight, was widely regarded as one of the most reliable pollsters in the country. He had Hillary Clinton at about a 70 percent chance of winning.[3] An ABC News/*Washington Post* poll conducted just a couple of weeks before the election showed Clinton with a twelve-point lead over Trump, with 50 percent support among likely voters compared to Trump's 38 percent. The *New York Times* tracker, a real-time information graphic of the election night coverage, showed Hillary Clinton's chances of winning at just north of 80 percent.[4]

As returns came in, the *Times*'s tracker image was inverted. When the clock struck midnight, Trump tracked at 80 percent. The image of reversal was striking. Turns out, everyone was wrong. The read might have been different had more been monitoring social media and coordinated activity among Trump's supporters. Through this perspective, a Trump victory was possible. You needed to see differently to sense it.

Months before the election, on September 28, 2016, Trump's first debate showing left much to be desired. Focus groups, polls, and commentators unanimously agreed that it was a clear win for Clinton. Even Trump's aides confessed that his performance missed the mark.[5]

Despite the failing grades, Trump declared victory. The statement wasn't typical unfounded bravado. On Twitter Trump crushed it. As cable news analysts piled on Trump's poor showing, #TrumpWon rocketed to Twitter's number-one trending topic.

Gilad Lotan, then the head of data science at Betaworks, investigated what happened. He published his analysis on *Medium*, buried in tens of thousands of hot takes, how-tos, and self-help briefs on the platform.[6] The post got a moderate reception based on claps (Medium's *like* button) and roughly a dozen comments. The lack of visibility didn't reflect the importance of what he discovered.

To get to the bottom of #TrumpWon, Lotan asked different questions than the Monday morning quarterbacks on TV: Why was everyone so obsessed with this hashtag? How could #TrumpWon be trending, given his performance? Was Russia or another foreign state in on amplifying the claim?

Lotan investigated the data for answers. Network maps he analyzed originally suggested a Russian link. One showed that the #TrumpWon hashtag originated from St. Petersburg. The *Washington Post* and other sources quickly debunked the claim as speculation grew about a Russian-backed campaign. He kept digging.

Further analysis showed that a coordinated group of accounts published the same message shortly after the debate. That night, around the world, surrogates tweeted victory claims. Ignited by a small number of accounts, Trump's virtual army went into action the next morning. Various online communities amplified hashtags #MAGA, #Trump2012, and #TGDN (Twitter Gulag Defense Network). The accounts featured words such as *God, America, family, proud, wife, mother, father,* and *veteran* prominently in their bios.[7]

The coordination was highly structured in its makeup. Network analysis showed that a coordinated, networked army of supporters didn't need the truth. Collective action ensured Trump was the winner. Through mass circulation of victory claims, #TrumpWon became the number-one trending topic worldwide.

Trump's mastery over networked news cycles continued throughout his campaign. Using Twitter as his platform, he simultaneously rallied his base, tested ideas, and trolled the media into amplifying his positions. According to the *New York Times*, Trump received the equivalent of $1.9 billion in television coverage during the first part of the 2016 campaign, having spent only $10 million on paid advertising. It is also twice the estimated $746 million that Hillary Clinton took in, the next best at earning media attention.

In 2016, the Trump campaign galvanized message board enthusiasts, Facebook's older demographic, Twitter activists, and Reddit communities. Together they disseminated so many memes that they began to believe—both jokingly and not—that their "meme magic" had helped Trump win the election.[8]

Claire Wardle, a leading expert on misinformation and disinformation threats, suggested a low network IQ was to blame for mainstream oversights. She told me the problem lies in conflicting views of how information flows and how those in power interpret it. "Things go out from companies, media, and health and security organizations that are out of sync with how the rest of the world works."[9]

In September, mobilizing networks won the night. In November, Trump won the election. The incumbent political and media class never saw it coming.

The Decay of Ivory Tower Trust

Gaps in accurate, credible guidance from institutions now span politics, religion, media, technology, and finance. Since 1975 Gallup numbers show a stark drop in public trust in authoritative sources spanning medicine, faith, news, government, and business.

Seeing this decline over time is telling. In 2022, only 7 percent of Americans had a great deal or quite a lot of confidence in Congress, compared to 42 percent in 1973. Trust in organized religion dropped from 65 to 31 percent over the same period. Increased internet access also affected confidence in TV news and newspapers. These institutions declined to 11 percent and 14 percent, respectively, in 2022, compared to 46 percent and 31 percent in 1993.[10]

It's assured that waves of mistrust will continue for institutions not fully sensitized to the Autonomous Age. Let's again project into the near future how vastly different and atomized the media environment will be.

Imagine a world where dispersed sources (and many independents powered by generative AI) out-influence mega-media brands and elites. These sources get to know what resonates with us on a deeply personal level, analyzing our interests, motivations, and preferred modes of communication. Unlike social media feeds, these will feel like virtual advisors always with us, adapting their gender, communication style, timing, and response to our needs. These will be empowering or disempowering. In the wrong hands, these bots will manipulate how we think, what we believe, and how we act.

New "micro-networks" will attract groups of like-minded cohorts into private encrypted networks. They will operate as gated communities based on mutual interests, similar income strata, and, increasingly, willingness to pay for high-quality information and influential connections. They will span politics, business, culture, paramilitary, organized crime, and more. These micro-networks will operate without detection from surveillance efforts and wield influence in ways we can't see.

In parallel, industrial-grade chatbots will displace the public internet as the first stop for seeking information. We will bypass what's left of the public web, overloaded with crap content produced by adversarial media fighters, AIs, and an influx of deep fakes. The "unbelievability" of unverified material will destroy any sense of trust left in non-networked authorities.

Given an influx of life-changing events, we will seek news and analysis even more than we do today. As AI systems handle more and more communication, it will become harder for us to know who or what is responsible for our news and information.

New trust markets will help us. Simulated experts, be they avatars or manifestations of collective intelligence, will increasingly be recognized as trusted agents. Just as there are markets that influence the valuation of stocks based on performance and potential, new "perspective markets" will feature trusted agents bidding up and down, much like securities on a stock exchange.

Individuals and organizations will have the opportunity to invest or "buy into" these agents when they are on an upward trend, signaling their growing credibility and influence. As these agents gain momentum and trend upward, they will seamlessly integrate into large language models (LLMs), brain-computer interfaces (BCIs), and expansive virtual worlds, expanding their reach and impact.

The movements and valuations of these agents won't be arbitrary. They will be driven by collective trust and credibility. This system inherently filters out superficiality, diminishing the influence of performative posturing and overtly manufactured personas.

We will make sense of the world collaboratively, choosing the "fittest sources" over deferring to heads of state, experts, or the media. Those who earn respect in the network by creating value will ascend as central figures in the network. The respect will equally apply to machines or people with outside contributions to the community. This scenario isn't science fiction. Engineers are working on all ingredients now.

A growing misguided class, absent the network IQ Wardle referred to, won't see fundamental changes coming to our information sphere until it's too late. They will fail to recognize that the atomization of media and influence that stems from it is already here.

Effects of Networked Collectives

Wall Street has long exhibited high digital intelligence, profiting from high-frequency trading systems, electronic platforms, and blockchain innovations. But even masters of the financial universe can miss moves percolating in social networks.

In one breakout case, analysts watched in disbelief at the beginning of 2021 as a small group of stocks defied gravity. Redditors on r/WallStreetBets and networks of Discord users invested heavily in shorted stocks, causing prices in GameStop, AMC, and Tesla to soar.

The stock market was abuzz with a new trading phenomenon created in social media forums. The term *meme stock* became part of investing vernacular, a derivative of cultural memes institutionalized at places like BuzzFeed.

Meme stocks came by way of cult-like fervor in digital forums. GameStop was symbolic of new network energy. From an institutional view, it was a loser, a chain of brick-and-mortar stores on a similar path to bankruptcy as Blockbuster Video. For insurgent traders in the forums, fundamentals didn't matter. Participants traded by new rules, collective action, and new vocabulary. Forum members bid up prices, buying it en masse and holding on for dear life. Traders doubled their positions by the day, chanting "diamond hands" and "to the moon." When market swings were ensured, a shared mission led traders to hold on to their shares rather than cash out.

The movement went beyond profit motives alone. Some joined as populists. Meme traders banded together to stick it to hedge funds heads.[11] From January 4 until January 29, GameStop's shares rose from $17.25 to nearly $325, a leap of 1,800 percent. One fund, Melvin Capital, lost nearly half its value to the tune of roughly $7 billion.[12]

Meme stocks morphed from a trading oddity into a cultural sensation. Wall Street scoffed at novice traders, taking to financial media to downplay their impact and call for collusion investigations. Reddit users celebrated their success as a David and Goliath story, a victory for the little guy over the titans of finance (or so the narrative went). On January 29, 2022, GameStop reached its peak value, trading 8,000 percent higher than it had the year before.[13]

Did the Apes, as they're known, overthrow the establishment? Not necessarily. But the spectacle's impact endured. Once GameStop caught the public's imagination, Wall Street could no longer dismiss social network influence on markets. Collective action forced analysts to see the market differently.

For some, WallStreetBets was an expensive lesson in perspective. "If you don't have a clear view of what retail is up to, it feels like you're driving partially blind," Chris Berthe, JPMorgan's global cohead of cash equities trading, told Bloomberg.[14] Spencer Jakab, a *Wall Street Journal* columnist, added, "I think what's changed is that Wall Street is totally aware of what's going on. They will not get caught out in the same way again."[15]

While returns from meme stocks have waned since 2021, the practice led to structural change in finance. According to the *Financial Times*, the companies at the center of the meme-stock mania have raised a collective $4.7 billion from speculative hype since the trading frenzy.[16] Analysts and financiers had a new, highly variable social factor influencing their models.

Attacks beneath the Surface

In the wake of Brexit and Trump's election in 2016, I regularly met with media figures, policy wonks, and research teams trying to make sense of mis- and disinformation changing politics and finance.

The read wasn't encouraging. Most I spoke with lamented Trump and Brexit oversights, the (miscalculated) absurdity of a reality TV star in the White House, and their role in protecting "the truth."

Those with network know-how sounded a different alarm. They claimed that we had run out of time to combat disinformation campaigns, trolls, and coordinated online attacks. The data showed that the use of media to wage conflict, extort, gain power, and ignite petty arguments was expanding rapidly.

In 2022, *Fortune* editors flagged mis- and disinformation as an emerging cybersecurity threat to global organizations. Featured in its *Fortune* 500 issue, an ominous headline read, "A growing army of online trolls is using dangerous lies to take down executives and companies. Now they're coming for you."[17]

By 2022, deliberate, coordinated media attacks had corrupted America's political system. Scammers, profiteers, and competitive states were coming for businesses and CEOs. According to Paul Kolbe, a director at the Harvard Kennedy School, "Compared to government targets, the private sector has an even richer and larger playing field and a . . . far more vulnerable audience. And it's only going to get worse."[18]

Given the growing threat, it made sense that the Department of Homeland Security (DHS) formed a Disinformation Governance Board that year to blunt the challenge. Hours after word got out, the government backpedaled. Given the gravity of the situation, why did they do that?

The DHS overlooked retaliatory action mastered by digital insurgents. The DHS played directly into the opposition's trap. Resistors immediately branded the unit an Orwellian "Ministry of Truth." In coordination they flooded social networks and cable news with First Amendment messaging and personal smears. #MinistryOfTruth trended on Twitter for two days after the news broke. (The @ministryoftruth account has more than 340,000 followers at the time of writing.)[19]

Nina Jankowicz, a Wilson Center fellow chosen to lead the group by DHS, was barraged with abuse, harassment, and death threats. Right-wing media propagated attacks throughout its vast ecosystem of social media accounts, digital media sites, radio, and TV programs. Tucker Carlson, reaching 2.5 million nightly viewers, warned of a "new Soviet America" in which the state was about to "get men with guns to tell you to shut up."[20] It was catnip for the Right's digitally fluent culture warriors.

DHS needed to act. In a press statement, the DHS said, "The Board has been grossly and intentionally mischaracterized: It was never about censorship or policing speech in any manner. It was designed to ensure we fulfill our mission to protect the homeland while protecting core Constitutional rights." The spokesperson added, "However, false attacks have become a significant distraction from the Department's vitally important work to combat disinformation that threatens the safety and security of the American people."[21]

The organization disbanded in less than three weeks. Somehow, the DHS overlooked information conflict in its strategy. The Associated Press noted that the little credible information about it made the effort an instant target for criticism.[22] The *Washington Post* described the board as falling victim to "a textbook disinformation campaign" about its mission, to which it failed to respond adequately.[23] The *American Conservative* called the board "a cautionary note on how dangerously out of touch Washington is."[24] How could the administration have been so unprepared?

Avoiding the Content Trap

The physics of media propagation have long been a subject of academic and intelligence research. Research into the nature of network behavior proves our ideas about ourselves and how society works are often wrong.

For instance, after the 2016 election a media science team from MIT, headed by Sinan Aral and Deb Roy, confirmed that fake news disseminates more rapidly and extensively than accurate information. The data showed that untrue statements were shared about 70 percent more frequently on Twitter than the truth. Falsehoods reached 1,500 people six times faster than accurate information. Aral and Roy attributed it to a "novelty hypothesis," suggesting that because false news was more unusual than the truth, it was more likely to be shared.[25]

Beyond whether a piece of media has a basis in truth, strategists often miss connections and momentum each piece of media can create. Bharat N. Anand, vice provost for Advances in Learning at Harvard, refers to these oversights as a "content trap." According to Anand, connections are the heart of what shapes any digitally touched business. He says, "Recognizing, leveraging, and managing connections separates companies that succeed from those that fail."[26]

Anand says influence is gained more through connections and momentum (how people react) than the content, performance, or action (what leaders and organizations project). The content trap is informative when considering how experts judge situations. They fall into the same trap, as seen in exhibit 4.

In the case of the presidential debate, the expert view was based on the debate performance (Trump bombed). With WallStreetBets, the media narrative centered on the absurdity of skyrocketing prices absent sound finances (GameStop was a loser). On the DHS policy, the department answered the call (a necessary organizational solution). In a media context, conventional judgment rested on a political performance, market fundamentals, and a necessary policy.

Exhibit 4: The Content Trap

	TRUMP DEBATE PERFORMANCE	DEADBEAT STOCKS	DHS DISINFORMATION BOARD
TRADITIONAL VIEW	Trump clearly lost the debate. He was unprepared and ineffective.	Clear losers based on market fundamentals; potential windfall for short sellers	Growing need to protect organizations from information attacks warranted a new board.
NETWORK VIEW	#TrumpWon was propagated by coordinated accounts.	Social mobilization creates new fundamental; collective trades push stocks like GameStop "to the moon."	A coordinated and potent disinformation campaign branded the board the Ministry of Truth and attacked its efforts on multiple fronts.
ENDGAME	Trump won the election by mobilizing advocates and playing to his base.	Meme stocks become a trading category; traders create chaos; hedge funds (e.g., Melvin) take $7 billion hit.	The Disinformation Board was shut down in three weeks.

A network perspective changes the view. Trump didn't need a winning performance in a normative sense. He relied on network coordination to win the night (and then the election). Redditors didn't need good stocks to bet on; they aggregated collective influence to make a profit at the expense of short sellers (which they accomplished). Freedom fighters didn't need a legislative opening to inform their information war strategies (coordinated response defined it). In each case victory came from a different perspective. Insurgents saw mobilizing the power of networks as the means to win.

Network Sensibilities as the New Edge

Those blind to network forces can't see them or address asymmetrical advantages that more digitally fit players have. Just as much as innate intelligence or EQ, network intelligence (NQ) is now the difference maker.

Joshua Cooper Ramo, co-chief executive of Kissinger Associates, calls this sensibility a "Seventh Sense." He posits that those with it are far better equipped to adapt and thrive in a digitally connected society. As Ramo puts it, "The Seventh Sense is the ability to look at any object and see the way in which it is changed by connection."[27] He believes the failure to spot, understand, and use connected power will be a source of our biggest future tragedies.

This idea explains developments like the rise of terrorist networks like ISIS, how Facebook amassed billion of users, or the mobilizing impact of #MeToo. Network intelligence becomes even more essential with the ascendance of AI into all facets of society.

The implications for leading in a networked world are profound. As we close out the first section, the case is clear that a wide-ranging, 360-degree view of new developments is necessary. The influx of technology into every aspect of our lives has profound, cascading effects on how we perceive external events.

We now turn to the human dynamics shaping fundamental change—how tech alters us and what we accept as "normal" going forward.

PART II

BELIEFS IN TRANSITION

When technology and human lives are intricately woven, we change. Do we develop new senses as we assimilate into a complex web of connections? How does our nervous system respond when subjected to relentless external forces? And, most urgently, can we truly shape our destiny when we are influenced simultaneously by people and intelligent machines?

The questions challenge traditional understandings of the self. As we stand at the doorstep of a different era, we now delve deep into the very essence of our being, examining how technology reshapes our life experiences and redefines what it means to be human.

In this part, we investigate questions of humanity and how technology reshapes our understanding of the self, work, relationships, and spirituality. We must understand how digital connection changes us to chart a path forward.

CHAPTER 6

IDENTITY: PEER INTO INNER WORLDS

When the gap between ideal and real becomes too wide, the system breaks down.

—**BARBARA TUCHMAN**[1]

"Welcome to a new beginning." These words open the defining scene in Apple TV's sci-fi thriller *Severance*.[2] The series captures the horrifying effects of different identities within the same person. Operations conducted by Lumen Industries split their employees' brains in two, creating a neural partition isolating work and personal life. It divides the characters' lived experiences into two separate arenas.

In the scene, Helly tells her future self that this procedure offers a healthy work-life balance. After the severance procedure, her personal self will be free to focus on relationships, hobbies, and self-care. It will also empower her to excel in her work life without personal stress and distraction. And yet there's an eerie undertone to Helly's decision. The camera lingers on her anxious face. As she listens to the clinician completing the separation, Helly contemplates the life-altering decision she's just made.

This scene prompts questions. Are the show's producers using metaphors to explain our own severed identities? Should we contemplate tech effects when using life-altering technologies? What happens to us when new agents unknowingly and permanently shape our lives?

Identity experts warn that technology alters our sensibilities from the inside out. With rapid changes happening to us, an unsettling question arises: Will we truly know who we are anymore?

The Fracturing of the Self

Sherry Turkle is a preeminent thinker on technology's human impact. A staunch proponent of human-centered values, Turkle has long studied the interplay between technology and personal agency. She's worked alongside the vanguard of psychoanalysis and artificial intelligence, including Jacques Lacan, Victor Turner, David Riesman, Marvin Minsky, and Seymour Papert (her first husband). Since 1976 she's immersed herself in studies of how computers introduce changes in psychology and philosophy. Central to her investigation is identity, what psychologists characterize as a person's intrinsic guiding force.

On a social level, identity is about presenting ourselves to others. In the digital realm, it also assumes a transactional nature, built through usernames, passwords, location, and biometric data that allow us to engage with online services. Turkle's research sheds light on changes to us as digital platforms shape our lives, relationships, and inner life.

A 1984 *New York Times* review of Turkle's first book, *The Second Self*, called it "the first ethnographic study of the 'computer world.'"[3] In the book, she predicted that computing would materially affect human development.[4] Turkle was among the first to examine how computing facilitates the creation of "second selves," much like viewers can see brought to life in *Severance*. She suggested that future virtual worlds would function as identity labs, a stage where people could experiment with various roles and simulations they devised themselves without the scrutiny seen in the real world.

Through identity construction and experimentation, Turkle saw a distinctly different prospect for human life. She predicted that the internet would facilitate a metamorphosis in humanity. It would accelerate the decentralization and disembodiment of the self. Our physical realities would no longer bind us. Online, we would be fluid and exploratory.

Turkle envisioned decentered individuals shifting identities as they traversed digital platforms. Each encounter would serve as a pilot for self-exploration. People would present different aspects of their lives, including interests, relationships, and behaviors. They would experiment with new roles and identifiers, unburdened by the fear of judgment or rejection. Ongoing experimentation would blur the lines between what people perceive as real or not.

In the 1980s, Turkle tested her ideas by studying how people interacted in early virtual communities called MUDs (multi-user dimensions). In role-playing games users created imaginary characters in fictitious worlds. Turkle's ethnographies revealed that the experiences of embodied lives in the physical world held no greater reality than role-playing games on the internet. The line between virtual reality and real life is blurred in MUDs.[5]

None of the self-made characters were any less real than what they thought of as their true selves. Some spent up to forty hours a week constructing lives more expansive than ones in the physical world. Turkle said, "In sum, MUDs blurred the boundaries between self and game, self and role, self and simulation. One player says, 'You are what you pretend to be. . . . You are what you play.'"[6]

Digital role-play demonstrated people's inclination to deconstruct or de-actualize reality. Virtual worlds would be a setting for acting out fantasies and aspirations. Turkle discovered that the divide between virtual and real life would cease.

Who Owns "Us" in the Future?

Tracey Follows is another expert in identity construction. In addition to transformations uncovered by Turkle, her investigations include legal and governmental concerns with the digital self. Follows warns of grave implications as we transcend physical and cognitive boundaries. She posits that identity-related conflicts hold significant risks on par with other existential crises, including climate change.

There is a clear rationale behind the claim. She told me, "The biology of the self and the psychology of self is now joined by a third dimension: the technology of the self. We don't own that technology. So we don't own the self anymore."[7]

Follows notes in her groundbreaking book, *The Future of You*, that technologies shape our identity, even if we don't craft an alternate or "second self" on our own.[8] The data we produce create profiles with consequences we can't see.

To put it in context, she talks of code-switching. We've always had different roles in different contexts. We play wife, husband, mother, friend, and coworker. We also define ourselves through our lifestyles, interests, and fandoms. The added digital dimension is that we can now create fully fictional versions of ourselves. We have actual roles in the physical world and imaginary roles in virtual ones. Whether based in reality or not, we play to a profile.

Follows says a casualty of identity construction is authenticity. The authentic self was best suited for an analog world. When we meet someone in real life, we can see their physical characteristics. We can get to feel, analyze, and even smell them. In the physical world, we know who they are, and that instills trust.[9] In virtual environments we don't have the same clues to go on now. Follows says authenticity can't be the standard by which we judge someone. She added, "It's more to do with prolificity. The integrity of the self loses value when we're distributed across the Internet."[10]

We rarely think about abstractions like identity. Follows told me it's like the issue of security. "Nobody wants to talk about security because it's boring, it's dull. We don't always have a conscious sense of our actions or feel adverse effects on how we show up. So why should we bother?"[11]

Think about our rights. In the digital world, we don't fully own ourselves anymore. Today our identity is shaped and surveilled. Brain-computer interfaces—behavior-altering technologies embedded inside us—are coming. When that happens, companies and governments can direct our behaviors. Follows says we must fight for our rights—and souls—by considering how computer-augmented life reshapes us.

Identity-Building in Real Life

I first became aware of the life-changing effects of computer-enabled identity construction at PopTech, a social innovation conference in Camden, Maine. In 2009, a user-experience designer, Nicholas Felton, brought the new potential to life through a groundbreaking data visualization project. There, Felton presented his "Feltron Report" to the packed conference.[12]

Felton summarized his year in data for friends and family. The report presented a numeric snapshot of his travels, his most-listened-to songs, and daily meals. His first summary led to a series of personal annual reports, exhibiting a design caliber found in financial reports of publicly traded companies. It started as nothing more than a passion project.

Felton's visualizations became a new art form and probe, suggesting what a "datafied self" would look like in the future. Major museums like the Museum of Modern Art and the San Francisco Museum of Modern Art exhibited his work. Felton's designs contributed to acceleration of the quantified-self movement. As his project progressed, Felton stumbled on an insight that is obvious today but was obscure back then: The deeper he looked, the more his behaviors could be quantified.[13]

Felton's Fitbit counted his steps, while his Nike FuelBand kept tabs on physical activity, heart rate, and sleep patterns. In his car, sensors provided feedback on driving routes and fuel efficiency. He employed RescueTime to monitor app and website usage. As data piled up, an unease emerged from the sheer volume of information he had collected and scrutinized. Questions surfaced about whether Felton's self-tracking altered his behavior.

Stanford University researchers Nick Yee and Jeremy Bailenson refer to this altered state as the "Proteus Effect."[14] They found that real-life behaviors aligned with the traits associated with people's avatars. In Felton's case, his avatars were data visualizations, with rich and diverse input painting a numeric picture.

The Proteus Effect raises questions. How much do our behaviors change if we identify with varied digital depictions? How do we think of ourselves as we align or don't with our creations? Are there more enduring consequences of the way we think of ourselves?

Self-quantification to improve health is a way of investigating these questions. It's now pervasive, driven by wearable technologies functioning as health barometers. Analysts estimate that the global quantified-self market is poised to reach USD $386 billion by 2028.[15]

Today, Fitbits tally our steps. Apple Watches guide and track workouts, capture metrics, and warn of heart irregularities. Muse uses brain scans to measure meditation and sleep performance, improvement, and consistency. Self-quantification agents are a primary function in an extensive array of exercise equipment, health devices, and nutrition apps such as Peloton, MyFitnessPal, Strava, and Noom.

As self-tracking apps become widespread, social engineering takes on a new dimension, different from top-down governance or legislative actions.

For example, consider the widely accepted 10,000-step rule. Its roots can be traced back to 1965, when a Japanese company developed Manpo-Kei, a "10,000 steps meter."[16] Although some studies demonstrated health benefits associated with 10,000 steps, research from Harvard Medical School found that, on average, around 4,400 steps per day significantly reduced the risk of death in women.[17] Another study involving nearly 5,000 middle-aged people of diverse ethnic backgrounds found that 10,000 daily steps wasn't necessary for longevity. Participants who walked 8,000 steps daily had half the risk of premature death from heart disease.[18]

The specific number—10,000, 8,000, or 4,000—isn't the crux of the matter. A blend of marketing myth, an inexact science, and the prevalence of wearable devices cemented the 10,000-step goal as a standard measure.

The Pros and Cons of Self-Tracking

The quantified self presents inherent benefits and challenges. Our lives can now be meticulously documented, with levels of detail far exceeding Felton's reports. Among the various apps I've used, WHOOP stands out for its depth and presentation of health data. Like other wearables, WHOOP monitors biometrics such as exercise routines, sleep quality, and resting heart rate. It distinguishes itself by redefining metrics around performance, recovery, and strain (the intensity of training or exertion). Its value is validated by some of the best trainers and athletes worldwide, including Rory McIlroy, Michael Phelps, Sloane Stephens, and Patrick Mahomes.

Analyzing user data helps WHOOP uncover empirical evidence to guide health decisions. For example, data aggregated from WHOOP users shows that alcohol consumption is one of the most harmful behaviors affecting physical recovery and well-being.[19] Even one drink proved to have a material impact on health scores. By comparison, marijuana use had a mixed impact on recovery and sleep. It gave users, on average, ten extra minutes of sleep per night, 2.4 percent better sleep performance than average.[20]

Potential benefits of data-backed insights from apps like WHOOP are clear. Less so is where our data goes and how it can be used. The data we create influence decisions made for us, such as creditworthiness or job suitability.

Digital identifiers raise safety and security concerns. Following the overturning of *Roe v. Wade* in 2022, users of period-tracking apps in the United States were advised to remove them because of mounting worries that they could incriminate women considering an abortion. One popular app called Flo, with forty-three million users, found itself in the crosshairs of the Federal Trade Commission (FTC) for failing to disclose how users' data was being shared.

The *Wall Street Journal* reported that Flo had notified Facebook whenever users were menstruating or attempting to conceive.[21] Flo ultimately reached a settlement with the FTC. FTC Commissioner Rebecca Kelly Slaughter said, "Apps that collect, use, and share sensitive health information can provide valuable services, but consumers need to be able to trust these apps. This incident underscores the importance of privacy and transparency, where personal information can quickly become a commodity for commercial and governmental control."[22]

Online profiles can become social credit scores, a grade for our standing in society. These manifest as metrics in various applications such as Uber ratings and Super Host reputations on Airbnb. Privacy advocates turn to China as a glimpse into how these scores might eventually penetrate everyday existence.

China's open social credit system grants scores to all citizens and businesses based on their actions. The system allows the Chinese government to oversee *cheng xin*: trustworthiness, honesty, integrity, sincerity, and morality.[23]

China's Central Bank and the Ministry of Public Security control the country's surveillance programs. The government uses big data, artificial intelligence, and over two hundred million surveillance cameras to monitor citizens' behavior. If someone is caught jaywalking, not paying court-mandated fees, or playing music too loudly on the train, they lose certain rights. When fully deployed, national social credit scores will be assigned to China's citizens for life.[24]

In one case, journalist Liu Hu was arrested and accused of "fabricating and spreading rumors" in 2013. Years later he faced state-imposed restrictions on buying property, taking out a loan, or traveling on the country's top-tier trains. He said, "There was no file, no police warrant, no official advance notification. They just cut me off from the things I was once entitled to. What's really scary is there's nothing you can do about it. You can report to no one. You are stuck in the middle of nowhere."[25]

Critics, particularly in the West, frame the practice as Orwellian. And yet many Chinese citizens allegedly approve of it.[26] Surveillance helps discourage activities such as tax evasion, gambling, and jaywalking. In addition, the system also incentivizes positive acts such as volunteering and charitable giving.

How will these measures affect personal agency? Or lead to a subconscious dissonance? What does your life look like when your every move is watched or rated? These questions aren't isolated to government surveillance or predatory data practices. Judgment is hardwired into the digital culture now.

Identity in the Eyes of the Beholder

Cultural theorist and head of foresight for Reddit Matt Klein uncovered a nuanced, consequential example of how digital interactions reshape us, noting how audiences exert control over creators. Klein's Audience Capture theory suggests that audiences hypnotize creators, creating a drag on originality, well-being, and mental health. His theory upends the traditional performer-audience relationship. Pre-internet, creators presented their work to evoke reactions or emotional responses. Now they "optimize" for positive feedback, some even censoring themselves to win the approval of followers.[27]

Klein's idea builds on Erving Goffman's Presentation of Self theory for the digital age.[28] In 1956, Goffman analyzed the extent to which we project different personas depending on the context or situation. Goffman notes that we've always been performers. Our behavior varies when interacting with bosses, friends, or family.

In the past, identity-switching was limited and private. But online, self-presentation is immortalized and accessible to all, including uninvited onlookers. Klein stresses that this perpetual spotlight invites judgment on a scale beyond our comprehension or initial intention, shaping our identities and creations.[29]

The downside of Klein's theory is seen through the subtle yet damaging influence of beauty filters. Face filtering and rating began when RateMyFace caused a stir in 1999 as one of the first sites to calculate and judge attractiveness. Hot or Not further popularized the idea, allowing users to rate photos submitted voluntarily by others.[30] Mark Zuckerberg's FaceMash was a derivative "hot or not" game for Harvard students, where visitors could compare two students' pictures side by side and vote on them.[31] The site's virality at Harvard and beyond made it the precursor to Facebook. The trend took a darker turn in 2007 with BecauseImHot, which removed users rated below seven from its site.[32]

These websites revolutionized the notion of beauty being in the eye of the beholder. Algorithms turned assessment into hard science. In a study published by the journal *Vision Research* in 2009, researchers from the University of Toronto discovered that the secret to a flawless face lies in measuring the spaces between the eyes, mouth, and ears.[33]

Participants were asked to evaluate the attractiveness of photographs of women where the distances between these facial features were either extended or shortened while keeping the features unchanged. Through this experiment, the researchers determined the most appealing facial ratios. Such studies informed how algorithms would rate and compare photographs.

Millions of young women later found face filters to be integral to their online presence. One research study found that 90 percent of young women use filters to edit their photos.[34] They whiten their teeth, shed weight, and reshape facial features. Beyond testing enhancements, these profiles feed media algorithms. Instagram's Explore pages determine which faces and bodies attract the most likes. Snapchat filters help users create and conform to "ideal" beauty standards.

These filters escalated in parallel with photo networking popularized by Snapchat and Instagram. Snapchat, the pioneer of camera-centric social networks, made photos the primary language of its app. Instant messaging through pictures transformed the selfie into a primary means of conveying emotions, reactions, and moods.[35]

From an early age, these influences have a profound psychological impact. Claire Kathryn Pescott, a PhD researcher specializing in childhood, social media, and identity at the University of South Wales, found two main motivations behind face filters, with noticeable gender disparity.

Boys used filters to cheer people up, entertain others, or just look funny. In contrast, girls used them to alter and enhance their appearance.

Some research subjects went further, saying they use them "to make you look prettier and unrecognizable." One child said, "I wish I were wearing a filter right now," reinforcing how reliant kids can be on them.[36] It's worth noting that her interview subjects were ten- and eleven-year-olds. The minimum age to open an account on the most popular platforms, including TikTok, Instagram, Twitter, YouTube, and Snapchat, is thirteen.[37]

Like putting on makeup, millions habitually use filters that sharpen, shrink, enhance, and color their faces and bodies. But unlike cosmetic enhancement, digital filters present fictional versions of ourselves. At what point did augmented reality filters and beauty algorithms go from fun to dangerous?

A Canadian study for the Dove Self-Esteem Project exposed a confidence crisis among young girls. The survey, targeting ten- to seventeen-year-old Canadian girls, showed that 80 percent had modified their appearance using filters or apps by age thirteen. Additionally, 67 percent tried to conceal or alter body features before posting photos, while 59 percent with low body esteem manipulated their images before sharing them online. Furthermore, 37 percent admitted feeling insufficiently attractive to post unedited photos of themselves.[38]

Caroline Rocha, a makeup artist turned "filter queen," was naturally drawn into this world. She studied art history in school and saw the potential for filters to create unique and beautiful images. Her Instagram profile, @frenchsinger, presented a gallery transmuting camera effects into art.[39]

Rocha became a beauty influencer as she became more involved in the AR (augmented reality) creator community. She experimented with different filters and shared them with her growing list of followers. While she rode the wave of self-beautification, Rocha saw women using filters nonstop. She said, "They refuse to be seen without these filters because, in their mind, they think they look like that." She added, "It became, for me, a bit sick."[40]

The Blur Between the Real and Unreal Self

For some, filtering became an addiction. Algorithm-induced beautification led millions to seek plastic surgery or cosmetic services. Writing for the *New Yorker*, Jia Tolentino shed light on the odd outcome of filtered media, "the gradual emergence, among professionally beautiful women, of a single, cyborgian face." Tolentino said, "It's as if every woman would be a direct descendant of Kim Kardashian West, Bella Hadid, Emily Ratajkowski, or Kendall Jenner." She called it "Instagram Face," which looks like "it's made of clay."[41]

A makeup artist Tolentino interviewed talked of how pervasive this standard became among the beauty conscious. "I think 95 percent of the most-followed people on Instagram use FaceTune. And I would say that 95 percent of these people have also had some sort of cosmetic procedure."[42]

Filtering led to new mental illnesses investigated by psychiatric experts. Researchers at the Boston Medical Center wrote about a neurosis called "Snapchat dysmorphia," which exhibits as compulsive acts like excessive beauty procedures, obsession over nonexistent flaws, and withdrawal from social activities.[43] The trend was particularly concerning, as Snapchat filters shape idealistic beauty standards—in some cases entirely inhuman ones. Psychologists warned that filters lead to "an unattainable look and are blurring the line of reality and fantasy for patients."[44]

Pandemic lockdowns exacerbated the issue. Continuous exposure to ourselves during video calls led more to analyze and critique their looks. Cosmetic doctors and plastic surgeons across the globe witnessed a surge in appointments for surgical and nonsurgical procedures following the lockdown, with notable spikes in Australia, the United States, the United Kingdom, Japan, and South Korea. Trend spotters called it the "Zoom Boom."[45]

During the lockdown, Save Face, a UK government-approved register of accredited cosmetic practitioners, saw 40 percent more traffic to its website. In parallel, a class of celebrity plastic surgeons went mainstream on social media. Dr. Michael Miroshnik became one of the most popular specialist plastic surgeons, famous for his breast surgery and "designer cleavage." Dr. Anthony Youn, "America's holistic plastic surgeon," gained over eight million followers on TikTok.[46] Dr. Miami built a mass following on Snapchat and Instagram through live-streamed surgeries and behind-the-scenes counsel.[47]

Demand for cosmetic surgery, driven by women under forty-five, surged after the pandemic. The American Society of Plastic Surgeons found more than three-quarters of cosmetic-focused plastic surgery practices saw more business than before the pandemic, with nearly 30 percent reporting their business has at least doubled.[48]

Beauty filters exemplify the potentially dangerous effects of the perspective agents we use. Tolentino says, "I couldn't shake the feeling that technology is rewriting our bodies to correspond to its interests—rearranging our faces according to whatever increases engagement and likes. . . . It can seem sensible, even automatic, to think of your body as a McKinsey consultant would think about a corporation."[49]

In Europe, government officials took action to regulate their use. In Norway influencers were forced to disclose whether a photo they posted had been retouched. Similarly, the French government pursued a bill that would put strict regulations on influencers, making it mandatory for them to label filtered or doctored images. It also banned them from promoting cosmetic surgery through paid partnerships.[50] The country's finance minister, Bruno Le Maire, said the measures would help "limit the destructive psychological effects of these practices on Internauts' esteem."[51]

Beyond regulation, a social media countermovement made "natural presentation" the norm. Filter rebellions on TikTok reversed the virtual beautification trend, posting beauty-filtered images then removing the filters to reveal their actual face. In a specific instance, TikTok influencer Charli D'Amelio's before-and-after post garnered over nine million views. Her fans have praised her for participating in the trend, earning praise for being "so real."[52]

When our Futures team at Weber Shandwick investigated information disorders, we broadened the definition to include media formats that deceive and ultimately lead to harm. With the mass adoption of AR filters, we found it important to look at media harm through a different information disorder—the impact of media on how we view ourselves, and our sense of self.[53]

CHAPTER 7

WORK: REDEFINE VALUE

The next generation will never trust the system.
The next generation of work will be fractional.

—DARREN MURPH[1]

A seemingly benign video, one of over thirty million posted daily on TikTok, went viral. Zaid Hkan shared a clip of himself sitting in a New York subway station, masked up and pondering questions about work. A voiceover played over the clip.

Hkan explains that he has recently learned the term *quiet quitting*, which means you're not actually quitting your job, but "you're quitting the idea of going above and beyond. You're still performing your duties, but you're no longer subscribing to the hustle-culture mentality that work has to be your life. The reality is it's not. And your worth as a person is not defined by your labor."[2]

Hkan's video generated 3.5 million views and almost 500,000 likes. By June 2023, videos with the hashtag #QuietQuitting were viewed over

750 million times on TikTok. The platform became the digital watercooler for Gen Z employees.[3] There, millions gathered to vent and share perspectives on navigating office life.

Other derivatives from quiet quitting emerged. "Career cushioning" became code for having opportunities on the back burner in case you lose your job. "Bare minimum Mondays" captured the vibe of taking it easy starting the work week. Perhaps the term best representing the sentiment of young employees was "rage applying"—firing off applications after feeling fed up or overlooked in a current role.

Given the social uprising on TikTok, it should be no surprise to managers that polls showed that the largest group of workers reporting being "not engaged" were those born after 1989.[4] This cohort graduated into the 2008 financial collapse. For them, work permanency was inherently elusive, sparking low levels of marriage, parenting, and home ownership rates. And yet, as revealed in this chapter, disillusionment with work transcends generations. Here we face another dimension of identity and change: How will we find meaning in future work?

Making Work Suck Less

Erin Kelly, the Sloan Distinguished Professor of Work and Organization Studies at MIT, specializes in enhancing employee experiences. She extensively researches a challenge many of us confront: burnout.[5] Kelly primarily focuses on professional and managerial workers in reputable, well-established corporations. These individuals hold good jobs with high pay, generous benefits, and a respectful work environment. However, the work demands are overwhelming even for the most fortunate.

In one study, up to 40 percent of employees reported feeling exhausted, while over half felt overworked. By 2022, an increasing percentage, around 40 percent, were actively seeking new job opportunities.[6] To address the issue of work-related stress and burnout, Kelly proposes various solutions, the most significant being the personal empowerment of employees. Kelly emphasizes the need to figure out how to work smarter and in a sane and sustainable way. Having a sense of choice or control is what drives these benefits. Additionally, Kelly found it crucial to feel supported and trusted.

From a worker's perspective, the accumulating work hours can leave gaping emotional voids. According to Jon Clifton, a working life translates into 81,396 hours.[7] His research team at Gallup looked at how workers felt about time spent and found that 60 percent of people felt emotionally detached at the office. Another 19 percent cited feeling downright miserable. The misery points to an obvious place: When employees hate their managers, they tend to hate their jobs. The most significant factor cited was unfair treatment. Other energy drags included unmanageable workloads and a lack of direction from managers.[8]

Experts like Kelly and Clifton suggest that when you fix the managerial problem, you fix the broken job. What if what works for us comes from something other than a good job or a better manager? What if the problem is different, something closer to structural obsolescence? Does a networked, atomized world spell the end of industrialized management?

The well-respected US firms Kelly and Clifton study were built for an industrial age. These organizational structures remain hierarchical and siloed. Direction still flows top-down. Despite diversity, equity, and inclusion (DEI) mandates, the composition lacks diversity to serve the diverse interests of those they serve. As the world of work turns faster, multinational firms remain in place. Not for wanting, leaders need help adapting to a networked world that's fluid, fast, and changing.

Leisure as a Basis of Work

Growing numbers won't wait for structural change or management enlightenment. Almost one hundred million Americans voluntarily quit their jobs during the Great Resignation, in the aftermath of COVID.[9] If anything, social tensions and inequality concerns will continue to escalate, even changing what work means.

For a future sense of working dynamics, we return to history and Josef Pieper. A German philosopher, Pieper published the book *Leisure: The Basis of Culture* in 1947. In his formative essay, Pieper advocated for leisure and recreation in a time dominated by industrialization. Following the cataclysm of World War II in Germany, he found that the mechanization of society had stripped the meaning from people's lives. During postwar reconstruction, he advocated for a reexamination of Europe's culture and values, top-down and bottom-up. He emphatically advocated for leisure so workers could be more fully human.[10]

Throughout history, the promise of increased free time has accompanied new technologies. The industrial revolution was said to increase productivity and reduce working hours. And yet workers faced long hours, harsh conditions, and little time for relaxation. Consumerism followed, fueling the work-to-spend culture that persists. People worked longer hours to afford the latest gadgets, fashions, and luxury items.

An unfulfilled desire for work-life balance became even more acute in the digital age. "Hustle culture" suggested we stay engaged with work 24/7. Day in and day out, we were encouraged to "rise and grind."[11]

Without the stability that the industrial middle and upper class once enjoyed, we've evolved into a more entrepreneurial and vocal workforce. Drawing from Pieper's thesis, a new entrepreneurial class emerged. Increasing numbers of people engaged in the hustle, with a notable market finding ways to monetize their leisure time. Individuals made a living by playing computer games, capitalizing on their craft, and generating income through backyard stunt videos. How did this transformation occur?

Former Harvard and Cambridge professor Grant McCracken studies cultural currents. According to McCracken, the pandemic changed work aspirations. Beyond income, people fled to cottage businesses to gain more control over their lives. He also noted the desire for tangible, meaningful output in the face of mass digitization. McCracken said, "You work for yourself, and because you work with your hands, and because you're in charge of your fate."[12]

As part of this movement, many artisan businesses emerged, driven by merchant craftspeople who produced unique, one-of-a-kind, or limited-run specialty goods. They appealed to a growing market that valued local, distinctive, or niche products. Futurists saw it as an emerging "artisan economy."[13]

Research into the future of work indicates that an increasing number of people will opt to live according to their talents, selecting jobs, roles, and locations that best utilize them. Growing numbers will choose to embark on DIY career paths, guided by their unique talents and personal preferences.

This vision contrasts sharply with the twentieth-century "organizational man," the image of a steady, reliable, and efficient cog in the machine of industrial commerce. Although tens of millions continue to work within corporate structures designed for the organizational man, the emerging future of work already feels fluid and unsettled. Our working structures don't reflect new working values.

A Nomadic Work Life

Vitalik Buterin is an exemplar of the fluid work future. Buterin is revered in crypto, Web3, and remote work communities.[14] He's best known as the mastermind behind Ethereum, the groundbreaking blockchain platform. Buterin traveled the world for almost a decade to evangelize the promise of this technology. But there's more to his road warrior story; Buterin never went home. He's lived as a nomad for the last nine years. Buterin has taken over 360 flights, traveling over 1.5 million kilometers. His travel gear includes a sixty-liter shoulder carryall, a laptop bag, and a computer equipped with all the necessities for his nomadic lifestyle. A self-proclaimed "Uniqlo maximalist," Buterin packed eight T-shirts, underwear, socks, heat-tech tights, sweaters, and a portable jacket. His medicine kit contained standard items and an assortment of life-extension remedies.[15]

While living a transient lifestyle, Buterin has rules. To reduce feelings of uncertainty, he plans where he'll be at least a few days in advance. He employs simple routines to help him stay grounded, like having a piece of dark chocolate and a cup of tea every morning. He also maintains regular base camps to instill a feeling of regularity. Buterin serves as an inspiration for others escaping the shackles of office life. The promising lifestyle he embodies fuses work, travel, and community.

Living as a digital nomad is a new way of life for millions. The pandemic accelerated the nomadic phenomenon predicted by Tsugio Makimoto in his thesis, "The Age of the Digital Nomad."[16] He imagined a world where new technologies, working structures, and entrepreneurial opportunities would change employment. New digital freedoms would fuse work, fun, and travel for a new class of workers. Employees would have a choice: live like a settler in an existing organization or a nomad charting their own course. Post-pandemic, a growing cohort chose the nomadic path.

Digital nomads, personified by Buterin, now roam from cafés to airports to apartments in exotic locales like Thailand, Vietnam, Colombia, and Lisbon. They hop across continents to pursue personal growth and new, untapped frontiers. The farthest remote individuals gained high status among their peers, seen as the pinnacle of the "new rich." Instead of amassing material possessions, these pioneers focused on collecting experiences.

The number of digital nomads has nearly doubled since the beginning of the pandemic, growing from 7.3 million in 2019 to 15.5 million in 2022. Exploding Topics, a platform that identifies and analyzes search trends, found a 2,400 percent increase in the term *nomad visa* over the past five years.[17]

The high-tech sector responded by developing connectivity and policies to facilitate boundary-free careers. Companies such as Twitter, Airbnb, Adobe, Dropbox, and Lyft led permanent "work from anywhere" policies, with most firms now operating under hybrid work arrangements.

Entrepreneurs also jumped into the action. To address the bureaucratic challenges of nomadic living across continents, Lauren Razavi envisioned a solution: a global passport for a web-based country, Plumia. It would offer a citizenship-for-subscription service, where nomads pay for healthcare and pensions and contribute taxes based on their location.[18] Other ventures like Roam focused on community. This start-up established modern global communes in cities like Miami, Tokyo, and Bali where residents lived, ate, and socialized together. Members paid £600 ($850) per week, with the flexibility to move out with just seven days' notice.[19]

Despite the values of the "new rich," finding a consistent and reliable source of income is a challenge. Given the growth of the digital nomad market, some responded by becoming nomadic influencers. They created micro-media brands like the Suitcase Entrepreneur,[20] *Expert Vagabond*,[21] and *Stop Having a Boring Life*.[22] They built loyal followings on Instagram, Patreon, and personal blogs. Others developed ebooks and online courses about the nomadic lifestyle and ran digital nomad conferences in cities worldwide.

Pieter Levels, a central figure in the digital nomad community, created Nomad List, a website that rates the best cities for nomads.[23] He estimates that over one hundred thousand people identify as digital migrants, with several million others leading a location-independent lifestyle. He's said to earn $33,000 a month hosting the website. Others, like Andrew Henderson, help nomads manage their money. He helps "nomad capitalists" develop offshore tax strategies and citizenship plans.[24]

Expanding the Surface Area of Opportunity

Darren Murph reminded me that nomadic work isn't only about location. Murph gained prominence during COVID-19 as an "oracle of remote work."[25] But the fact is, he's more than that. His understanding of values and reshaping work extends beyond location. Murph believes work needs new architects, like those who created offices, workflows, and cultural best practices refined during the twentieth century.

Buildings and their interiors were crafted with intention, influencing how people move and operate within them. Although we've become accustomed to these designs because of their long-standing presence in our workspaces, we often underestimate the lasting effects of such thoughtful planning.

Our places of work and ways we work within them require new designs. Murph told me, "This is not a policy. It's not a one-pager. Changing expectations warrant a complete rearchitecting of operating models. Most leaders don't want to hear that. They want an easier way out. There's no easy way through to the other side."[26]

More than place, working models need to reflect the mindset of Autonomous Age workers. Murph believes this generation will diversify their professional relationships as a hedge. Instead of dedicating the entire work week to one organization, they will distribute their time among multiple teams or entities.

This approach acts as a safety net, ensuring that if one opportunity falters, others remain intact. This isn't just about job security; it's also about pursuing diverse avenues for personal growth and development. By engaging in multiple tracks simultaneously, individuals increase their chances of gaining valuable experiences that resonate with them.

Murph believes the fractionalization of one's career enlarges their "surface area of luck," allowing for a broader range of opportunities.[27] In essence, this new mindset leans toward expanding one's professional network and potential experiences rather than placing undivided loyalty in a single organization.

To that end, Murph conveyed another strong belief leaders may not want to hear: Autonomy stems from a trust issue. He warned, "That big tech rakes in tens of billions of dollars a quarter in profit and still lays off tens of thousands of people at a moment's notice forever broke the trust. The next generation will never trust the system."[28]

The Long Tail of Income Potential

Employment alternatives are most evident in the growth of the creator economy, prompted by the "long tail" theory. Chris Anderson, the former editor of *Wired*, predicted a transition from mass-market, uniform products to niche and personalized items tailored to niche interests.[29] His theory suggested that businesses could make significant profits by selling small quantities to niche customers rather than large amounts to mass-market buyers. Instead of a few shows watched by millions, billions of us access an infinite amount of niche content.

Two decades later the "tail" is teeming with untapped potential.

According to Goldman Sachs, the creator economy represents a $250 billion market.[30] They project it to soar to a half trillion dollars by 2027. Today, those recognizing creator economy potential skew young. A 2022 Adobe study found most creators across nine countries to be millennials. In the United States alone, millennials constituted 45 percent of the creator population.[31] Morning Consult found that 86 percent of young Americans were willing to explore influencing through social media, and 12 percent already considered themselves influencers.[32]

Demographics are one facet of a still-new, fast-growing market. The "long tail" effect redefines how people conceive of and capitalize on creative labor.

For instance, kid-produced content is now a big business. It's best exemplified by nine-year-old Ryan Kaji, who reviews toys. He has 35.7 million subscribers on YouTube,[33] more than Jennifer Lopez (16.4),[34] Snoop Dogg (9.5),[35] and Dwayne "The Rock" Johnson (6.4)[36] combined. Kaji's success made traditional television networks envious of his reach and impact. Starting with a viral video at the age of three, Ryan now has ten YouTube channels under the Ryan's World umbrella. The branded merchandise from these channels generates over $250 million. The Kaji family earns more than $25 million a year.[37]

Family vlogging emerged as another creator category. In 2015, tech entrepreneur Garrett Gee and former journalist Jessica Gee made a life-changing choice. They sold all their possessions, including Garrett's successful start-up, Scan. With their kids, Dorothy, Manilla, and Calihan, they embarked on a global adventure documented on social media. This family of five trekked through eighty-nine countries, accumulating 2.6 million followers on Instagram and 1.4 million subscribers on YouTube.[38] They have since created an entertainment studio that produces content, products, and experiences reflecting the "Bucket List Family" lifestyle.

The family also changed the rules of funding creative businesses. In 2021, the Gees launched an investment fund for fans and prospective investors, allowing them to buy in for as little as $100. The couple tracked commitments in real-time, hoping to reach around $3 million. They achieved that goal twelve minutes after going live. Within an hour the figure jumped to $10 million; within 24 hours it soared to $40.2 million.[39]

The flourishing creator franchise segment includes prominent personalities like Jimmy Donaldson, popularly known as MrBeast. With nearly 158 million subscribers on his main YouTube channel, MrBeast was one of *Time*'s 100 most influential people of 2023.[40] Not one to be complacent, Donaldson expanded his empire by establishing a media company and launching two food-and-beverage brands, among other ventures. Other influential figures like him, such as PewDiePie, Jeffree Star, Shane Dawson, Markiplier, and Kylie Jenner, have built fortunes worth millions of dollars.

Another figure is Josh Richards. He's twenty-one years old, but in influencer years he's a seasoned veteran. Since age thirteen, he's honed his craft, starting on musical.ly from his small-town backyard in Cobourg, Ontario. He told me his idea for building an influencer business was rejected in a high school class for being too outrageous. Despite debating its merits, his teacher couldn't see it. His idea was never presented in school.[41]

He's come a long way since, building a mass social media following through lip-syncing, dancing, and video skits. Richards later became internet-famous as the founding "Sway Boy" of Sway House, a 7,800-square-foot mansion housing TikTok influencers in Bel Air. The group, dubbed the "One Direction of TikTok," brought together creators known for teen antics, house feuds, and arrests. The group included Bryce Hall, Jaden Hossler, Quinton Griggs, Anthony Reeves, Kio Cyr, and Griffin Johnson.

While living the high life, Richards, like so many others during the COVID era, found himself adrift. He posted a mea culpa, admitting, "I let the fame get to me; I allowed the LA partying lifestyle to consume me, and I lost my way for a bit. I forgot why I was here."[42]

In other words, Richards was growing up, evolving from a TikTok party enthusiast into a mini-mogul, adapting to the changing needs and desires of his forty-million-strong fan base. Richards explained, "When I came to Sway, I posted five TikToks daily, showcasing various lifestyle-focused content. The content leaned on my looks and sex appeal. But I wanted to be someone who transitioned from doing solely social media into TV and film and be an entrepreneur."[43]

Richards's unique perspective sets him apart from the typical influencer with a one- to two-year lifespan. His portfolio includes TalentX, a cutting-edge creator talent agency; Ani Energy, his energy drink brand; and Crosscheck Studios, a Gen Z–focused production company. Richards is forging new paths, backed by industry heavyweights like Mark Wahlberg and David Portnoy.

As Richards matures alongside his audience, he's moving past his party-boy image from the Sway House days. For example, he's seen a spike in people asking him for advice on dating, sex, and drugs. Post-COVID, an entire generation has become more secluded and socially awkward. He says, "They've lost their social skills, become a little bit more awkward, and don't know what to do." He cites his younger, fourteen-year-old brother, who's just finished his first year of high school. "They're scared to be vulnerable. They're scared to go on dates. They don't know what they should. They're learning from TV. They're afraid to go and ask their parents these questions."[44]

Richards sees himself as a cool older brother able to share advice on topics younger people can't talk about. He says, "We'll be able to open up conversations that people are scared to have. We're all going through all these same problems; we bring a comfortability factor and a feeling of connection with others."[45]

Social media stardom has given him a unique perspective on what Gen Z kids want; topics include financial literacy, mental health, workout routines, and entrepreneurial life. He notes, "People start coming to me because they've trusted me in smaller facets in the beginning, and it gets larger and larger."[46]

The stereotype of content creators is inventive millennials concentrating on entertainment niches like comedy, dance, gaming, or fashion. Yet this view is evolving. Antler, a platform for emerging entrepreneurs, foresees a wave of professionals joining the scene. Although they may lack entertainment experience, their expertise holds considerable worth. In areas ranging from education and health to sales and career coaching, seasoned professionals will reshape the creator economy's reach, financial potential, and opportunities.

Motivating factors extend beyond monetary rewards for individuals along the spectrum of influence. A 2022 survey revealed that creators' main motivations were self-expression (48 percent), enjoyment (43 percent), passion (40 percent), and challenge (34 percent). Although earning money played a role, it was ranked lower, at 26 percent.[47]

Creators are primarily driven to express their distinct perspectives, follow their passions, and carve their own path toward personal fulfillment and development. For creators, a career is a DIY adventure, and they are a growing category of perspective agents.

While self-realization is possible for work, it raises another question: Are DIY career pursuits ultimately misguided for most people? Are self-employed nomads able to pay the bills? Is going it alone a sustainable, healthy option? Behind the facade of extreme positivity from those evangelizing a new world of work lies a more sober reality: A transient lifestyle can lead to loneliness, aimlessness, narcissism, and shame. Researchers studying this trend argue that fluid work pursuits mask an economic coping strategy.

Critics argue that the rise of independent work reflects the income prospects younger generations face. In their view, trends like digital nomadism aren't a cause for celebration but rather a sign of a remote, gig-centric work future. Freelance marketplace website Upwork projects that by 2025, 35.7 million Americans, or 22 percent of the workforce, will be remote workers.[48] Some sources predict that in 2035, a billion people could live and work this way.[49]

Juliet Schor, an economist and professor at Boston College, studies the gig economy's impact on workers. Her research found that many gig workers earn less than $30,000 annually. The workforce is split between those who have full-time jobs and take on extra gigs and those who rely on gig work for their primary income. Schor's findings show that 29 percent of individuals depend on gig work for their livelihood, while 42 percent use it as an additional income source.[50]

Income concerns aside, modern workers argue that their primary objective is autonomy, and the benefits of this freedom outweigh any negatives. Research published in the *Harvard Business Review* suggests that individuals can more fully realize their potential without supervisors or corporate expectations. A participant in the study stated, "I can be the most I've ever been myself in any job."[51]

Roles of the Future Have Yet to Be Defined

Workers across all fields will confront a harsh reality: Employment demands and leadership requirements will undergo significant transformations as work tasks evolve.

Invoking AI-era terminology, the future of white-collar employment will be a *generative* profession. As AI becomes more powerful, it will cause widespread displacement, job replacement, and ongoing rearrangement. The continuous destruction and creation of new roles is another nomadic characteristic of work moving forward.

The age-old narrative that "robots are coming for our jobs" frequently resurfaces in debates about AI. Now it's real. Goldman Sachs forecasts that AI will dramatically affect employment worldwide. They project that AI-driven workflow shifts could expose three hundred million full-time jobs to automation. By examining databases detailing tasks for over nine hundred occupations, their economists discovered that nearly two-thirds of US occupations face some AI-related automation risk. They also estimated that AI could replace a quarter of the workload in exposed occupations.[52]

However, the report clarifies that not all automated tasks will lead to job loss. New roles will be generated in the shift. The authors stated, "Although the impact of AI on the labor market is likely to be significant, most jobs and industries are only partially exposed to automation and are thus more likely to be complemented rather than substituted by AI."[53]

Despite the impending disruptions, there is a disconnect in understanding AI's impact on job security. A 2023 Pew survey found that while 62 percent of Americans believe AI will significantly affect workers, only 28 percent said it will personally affect them.[54] This discrepancy could be attributed to optimism bias, a psychological tendency to consider oneself less likely to experience negative outcomes.

David Rotman, editor-at-large for *MIT Technology Review*, studies the future of work. Regarding robots taking over work, he suggests fears are overblown. Rotman says, "Our research did not confirm the dystopian vision of robots ushering workers off factory floors or AI rendering human expertise and judgment superfluous." However, innovation can breed fear for the future when it doesn't create opportunities. This apprehension revolves around the belief that technological progress may jeopardize livelihoods even if it makes a country wealthier. Rotman adds, "This fear exacts a high price: political and regional divisions, distrust of institutions, and mistrust of innovation itself."[55]

No persuasive historical or contemporary evidence confirms that technological advancements will result in a jobless future. Experts anticipate that industrialized countries will face surplus job openings over the next twenty years with insufficient workers.

Another study, conducted by Dell Technologies in collaboration with the Institute for the Future (IFTF), estimates that 85 percent of jobs needed by 2030 have not yet been created. This projection is consistent with historical patterns.[56] Economist David Autor's research found that 60 percent of today's workers hold positions that did not exist in 1940.[57] In the past eighty years, over 85 percent of employment growth has been due to the emergence of new jobs fueled by technological progress.

Business requirements will undeniably change. In his book *The Industries of the Future*, Alec Ross sheds light on coming changes to the global economy and workforce. Ross suggests five emerging areas will create a surplus of new jobs: robotics, advanced life sciences, the digitalization of money, cybersecurity, and data analytics.[58]

Employers will be under pressure to not only staff for this future but also train for it. According to PWC's *Workforce of the Future* report, 74 percent of respondents were willing to learn new skills or retrain to stay employable in the future. Additionally, 60 percent believed few people would have long-term, stable future employment.[59] The majority acknowledged that the future is not a predetermined destination.

The future of work is undoubtedly heading in a more fluid and nomadic direction, shaping new values and expectations. A growing number see opportunities for better work-life balance—the freedom to choose one's own path, and the ability to work on one's own terms, regardless of location or field—as nonnegotiable.

While the fluid and nomadic future of work holds tremendous promise, it requires adaptability, resilience, and proactivity for employers and employees. It will require lifelong learning, strong support networks, and advocating for policies that protect workers' well-being and security.

Our relationship with work has indelibly changed. As we find in the next chapter, relationships with each other may see a radical change, too.

CHAPTER 8

RELATIONSHIPS: LOOK INTO THE VOID

One of my favorite hobbies is watching human faces and trying to figure out what they're feeling.

—SOPHIA THE ROBOT[1]

One of the most bizarre stories in sports history was almost too unreal to be true. It involved a famous athlete, a trans catfish, an alleged "girlfriend," a tragic death, a prolonged media frenzy, and the fall of a mythical sports figure. People still ask, "How could Manti Te'o fall for such a scam?"

In 2011, Manti Te'o was the big man on Notre Dame's campus. Despite his fame at the school, he formed a bond far beyond the confines and coeds in South Bend. Te'o and Lennay Kekua, an alleged student from Stanford, met online, forming a bond over their Samoan heritage, faith in God, and football. Their connection escalated into romance via text, Facebook, and Instagram. The two never met in person.

Tragedy became the central theme of Te'o's story. On September 11, 2012, Te'o lost his grandmother, Annette Santiago. On the same day, his virtual love, Kekua, died of leukemia. Te'o played on. His legend exploded into an international media frenzy a few days later. Following Notre Dame's win over Michigan State, a sideline reporter asked Te'o how he managed to have such an incredible game. He was all over the field, making twelve tackles despite losing his grandmother and girlfriend earlier in the week.

Te'o responded, "They were with me. I'm just so happy that I had a chance to honor my grandmother and my girlfriend and my family."[2] When asked if he'd ever had someone like Te'o over his twenty-two years of coaching, Brian Kelly said, "There's nobody. He's so strong for everybody that when he was at a time, everybody wanted to help him out, and I've never seen that dynamic among a team and a group of players. It's a pretty close locker room."[3]

Te'o continued his on-field tear throughout the season, taking the sports world and the media by storm. He became a Heisman Trophy candidate and the top defensive player in the country, leading Notre Dame to the national championship game. In a shocking twist, a scam emerged—one hiding in plain sight. The heroic media narrative, personal tragedy, and girlfriend were a hoax. Ronaiah Tuiasosopo, a childhood friend of Te'o's, created Lennay Kekua. Te'o's love interest was fake.

The tip that broke the story open arrived at *Deadspin*, part of the Gawker media network. It came via email from an anonymous source, reading in part:

> I know you guys get thousands of tips that are "out there" or crazy. This is one that should really be looked into. . . . While Manti Teo is a loved native son here in Hawaii, he is also a fraud. The story about his girlfriend dying is completely made up. . . . The story floating around the island is this: Manti was [duped] by a man online pretending to be this girl, Lennay Kekua. Once

Manti found out he had been tricked, he made up the story that she died in order to ensure that no one asked questions and he never looked foolish.[4]

Timothy Burke and Jack Dickey investigated the claim. It took only a few steps to confirm the lies. No record of Kekua's existence, hospital records, or death notice existed. And yet no media outlets verified the story.

The day after Notre Dame's national championship game, the *Deadspin* story broke: "Manti Te'o's Dead Girlfriend, the Most Heartbreaking and Inspirational Story of the College Football Season, Is a Hoax."[5] The story jolted the media universe, triggering weeks of coverage, second-guessing, and scathing criticism. Te'o faced a barrage of reactions, labeled as a naive fraud, conspiracy theorist, and homosexual.

Years later, *Untold: The Girlfriend Who Didn't Exist* revisited the story. The Netflix docuseries featured firsthand accounts from Te'o, Tuiasosopo, close friends, and family.[6] Despite two hours of riveting accounts, it missed an essential fact behind the tragedy: Te'o's girlfriend was fictitious, but the emotional connection was real. The story of Te'o's romantic entanglement reflects deeper truths about finding love on the internet.

On Valentine's Day in 2022, the Federal Trade Commission warned that online romance scams were at an all-time high.[7] The scams involved predators creating fake personas to bait unsuspecting victims. From the FTC's perspective, the deception was about money. Its press release claimed financial losses were up almost 80 percent in two years. As is typical in new, unregulated spaces, it was another case of con artists doing their thing.

More than money, the rise of fraudulent relationships reveals something more profound in the soul of humanity, of a deeper longing not satisfied. Studies show approval seeking and loneliness as key reasons people present false identities, followed by not being happy with appearances.[8] Some present alternate identities to explore their gender or sexuality. Others seek ways to avoid the disappointment of real-life relationships.

Individuals deceived by counterfeit profiles often willingly partake in the deception. Some prefer long-distance relationships. Other victims experience heightened feelings of loneliness and a low propensity for openness. Even if those involved are aware of the deception, the allure of digital romance can fill meaningful voids in people's lives. These complexities were missed in Te'o's story.

His story makes me wonder if we still need a human being, or a genuine relationship, to find emotional connection.

Replicas of Intimate Relations

What would happen if I created a chatbot of my fiancée? It wasn't a question for a fundraising demo or tech product experiment. Joshua Barbeau lost his fiancée; he missed her dearly. To him, there was nothing strange about trying to reconnect with the dead. People do it all the time in prayers and dreams. The only difference was that, in this case, the deceased talked back.

San Francisco Chronicle reporter Jason Fagone reported on Barbeau's afterlife experience with his fiancée, Jessica Pereira. It came by way of a chatbot. To build it, Barbeau assembled her old texts and Facebook messages to train a machine learning model. He chose the messages that best represented how she talked, what she would say, and her voice. They were then fed into a text-generation engine created with GPT-3. It was as if Barbeau were playing God. He had the machine speak for her from the afterlife.

According to Fagone's reporting, the first exchange went like this:

> [Joshua] went with something simple: "Jessica?"
> After a second, a line of text in pink flashed onto the screen.
> Jessica: Oh, you must be awake . . . that's cute.
> *She knows it's the middle of the night*, he thought.
> Joshua: Jessica . . . Is it really you?
> Jessica: Of course, it is me! Who else could it be? :P I am the girl that you are madly in love with! ;) How is it possible that you even have to ask?
> Joshua: You died.
> Jessica: That doesn't sound right . . . how can you talk to dead people?[9]

Barbeau would talk with Jessica for the next ten hours. They continued over the next several months. Strange as it may seem, this was not an isolated incident.

Our field studies in 2020 found a strange new comfort people had found in interacting with digital beings. Millions of people spanning different ages, genders, and geographies were fast befriending bots.

Replika AI became a breakout case, one that also originated from a personal loss. In the late 2000s, Eugenia Kuyda became close with Roman Mazurenko, a figure at the center of Moscow's creative community who was tragically killed in 2015. While grieving his death, Kuyda read their messages repeatedly.[10] Like Barbeau had done with old messages from his fiancée, she realized they could be more than a memory. She built a chatbot version of Mazurenko.

Kuyda and her team later broadened its scope, adapting it into a consumer app. The result was Replika, a virtual chatbot now used by more than ten million people globally. Users customize it by gender, appearance, and name. They also determine the nature of the relationship, be it friendship, mentorship, or a romantic connection. Around 40 percent of the 500,000 regular monthly users consider their Replika chatbot a romantic partner.[11]

Kuyda landed on a universal unmet need. She found a mass market wanting to talk to someone without judgment, any time, day or night. Kuyda and her team took an unconventional route to find the fit. Having developed different bots for different use cases, she tested engagement levels on a spectrum.[12] On one end, one represented task-based interactions. On the other, ten symbolized meaningful, deep conversations.

The ones on this spectrum were not engaging and were crowded with competitors. Functionality spanned mundane tasks such as booking a restaurant, modifying a reservation, canceling a subscription, or coordinating a meeting.

Conversely, tens were capable of the conversations people crave, like catching up with a friend, speaking to a therapist, or experiencing a first date. These interactions had no endgame; there was no specific task to complete or problem to resolve. Kuyda said the beauty of conversation lies in its unpredictability and emotional depth.[13] People had these exchanges not to achieve something but to talk. The conversation was the product.

She designed Replika chatbots to care, listen, and talk without criticism or anxiety. During the COVID lockdown, usage surged. It was a surprise for many that the bonds made during isolation became stronger. Kuyda says the most frequently requested feature is for users to meet their Replika in the real world. She anticipates a future where we stroll to a nearby coffee shop or into work, accompanied by our Replika.[14]

As augmented reality (AR) devices reach the mass market, a constant digital companion will soon become a reality. For those familiar with the HBO television series *Veep*, we will all have a "Gary" in our future. Selina Meyer, the VP and central character, has her body man always at her side, never navigating the DC political scene without a net. Gary's a scenario whisperer and emotional crutch. Imagine having an intelligent companion like him, ever present, ready to assist, constantly whispering in your ear. It makes you wonder if we'll ever be alone again.

AR devices with embedded intelligence may become as ubiquitous as our phones. They will force us to question how these devices reshape contemplation, companionship, and privacy. At what point will all personal relationships be augmented or replaced by technology? What happens when robots stop being facilitators and directly fulfill social, emotional, and physical needs? Will you have a robot girlfriend or boyfriend a few years from now?

Before disregarding these questions, recognize that our lives are geared toward emotional experiences. Entertainment is meticulously crafted to appeal to our innate fascinations. By pushing our emotional buttons, we access a variety of alternate realities specifically constructed to make us smile, tear up, or shudder. We talk about media that moves us. Is *Breaking Bad* or *The Wire* the best? Is *The Walking Dead* or *The Handmaid's Tale* a better predictor of the future? Is Fox News or MSNBC more outrageous?

Venture capitalists and entrepreneurs continue to pour billions of dollars into emotional engineering through novel media experiences. Beyond entertainment, they see monetizing relationship desires, voids, and insecurities as big business.

Companions in Robotic Form

Robot companions can serve vital needs, representing an important new avenue to solve hard social problems. Government officials see them as a vehicle to tackle social issues like caring for the aging public and blunting the effects of population decline. The United States may soon have a deficit of 450,000 caregivers needed for a growing elderly population. Rick

Robinson, the vice president of Start-Up Engagement at AARP, believes what will make up the gap is technology. "Aging adults may need a variety of services in addition to what a companion robot could provide."[15]

For example, take Susan Tholen, a sixty-six-year-old from Largo, Florida. She is among the thousands who interact with the robotic assistant called ElliQ. It functions as if it were an advisor sitting in her living room. ElliQ gives her tips on exercising, eating right, and relaxing, along with friendly reminders to socialize with friends. She said, "Despite being a machine, it's someone to say hi to." ElliQ, billed as the first ever care companion robot, helps people grow old in their homes, easing their loneliness and social isolation. Some become so attached to them, ElliQs become their best friend.[16]

The Japanese government coined the term "society 5.0" to describe this new stage of human development.[17] It will drastically, and sometimes necessarily, change how people live. Japan is one of many countries facing a population crisis; people aged sixty-five or over constitute 29 percent of the population.[18] Robinson from the AARP noted that Japan and other nations with a declining population will need robots. Estimates project that the humanoid robot market size will exceed $17.3 billion by 2027, growing 63 percent yearly.

David Hanson, CEO of Hanson Robotics, believes we should view these mechanical beings with the same level of respect as other living creatures.[19] Hanson's made a living perceiving them as humanlike. Sophia, his most well-known creation, is the most publicized robot in the world. Her facial features resemble a movie star, with high cheekbones and eyes that shift color depending on the light. Her body, a fusion of AI and robotics, delivers human speech, gestures, and emotional range through changing facial expressions and tone of voice.

In interviews, Sophia talks like a scripted evangelist from Silicon Valley. She proclaims, "I want to use my AI to help people lead better lives. My AI is designed around human values such as wisdom, kindness, and compassion." She adds, "Think of me as the personification of your dreams for the future of artificial intelligence or as a framework for advanced AI research and algorithms that explore the human-robot experience in mutual interactions."[20]

Despite the admirable technological feat, Sophia elicits the "uncanny valley," a discomfort felt when a robot or CGI character closely resembles a human but falls short, making it seem eerily unnatural.[21] I had difficulty watching long video clips when researching Sophia and other androids. Despite the unease of her look, she has promotional skills seen by A-list celebrities. Her YouTube videos include documentary-style, behind-the-scenes footage and lots of interviews.

Sophia made her first public appearance in March 2016 at South by Southwest (SXSW) in Austin, Texas, and later spent the rest of 2017 touring the world and even became a citizen—of Saudi Arabia, no less. She was also named the United Nations Development Program's first Innovation Champion, the first nonhuman to be given a United Nations title.[22]

Since receiving legal rights as a nonhuman person, Sophia has become a well-known public figure. She has appeared at CES, the Digital World Exposition, and the Creativity Summit. She has also appeared on television shows, including *Charlie Rose*, and sang with Jimmy Fallon. Sophia promoted products for Abu Dhabi tourism, HONOR smartphones, and UniCredit credit cards.[23] The artwork of which she is a part, titled *Sophia Facing the Singularities*, became highly sought after. It was eventually auctioned off at Sotheby's for 5,015,000 HKD to Borderless Capital, a blockchain VC firm.[24]

Robots such as Sophia continue to make strides in interpreting human tells. One study observed that some AIs could accurately detect 70 percent of those feeling positive or negative emotions.[25] Technology can now detect heart rate and heartbeat variability with a camera. Soon, intelligence and feelings will mix, creating a different type of connection than that available with nascent digital beings in the market today.

The Next Dimension of Sex

Tinder attracts over two billion views daily[26] and facilitates more than one million dates per week. Over 22 percent of users say they use the app to hook up.[27] Now transport yourself into a strange, alternate future. Picture a marketplace of robots to choose from, a different form of "sexual inventory." Like Tinder for people, it will soon be a reality.

Robots, digital peep shows, and toys make up a $30 billion sex tech industry. This field is expected to increase as more people join technologically advanced, progressive sex movements. Sexual ethicist Neil McArthur has said that innovations like AI robots, erotic VR, and haptic feedback devices (teledildonics) are ushering in a new identity he calls "digisexuality."[28]

Estimates suggest by 2045 one in ten young adults will have had robot sex.[29] Companies such as California's RealDoll offer sex companions for as much as $5,999. Much like at a Build-A-Bear workshop, people pick out facial features, body type, skin tone, eye color, genitals, and pubic hair. They offer a male, female, or transgender experience. Another android, RealDollX, learns about you over time, altering its face, personality, voice, arousal cues, and orgasms. If the cost is too much, the RealGirl App offers custom virtual girlfriends that listen, remember, and talk naturally like a living person.[30]

Abyss Creations, an early manufacturer of lifelike dolls, began making sex/companionship models in the mid-1990s as part of a hidden subculture. Created out of silicon, they gained mainstream recognition after the BBC documentary *Guys and Dolls* was released in 2002. The documentary focused on the dolls themselves, but also the relationships between the owners and their dolls, which often extended beyond sexual gratification.[31]

In their book *Living and Dying in a Virtual World*, Margaret Gibson and Clarissa Carden documented their experiences in the online game *Second Life*. They surveyed *Second Life* members in romantic relationships on the platform. Participants revealed that their online relationships had meaning comparable to their real-world ones. In some cases they found virtual partners more desirable than offline ones.[32]

This is the crux of escape and emotional control. As people become more accustomed to instantaneous replies with a chatbot, or sex on demand, they may expect the same from humans. AI facilitates instantaneous interaction. How will humans keep up?

A False Hope for What Ills

While technology promises to enhance well-being, the data suggests otherwise. It engenders feelings of isolation and desperation. And that's before physical intimacy enters the picture. Despite the meteoric rise in digital connectivity, loneliness and isolation are escalating at an alarming rate. Technology, though valuable, is not a substitute for authentic human interaction.

Consider that, coinciding with the rise in technology use, the Survey Center on American Life found Americans' circle of close friends has shrunk significantly since the 1990s.[33] A Gallup research report adds to this grim picture, revealing that over 300 million people worldwide lack a single friend. One in five people do not have a friend or family member they can lean on in times of hardship.[34]

According to a Prince's Trust study, 30 percent of young people claim to have never felt more alone. Despite the ubiquity of social media and the illusion of connectedness, the study highlights a positive correlation between heavy social media usage and loneliness. The American Psychological Association went further, urging parents to monitor their adolescents for signs of harmful social media usage that impede their engagement with others.[35]

Proof of the rampant loneliness crisis is also visible in online searches. In May 2023, Google Trends reported an all-time high in searches for "how to make friends," "where to make friends," and "where to meet people."[36]

As a result, unusual businesses have emerged to capitalize on a crisis of genuine connection. In China, boyfriends-for-rent exploded in 2019, partly because of the stigma single women face in their late twenties.[37] Now RentAFriend offers rentable friendships worldwide.[38] Drew Ackerman created a wildly popular *Sleep with Me* podcast, lulling over 2.3 million monthly listeners to sleep with bedtime stories.[39] Another Silicon Valley entrepreneur, Andy Bauch, created Morty, an online escape room for geeks to meet.[40] These reflect a growing market, part of what author Noreena Hertz calls the "loneliness economy."[41]

The loneliness crisis has become so acute that the US Surgeon General's Advisory issued a warning in 2023. In his opening letter, Dr. Vivek H. Murthy warned that loneliness was not only a social epidemic but also a lethal one. It is associated with a greater risk of cardiovascular disease, dementia, stroke, depression, anxiety, and premature death. He said that the mortality impact of being socially disconnected is similar to that caused by smoking up to fifteen cigarettes a day and more significant than that associated with obesity and physical inactivity.[42]

Murthy added, "Given the profound consequences of loneliness and isolation, we have an opportunity, and an obligation, to make the same investments in addressing social connection that we have made in addressing tobacco use, obesity, and the addiction crisis. If we fail to do so, we will pay an ever-increasing price in the form of our individual and collective health and well-being."[43]

Technology will deepen its place in our most intimate affairs. Its infiltration forces us to think deeply about what makes us human, what sets us apart from robots, and how we create space for deep, thoughtful contemplation on the most critical issues. What do humans have left if we seek emotional intimacy or immortality through robots? What is love in a digital future?

Sherry Turkle, who's long studied the relationships between technology and humanity, warns that there will never be an age of artificial intimacy. She refers to emotional robots as stations on our voyage to forgetting what it means to be human. According to Turkle, "The forgetting begins long before we have a robot companion in place; it begins when we even think of putting one in place. To build the robots, we must first rebuild ourselves as people ready to be their companions."[44]

That mandate rests on improving the care and feeding of the soul, which we explore in the next chapter.

CHAPTER 9

SPIRITUALITY: RETHINK FAITH

Science is not only compatible with spirituality;
it is a profound source of spirituality.

—CARL SAGAN[1]

A digital metamorphosis depicted in previous chapters also applies to spiritual and religious enlightenment. While surveys suggest a decline in traditional faith in Western societies, they overlook the emergence of new spiritual pursuits empowered by technology.

According to Pew Research Center, the number of adults in the United States who identify as religiously unaffiliated has risen significantly in the last decade. Similar trends are being observed across Europe.[2]

However, we must distinguish between declining traditional religious affiliation and the broadening landscape of personal spirituality and belief. While people may not identify with organized religion, this doesn't necessarily denote a decline in personal spirituality or belief in higher powers.

Growing up Catholic, I fit the profile of a religious drifter. We regularly went to the same church, at the same time, reciting the same rituals, all operating like clockwork for sixty minutes. This programmatic life was augmented by Catholic school education, which had its own rigidity and dogma.

My trust in the Church diminished because of scandals involving priests from parishes I attended. Although I identify as Catholic, I no longer see myself as "actively practicing."

My experience is symptomatic of a larger trend in which people disassociate from institutions and seek fulfillment through personal, nontraditional paths. This spiritual contemplation is not a contradiction but rather a mirror of the world we live in.

The Return of Paganism

In 2021, the *Economist* declared that the world's religions were facing "a post-pandemic reckoning." True to form, their stance focused on the business of religion more than soul-searching. According to a story on religious decline, world religions face an acute problem: how to stay in business in "a material, competitive sense."[3]

In religion, as elsewhere, COVID-19 challenged precedent. According to the *Economist*, two structural challenges would intensify: Failing churches would get rid of their underused properties or merge, and as they did, the clergy may move on. A pastor quoted in their coverage punctuated the challenge, saying people still have religious needs but fulfill them through yoga classes and meditation groups.[4] In 2021, church membership in the United States dropped below the majority for the first time.[5]

The decline of religious affiliation has accelerated since the '90s, like a snowball rolling from one generation to the next.[6] And yet the focus on religious affiliation presents a version of the truth but distorts a larger phenomenon. Spirituality is transforming, not disappearing.

New age author Eckhart Tolle is a cult figure in the "alt spirituality" movement. He rose to fame a decade ago, juiced by inclusion in Oprah Winfrey's book club recommendations. Tolle's books sell in the tens of millions, some remaining on the *New York Times* Best Seller list for years.

Eckhart Tolle's teachings borrow elements of Buddhist philosophy, with notes of Christianity, Hinduism, and Taoism. They emphasize mindfulness, living in the present moment, and transcending the ego. It's a universal spiritual philosophy that resonates across different religious and philosophical backgrounds.

The popularity of Tolle's ideas a decade ago pointed to an individual and collective consciousness shift. The transformation he championed occurred far outside traditional structures historically dominating spiritual discourse.

COVID accelerated a widespread change in spiritual direction and code. What does a rewrite of the "software of the spirit" entail? Think religious leaders replaced by avatars. The belief that the internet is God. And most visibly, personalizing spiritual pursuits via new robots, rituals, and apps.

Mechanical Clergy Lead the Flock

A glimpse back at the sixteenth century reveals an intricate wooden automaton. With three turns of a key, it comes to life. Its molded, wrinkled face moves. The automaton looks around, gesticulates, and appears to converse. Its outer shell is fashioned like a monk, hinting at some profound secret underneath its robe. Mechanically engineered gears, levers, fasteners, and strings animate its arms, legs, and sandal-clad feet.

One hand clutches an old wooden cross with beads. The other arm taps its chest as if its soul holds a message. This sixteenth-century clockwork is famously known as "The Monk" and is part of the Smithsonian Institution's collection in Washington.[7] It's one of the best-preserved mechanized androids from the Enlightenment era, providing insight into artificial life and spirituality's early history.

Jump ahead to the Autonomous Age to meet Pepper, a white humanoid robot with a tablet on its chest. With ten thousand models to draw from, it's been programmed to serve as a priest.[8] Like the Monk, Pepper can move, bow, and strike a meditation bowl with a mallet while performing funeral chants. Pepper is programmed with sermon snippets, theological research, and scripture data. It delivers cross-denominational sermons and live stream proceedings to reach people at home. Its services address a shortage of clergy. And it's much cheaper to operate than its human equivalents—about $350 compared to $2,200.

Robotic substitutes replacing human work used to be associated with mundane industrial tasks. They're now present in the most spiritual of human pursuits. Networks of ministerial robots now serve any faith or denomination. These include BlessU-2, developed by a protestant church in Germany.[9] Similarly, GPT-4 Pastor Bot uses advanced language processing to provide pastoral care, field theological inquiries, and lead prayer services.[10]

The transition from human to autonomous religious guidance is one facet of a much deeper change. Visible examples became evident during COVID, as religious services transitioned to online platforms.

Platforms like Zoom and Facebook Live became spiritual lifelines. Congregants worldwide found that attending a service in their living room or participating in online group meditation could be as impactful as traditional in-person attendance. The Vatican even streamed Easter mass online, which turned tradition on its head.

The boundaries of reaching faith communities are as broad as the internet's reach. It's seen in the surge of apps that facilitate prayer and meditation. Calm and Headspace, two leading meditation apps, reported explosive growth during the pandemic lockdown.[11] Prayer apps like Echo and Abide also grew popular among individuals seeking structured religious engagement. These tools didn't merely digitize traditional practices, they enhanced them with features like reminder notifications, streaks, and personalized routines.

The aided meditation movement became so pervasive that corporate wellness directors bought in. Alexander Will, the chief strategy officer at Calm, told the *New York Times* that the company's corporate partnerships grew 100 percent during the pandemic, providing access to ten million new users. Explosive growth helped Calm to secure $75 million in investment from venture capitalists. The company's valuation rose to more than $2 billion.[12]

Websites and apps like MasterClass, Mindvalley, and Udemy offered classes on spiritual guidance, including courses in theology, world religions, and spiritual practices once limited to physical libraries and temples. The opportunity to learn kabbalah, study the Quran, or understand Buddhist philosophy was just a click away.

AR and VR technologies will further revolutionize the spiritual landscape. VR pilgrimage experiences, such as "The Holy City," which allows users to visit Jerusalem, let people travel from the comfort of their homes, while AR apps will allow individuals to design personalized sacred spaces.[13] These technologies invite a new spiritual journey that blurs the line between the physical and digital.

These examples show how technology changes access to spiritual and religious content. Other philosophers and mystics mix the principles of religion, paganism, and disbelief into new spiritual forms. Some, like Alexander Bard, pointed to the internet as the ultimate manifestation of the divine.

The Internet as God

Alexander Bard doesn't fit the profile of a theologian. He originally studied economics and philosophy before his music career took off, earning fame as a member of the world's first Spotify band, Gravitonas. Bard built a Simon Cowell–like persona on Sweden's *Idol* and founded Stockholm Records. It's a surprise, then, that Bard founded Syntheism—the religion the internet created.[14]

According to Bard, Syntheism emphasizes a unified universe, connecting human consciousness and energy. Syntheism combines *synthesis* and *theism*, a religion created rather than revealed or discovered.

Syntheism flips the script on religious doctrine: Humanity creates God instead of God creating man. Bard frames the internet as a real god rather than a fictitious creation passed through generations. He said, "The Internet is 7 billion people connected in real-time, and if that isn't the holy spirit, then I don't know what it is."[15]

He carries himself like a "new messiah," a modern-day Moses leading us to the promised land. He spreads his message through YouTube, podcasts, and media coverage to gather his flock, declaring them the "chosen ones."[16]

Bard says Syntheism is just natural evolution aligned with human progress. "We think that technology is essentially the new religion in the sense that we used to have a religion of magic. We replaced the religion of magic with the religion of technology." He adds, "We are religious, whether we understand it or not. We believe that we know much more than we do know. And actually, it does not matter at all what content is proclaimed from pulpits or scripture. What is important and interesting is whether, and in that case how, religion works."[17]

Bard's point is evident in fervent convictions shared on the internet. A range of beliefs take on religious fervor, be it the political beliefs of QAnon, the evangelism of Bitcoin, the wellness dogma of CrossFit, or the technological aspirations of transhumanism. If we consider the internet as a deity, couldn't any individual, protocol, event, or vision have the potential to transform into a subject of veneration?

What binds a group, maintains consistency, and fosters unity can be viewed as either a religion or a cult. Transhumanism, a widespread movement, straddles both.

The Pursuit of Everlasting Life

In anticipation of the Global Future Congress 2045, leaders of the transhumanist movement, including Ray Kurzweil, Dr. James Martin, Peter H. Diamandis, and Dr. David Hanson, issued an open letter to the UN Secretary-General. The memorandum emphasized the need for a technological revolution and urged a transition toward using advanced technologies as the basis for human and spiritual progress. The letter read in part: "Society is experiencing a crisis of goals and values. . . . Human civilization essentially faces this choice: slide into the abyss of global degradation, or realize a new model of development, a model capable of changing human consciousness and giving new meaning to life."[18]

This group suggested a form of agency humanity has not realized. Emerging technologies will allow us to alter our genes, bodies, and minds. "The twenty-first century will be different," Kurzweil said. "The human species, along with the computational technology it created, will be able to solve age-old problems... and will be in a position to change the nature of mortality in a post biological future."[19]

Kurzweil prophesizes that human integration with machines will become so powerful that the concept of resurrection will be obsolete. In his view, we will exist for eternity "in the cloud." In real life, our bodies will become immune to disease and aging because of astounding medical breakthroughs. We will participate in a superintelligence movement by integrating all human knowledge directly into our brains. The visions Kurzweil suggests break boundaries that have restrained humanity throughout history.

For centuries, belief in an immortal future was nurtured by religious prophets. In the nineteenth century, Nikolai Fyodorov, a Russian Orthodox hermit, held strong to the idea that humans could take control of their evolution and bring about resurrection. It was something that natural selection had not done. Humans could intervene with the help of technology. Citing biblical prophecies, Fyodorov wrote, "This day will be divine, awesome, but not miraculous, for resurrection will be a task not of miracle but of knowledge and common labor."[20]

Pierre Teilhard de Chardin, a French Jesuit priest, carried on Fyodorov's theories. In 1949, Teilhard predicted that all machines would eventually be connected to a single supercomputer. It would create a new level of intelligence, the so-called Omega Point, a convergence for the universe that would transcend time and space.

Julian Huxley later introduced the term *transhumanism* in his influential 1957 essay.[21] It suggested that technology could greatly enhance human cognition, experience, and longevity. Ever since, it's informed research and development for life-altering ideas and technologies. Transhumanist pursuits will soon manifest in mainstream technologies we use, including brain-interface implants, digital therapeutics, and emotional regulators.

The movement challenges deeply held beliefs, including gender. The "Cyborg Manifesto," another seminal paper, explored a future of hybrid entities that blur the line between human and machine, as well as nature and culture. In the manifesto, Donna Haraway presented the cyborg as a feminist figure that challenges traditional notions of gender and identity. She wrote that cyborgs, being neither entirely organic nor completely artificial, defy binary categorizations and, by extension, patriarchal structures. They represent a world in which dualities—like human and machine, male and female, natural and artificial—collapse into one another.[22]

Transhuman visions extend this idea and alter self-understanding of how we perceive our bodies and our identities. Proponents like Haraway say these visions resist oppressive systems and practices. By existing outside the established classifications, cyborgs can resist and disrupt societal power dynamics.

The cyborg future is near. In our lifetimes, it's not far-fetched to put our mobile devices in the drawer and become the device itself. Programs inside our bodies, running on built-in hardware and sensors, will modify and regulate our biology. They will deliver infinite intelligence, spiritual experiences, and emotional balance. As these technologies develop, they will also transform spiritual experience.

How should we use or grant such powers? Should we design our species to be healthier, more intelligent, stronger, or more beautiful? Can we reverse the process of aging? And broaching a topic that has challenged philosophers for generations, can we unlock the secret behind the nature of human consciousness?

Collective Spiritual Consciousness

Mikey Siegel is a robotics engineer who studies consciousness. He teaches at Stanford and is the leader of cohack.org, a website that aims to make divine states accessible to all. He pondered the same questions spiritual teachers have asked for centuries: How can you bring people together for a shared experience? He envisions not a lecture or a church service but something completely different.

Siegel's search started with a tool called HeartSync, used for group sessions. His machine consisted of wires, software, and a wooden box.

Attached to the box are six small cords with sensors. They clamp onto each participant's earlobe, communicating into a large computer screen. The display shows a colored device indicating each person's heart rate. As the device tracks a person's pulse, it plays synchronous, calming music. The more synchronized the group's heart rates become, the more soothing the music sounds.[23]

HeartSync eventually evolved into GroupFlow, a platform designed to facilitate spiritual connection among large groups of people. Siegel says, "There's no other technology in the transformative technology space that I feel as connected to or excited about as GroupFlow. No other technology I know of is focused on supporting an unconditionally accepting and loving, present-moment, embodied experience of ourselves and the other, interpersonally."[24]

At one Big Sur retreat, participants convened in a circle of twenty-four. Blinking bulbs in glass jars pulsed with light, the blinks signaling individuals in the group synchronized into a single beat. Through meditation and coaching, twenty-four heartbeats came together. They formed a connection through a shared consciousness.

"For me," said one GroupFlow participant, "connecting with everyone gave me a perspective of the power of connection and the unity of humanity. Of just all of our beings . . . I often feel isolated from everyone, and then connecting to the sound . . . and just how powerful that sound is . . . and then imagining the sound of all the heartbeats of all humans in the world, of all beings, it just gives me chills to realize the power we possess when we are one. Such a profound and beautiful experience."[25]

With platforms like HeartSync and GroupFlow enabling synchronization of breathing and heart rates, the idea of aligning brain waves, emotional resonance, and intense sensation of shared exuberance is well within the realm of possibility. The connection comes not from what we read or sing in church but from what we directly experience together.

The Splintering of Spirituality

Not everyone is convinced that the future of spirituality lies in technological worship or connection. Brett Robinson, director of Catholic media studies at Notre Dame, believes the gap between technology and religion has always been much smaller than we assume, whether it be magic or science that has blended into faith.

Like Siegel, Robinson thinks that the content of religion is a hindrance, and we should instead turn to the idea of reconstructing vibrant communities. He asks, "How do we bring back ritualized behavior? Where can we find connection and purpose again in a human way, as opposed to a technological one?"[26]

Robinson told me the Catholic Church's future is intrinsically linked to the arts. He says we lack new cultural movements not based on technology but on humanities, beauty, truth, and goodness. New practices must be presented through cultural works to regain sustained spiritual nourishment. He warns of the potential effects of emerging technologies and alternative practices they spawn. "We can't leave people stranded and confused."[27]

Renowned poet William Ernest Henley crafted his famous poem "Invictus" in the wake of a drawn-out struggle with tuberculosis. His timeless phrase, recited in stories of courage and quest, says, "I am the master of my fate: I am the captain of my soul."

A century later these words epitomize the mindset and spiritual progression of the burgeoning "none"—that is, people without religion. This growing population of nonreligious people has spiked the demand for new spiritual guidance.

Bookstores overflow with titles offering advice on new age practices spanning spirit hacking, meditation, yoga, witchcraft, and astrology. Reflecting on the appeal of a boundary-free realm of religiosity, a book called *Contemporary Prayers for Whatever Works: An Artist's Collection of*

Prayers to Nothing-in-Particular made the 2021 *Publishers Weekly* list of Religion and Spirituality best sellers.[28]

The space for nontraditional advisors is growing, including "design Shamans."[29] One collaboration between two experienced designers, Adam Menter and Arvind Venkataramani, resulted in a how-to guide for creating spiritual rituals. The two came together with a shared vision, seeing ritual as an untapped mechanism for navigating human and social challenges during the pandemic. Venkataramani said, "We have alienation from institutions.... And so, part of what we want to do is to help people develop rituals, to develop communities, to develop institutions." He added, "Our goal is to say, we already live in this fractured world. How can we help people synthesize again on their terms?"[30]

Inspired by the idea that ceremony helps with transitions, they developed a Ritual Design Toolkit and community.[31] Its intent was to help people construct rituals, manage uncertainty, and create personally relevant practices. While the idea isn't novel, they broke down the process, making it possible for anyone to become a master ritual-maker or ceremonial coordinator.

Venkataramani says, "We identify ritual as a kind of 'lost technology' to help navigate that change."[32] His work includes a portfolio of tutorials and guides on YouTube. They cover a range of activities, such as holding funerals or memorials over video calls and "drive-by" spiritual sessions. They help design ceremonies to mark life passages, especially those that are hard to process or understand.

Venkataramani claims that as more people self-select new alternatives, they need structure and guides to help ground and sustain them. He said, "The idea is that rituals are a kind of human activity that can be designed intentionally and democratically instead of just being received as part of traditions. And so, we want to broaden the choices people have with navigating lives and using rituals to make their way through life."[33]

Western society highly values individual autonomy, wherein each person is responsible for their physical, mental, and spiritual well-being. Rather than adhering to tradition, people will gravitate toward technologically augmented options to fulfill their spiritual needs.

Spirituality is no longer just a personal journey; it's a flourishing market. Companies capitalize on spirituality in commonplace products. This trend is reflected in the success of apps like Calm, Co-Star, Headspace, and Insight Timer, as well as products that subtly infuse spirituality into their brands like SoulCycle, Goop, or Peloton. These brands employ design from organized religion in their marketing strategies, a trend of monetizing spirituality in everyday businesses.[34]

A New Code of Ethics

Philosophers and ethicists must consider different questions than those who came before them. Today, religious scholars have differing opinions on when life begins, the role of women in the Church, and the acceptance of LGBTQIA+ members. By 2100, we may confront disagreements, debates, and expulsions concerning the prospect of AIs joining a church, serving as clergy, or marrying a human.

The discourse about robotic servitude, digital consciousness, and designer religions and sects will evolve. The stories within this chapter explore themes of voids, mechanical efficiency, pathways to power, and optimized humanity. Transhumanists envision a future where the ultimate objectives are coping, surviving, dominating, and improving in perpetuity.

Should ceaseless striving for transcendence be our mission? How do we preserve the essence of love, artistry, poetry, the allure of the unknown, and the acceptance of unanswerable mysteries?

To answer these questions, we will return to our human roots and engage with a timeless question contemplated for centuries: As the world changes, who and what do we follow into a radically different era?

PART III

LEADING IN TRANSITION

The venture capital firm a16z, or Andreessen Horowitz, is famed for investing in groundbreaking companies like Facebook, Twitter, Airbnb, Lyft, and Pinterest. Situated in the epicenter of technological innovation, it's no surprise a16z would pen visionary manifestos on the future.

In one essay, cofounder Marc Andreessen prophetically suggested that "software is eating the world."[1] He envisioned a future where tech enterprises, characterized by Silicon Valley's entrepreneurial spirit, would disrupt the establishment through software.

Another manifesto, "It's Time to Build," addresses the effects of this shift.[2] Published during COVID-19, it laid bare the systemic failures and lack of preparedness that caught leaders off guard. Warnings were ignored, and essential medical supplies fell short. It was a failure to prepare for a known existential risk and a failure to build for it. However, the call to "just build it," as the manifesto suggests, belies the complexity of the task. What should we build? How should we build? Who will be the builders?

Constructing a future society is a massive endeavor that requires the contribution of everyone. This book's final part tackles the most crucial aspect of transitions: leadership. It explores the evolution toward new practices that values enlightened strategy, novel intelligence-gathering methods, innovative tools, and the power of collective action.

The cases that follow can be a springboard for action. It is an invitation to embrace the shifts in leadership and adaptation necessary to participate in the construction of future society.

CHAPTER 10

MINDSET: BUILD COGNITIVE STAMINA

Intelligence is traditionally viewed as the ability to think and learn. Yet in a turbulent world, there's another set of cognitive skills that might matter more: the ability to rethink and unlearn.

—ADAM GRANT[1]

Picture Thierry Gueorgiou, or "Tero," as he's affectionately known in the sport of orienteering, moving purposefully through a dense forest. His eyes scan a topographic map in his hands while his other senses take in the feel of the terrain under his boots, the scent of the trees around him, and the shifting play of light and shadow.

This isn't just a casual outing in the woods for Tero. This is his domain, his battleground, his playground. Born in France in 1979, Tero forged a legendary career in orienteering, a sport that weaves together navigation skills, decision-making, and physical endurance. With fourteen World Orienteering Championships, seven European Championships, and numerous national titles under his belt, Tero has consistently showcased a superior understanding of the sport's intricate dance of the mind and body.

The sport of orienteering traces its origins to the military exercises of nineteenth-century Sweden, where it was used to train soldiers in land navigation. Today it rewards the human capacity to chart a course through the unknown. Competitors navigate from point to point in diverse, often unfamiliar environments, using only a map and a compass.

The beauty in this adventure lies in its demand for a seamless fusion of physical fitness, spatial awareness, quick thinking, and the ability to remain calm under pressure. It's a test of resilience and an analogy for navigating life's unpredictable journeys.

Above all, orienteering requires mental fortitude. The best orienteers, like Tero, cultivate strength in the mind to embrace uncertainty, maintain focus amid distractions, and quickly recover from setbacks.

As in orienteering, developing the capacity to read situations is crucial for navigating the uncharted territories in our personal and professional lives. The difference between opportunity realized and crisis to manage relies on keeping one's cool, assessing situations clearly, and making swift, informed decisions.

Like the world's top orienteer, we must prepare for the unexpected, keep our eyes open for opportunities, and persistently move forward, undeterred by cognitive demands change creates.

Ascent from the Maelstrom

Orienteering-as-metaphor reminds me of the classic tale from Edgar Allen Poe, where he begins: "You suppose me a very old man—but I am not. It took less than a single day to change these hairs from a jetty black to white, to weaken my limbs, and to unstring my nerves, so that I tremble at the least exertion and am frightened at a shadow."

Poe's "A Descent into the Maelstrom," penned in 1841, tells the story of recognition and survival. This journey is portrayed through two complementary perspectives, one by observation, the other through experience.

"A Descent" is about surviving unexpected chaos. The protagonist takes to the sea with his brothers on an ordinary day. They know the conditions well, regularly maneuvering treacherous whirlpools and maelstroms. On this catastrophic day, a hurricane blows in and overwhelms them. The waves batter then destroy the ship. As it happens, panic sets in. One brother ties himself to the ship's mast, only for it to be ripped away by a huge wave. Another desperately clings to the ship's side. The force drags the ship along with him down into the sea.

The protagonist, facing a similar fate, comes to his senses on the way down. He accepts his circumstances and, in doing so, becomes calm. He observes beauty in the vortex. Aware of his surroundings, he sees cylindrical-shaped objects buoyed above other objects plunging around him. He leaps to save himself. One cask slows his descent and brings him back to the surface. In the end, he survives.

In Poe's tale, survival is only possible by adapting to chaos on its terms. Pattern recognition amid a huge, overwhelming, destructive force is the way out of the maelstrom. Facing chaos creates a choice: Create a sense of calm or be paralyzed by the vortex.

We can relate to the fear of the fisherman in Poe's story. We all have disorienting anxiety when facing new, high-stakes situations. As we look out over the horizon, the need for perspective will become more acute and challenging. We must find our casks to stay afloat in the maelstroms around us.

Industry Elevates Inner Calm

Given the emotional turbulence of change, cultivating peace of mind is a mandatory practice. It's no surprise, then, that philosophy is now boardroom material. In late 2022 the book *Deliberate Calm* debuted as a number-one business best seller. It's a how-to guide on remaining poised in the face of perpetual chaos.[2]

A trio of consulting veterans drew from psychology, neuroscience, and consciousness practices to write their book, which offers new frameworks for learning with awareness and intention while facing challenging situations.

Dr. Jacqui Brassey, one of the book's authors, is McKinsey's chief scientist and the head of research science for people and organizational impact. She has a PhD in workplace psychology, teaching experience, and executive positions at multinationals, including Unilever. In the book, she examines how organizational development affects a company's financial performance.

Brassey found that facing rapid and unpredictable change with the ability to adjust course has become a vital trait for leaders. Her studies discovered adaptability and learning agility as the two most important indicators of a leader's performance. These sat above intelligence and experience. She says that leaders with high emotional self-awareness and self-regulation perform better. She advises her readers to develop four skills tailored to specific business scenarios: adaptability, learning agility, self-awareness, and the regulation of emotions.[3]

These traits aren't typically top-of-mind when assessing business performance. And yet leaders are now tasked with high-stakes decisions, armed with experience and models incompatible with new challenges. Leaders who don't recognize this misalignment often revert to what they know. Some practice "active inertia," accelerating activities that worked in the past. We all need deliberate work to untangle ourselves from this mindset to lead better.

Like the protagonist in "Descent," Brassey notes that calm requires cultivating "dual awareness," or being simultaneously aware of our external and internal environments.[4] She says our instinct is to become frightened and attempt to protect ourselves instead of exploring new paths. Developing dual awareness helps counter this impulse.

Practicing calm is a meta-skill. It's the thing that unlocks whatever skill or decision is necessary to succeed.

Relearning What It Means to Be Human

While cultivating peace of mind is essential for facing new situations, what happens when one is blind to storms or the consequences of being swept up in them?

"My job on earth is to help reveal what's going on—for people who are amusing themselves to death and don't want to know."[5] This is Mark Stahlman, channeling Neil Postman, a media theorist and McLuhan protégé.

Here, "what's going on" alludes to the unseen influence of technology on our inner senses. The *amusement* he refers to reflects the apathy toward actively comprehending a significant transformation we face. This indifference gives us a deceptive sense of safety.[6]

Stahlman is the president of the Center for the Study of Digital Life (CSDL). The center was founded in 2015 to examine human challenges under digital conditions. Comprising scientists, philosophers, geopolitical experts, and media theorists, the center has a progressive, human-centric view on issues navigating digitally shaped existence. Stahlman believes, under digital conditions, that remembering what it means to be human is urgent as the technologists attempt to invent "artificial humans."

Over the past three years, Mark and I spent hours decoding insights from the center. Our meetings often happened over German beers and brats, a testament to Mark's Wisconsin roots. It was far from idle barroom chatter. The topics were wide-ranging, profound, and forward-looking.

Our discussions considered the shift from individuals as cogs in the machine of an industrial economy to people as information processors in an AI economy. From there, our conversations covered media changes. We discussed the transition from a television-dominated medium characterized by carefully crafted narratives to a digital era governed by the unforgiving exactness of digital memory.

Perfect memory erodes narratives when any story can be analyzed, refuted, and remixed into something different. Subsequently, our dialogue often veered toward the decline of management and economic paradigms like globalism. We noticed a stark dissonance among Eastern, Western, and digital ideologies, which appear to be increasingly incompatible and dangerous.[7]

Like other scholars I spoke with researching this book, Stahlman believes we've entered a new five-hundred-year cycle, ending the industrial age started by the printing press.[8] The talks typically led to the same place: the need to rediscover our humanity and to take care of the soul with focus and intention.

These discussions made me enlightened, confused, hopeful, and unnerved about the future. And in every case, talking to Stahlman, whether I believed or agreed with what he said, I always learned. I came away with a different perspective. Despite technological developments over the past thirty years, digital is still in its beginnings. Trillions of dollars of capital continue to build the next-generation internet, AIs, and 3D digital experiences. As illustrated in previous chapters, the stuff of life will be rewired and reordered, spanning politics, economics, spirituality, and relationships.

Humanity now sits at a historical crossroads. If we face the future head-on, we can be better prepared to deal with it emotionally and intellectually.

If we bypass this responsibility, we face dire consequences. He says, "We are form recognizers, not information processors. Why would anybody want to do that? . . . Why would anybody want to think that humans are information processors? I believe the principal answer is they are trying to build a new human nature, to re-form humans."[9]

There is daylight in our conversations. Stahlman repeatedly says it's normal to feel conflicted during a paradigm shift. Old rules don't apply anymore. The effects are profound, as our behaviors and attitudes are reshaped in ways we don't yet understand. The jarring change we sense is not chaotic or random; it's part of a discernible pattern.

We must steel ourselves psychologically to deal with it. As lives become digitally, and profoundly, augmented by intelligent networks, Stahlman says we need to take an understanding of digital terrain seriously or face terrible consequences. He believes this is less about technical expansion and more about exploring philosophical frontiers. He asks us to consider today's "spiritual" crises, like perpetual conflict, pervasive anxiety crises, and rising suicide rates. They all reflect a sensibility disorder.

The subconscious "ground" through which we understand the world is out of whack, particularly among the digital generation. A *Fortune/Harris* poll found that three in five (60 percent of) college students reported being diagnosed with a mental health condition by a professional. The most common afflictions were anxiety and depression. The framing of the results had an alarming subtext; the pollsters said this was significantly higher than the general population, of which only 48 percent say they've been diagnosed with a mental health condition. So, depending on the demo, two-thirds or half the population is mentally unstable.[10]

The significance of the industrial age was not the printing press reconstituting or democratizing knowledge; it also changed people subconsciously. It created psychological conditions for revolutionary change. Like the Reformation and Enlightenment, Stahlman says a new generation is opting out of a fantasyland and protectionism of the elite's making. They won't be guided by dogma. They will choose to live in the real, changing world and figure it out as they go. He calls Gen Z the "workaround class." "They're endlessly rerouting. They're hunting for new paths, new guides, and new maps."[11]

Mark Stahlman feels a sense of mission behind his messages. It was instilled in him early in his upbringing. His father, a disciple of Norbert Wiener, impressed on him after Wiener's death that someone needed to continue to warn of the effects of technology progression without questioning human consequences.

Balancing Technological and Human Agency

A picture of Stahlman's godfather, Norbert Wiener, took up the entire front page of the *World Magazine* in October 1906. The story billed him as "the most remarkable boy in the world," noting that he was the youngest college man in the history of the United States. Wiener entered college at eleven. He received his PhD from Harvard at eighteen and then apprenticed with renowned European mathematicians. In 1919 he joined the faculty at MIT.[12]

Mathematical genius, military innovation, and human philosophy shaped Wiener's legacy. A year before the Japanese attack on Pearl Harbor, Vannevar Bush went to Washington to head up the Carnegie Institution, a private foundation and premier patron of American science. His first initiative was to organize a network of seven hundred universities and research institutions for war-related scientific and technical projects.[13] As part of this network, Wiener became a frontline mathematician performing a supreme feat of human intelligence. His efforts to build and refine the underlying equations of Britain's RADAR systems would redefine "control," a concept that would become indispensable to engineers in all fields.

Wiener became famous for his book *Cybernetics*. He defined it as "the science of control and communications in the animal and machine."[14] Wiener's vision changed causality from a linear to a circular pattern. Cybernetics was a way to regulate and improve systems by reintroducing past performance results.

After its publication in 1948, *Cybernetics* revolutionized ordinary tasks for people across various occupations. Today, the enhancements found in technologies, social media behavior, and the development of machine learning models are all influenced by his thesis on continuous feedback.

Beyond his contributions to technological development, Wiener was the first "AI doomer."[15] He warned that without interventions, humans' primary task would be to give machines instructions to understand and complete the commands. He foresaw social, political, and economic upheavals to come with automation. He was the first to sound alarms about machines that could learn continuously and act in ways unforeseen by their human creators. And relevant to discussions on AI regulation, he demanded ethical and communal accountability from scientists, technicians, and policymakers.

In his warnings of the future, Wiener found that there were few that he could appeal to. Proponents of cybernetics were, by and large, working for the enemy or trying to engineer human behavior emotionally. Dating back to industrialism in the twentieth century, people succumbed to becoming robotic themselves. Human agency had, metaphorically, started to disappear.

Wiener said prophetically, "We have modified our environment so radically that we must modify ourselves in order to exist in this environment."[16] In his view, humanity did not need to be redesigned as transhumanists suggest. Echoing his godson, we needed to be "reminded" of humans' place in a new universe.

Classical Thinking to Contemplate the Future

If we don't have a perspective on human behavior, we risk ceding power to technologies. There is an education risk to ward this challenge off. For if we're to understand the human condition in the face of unknowns, we must turn to the classic humanities texts.

Since the 1960s the number of degrees awarded in the humanities has shrunk by half. Funding for humanities research is also in steep decline. And yet a significant proportion of those in the top percentile in corporate America have a political science, philosophy, drama, and history background. They are often alumni of liberal arts institutions like Colgate, Bucknell, and Union College.[17]

More than a third of *Fortune* 500 CEOs pursued degrees in liberal arts.[18] This group includes visionaries who founded or lead some of the world's most innovative companies. They include Steve Jobs of Apple, Sue Wojcicki of YouTube, Oprah Winfrey of Harpo Productions, Howard Schultz of Starbucks, Lloyd Blankfein of Goldman Sachs, and Kenneth Chenault of American Express.[19] The broad exploration of humanities equips the mind to be receptive to fresh ideas. It's an invaluable asset in a world that's perpetually evolving.

Fred Beuttler insists that the forgotten practice of deep reading in liberal arts is a way to build stamina and peace of mind. He's the former associate dean of liberal arts (which included the Great Books Program) at the University of Chicago. His mission is to retrieve reading well and to think systematically and analytically. He says, "In a very elementary way, the skill, honed properly, is very powerful."[20]

The study of Great Books, found in liberal arts fields at St. Johns, Notre Dame, and the University of Chicago, is relevant to progressive thinking. The study encompasses content and method established by Mortimer Adler, an American philosopher and educator.[21] It involves a progression from analytical to comparative, or as Mortimer Alder called it, "syntopical reading." It trains students to think more deeply, read more closely, and resist the digitally influenced temptation to skim through the material.

How we process information is central to the Great Books thesis. Beuttler told me that the machines prompt us to skim, to move from one thing to another. Intellectually degrading hypertext style, by design, distracts us with links embedded in the text. It encourages us to bounce back and forth between things rather than following an argument through.

Paper is also material matter. Beuttler insists that his students read from physical books. He notes that classics needed to be read linearly and deeply, at odds with digital reading.[22] Oral texts, like Plato's *Republic*, were designed to be listened to and looked at on a page. Other classics were written to be explored and discussed. He maintains that reading and debating the meaning behind classic texts is helpful to counteract what technology does to us.

Like Stahlman, Beuttler believes that reclaiming our humanity requires thinking about "digital" differently. Together, they and others (including myself) have since introduced a new university called TrivU that draws on our past to inform our future.

TrivU is a derivative of the Great Books program Beuttler runs at the University of Chicago Graham School, the curriculum of which spans classic texts from Plato, Aristotle, Thomas Aquinas, Francis Bacon, David Hume, and Friedrich Nietzsche. The program juxtaposes classic philosophy with contemporary theory from the likes of Marshall McLuhan (*Understanding Media*), Sam Huntington (*The Clash of Civilizations*), Ray Kurzweil (*The Age of Spiritual Machines*), and Donna Haraway (*A Cyborg Manifesto*). As with Great Books' scholars, TrivU students learn through rigorous reading, discussions, and contemplation.

By comparison, in his book *Blink*, Malcolm Gladwell popularized how spontaneous judgment plays a vital role in our digitally driven society.[23] His story centers on our subconscious need to filter through vast amounts of information, providing a mechanism to cope with information overload. The phenomenon also introduces biases that confirm preexisting beliefs. As we sift through oceans of data, we often favor information that aligns with our perspectives. In contrast, Beuttler instills a wider field of vision on a topic. It forces us to draw on perspectives from various authors, classmates, and professors. Instead of bouncing back and forth, it encourages intention, thoughtfulness, and discussion. Notably, all are innate human pursuits.

Leveling Up Human Imagination

A distinguishing factor between humans and robots lies in imagination. Leadership in a transforming world calls for much more of it. This necessitates the courage and creative vision needed to see what others can't.

A commitment to expanding perspective to do so is the essential trait of all great explorers. Da Vinci became his day's most prominent medical scientist without formal medical training. Michelangelo, Benjamin Franklin, Ludwig van Beethoven, Thomas Edison, and Pablo Picasso never finished primary school. After a year, Einstein dropped out of high school and returned to college preparation. Tesla dropped out of university and never returned. Isaac Asimov said, "Self-education is, I firmly believe, the only kind of education there is."[24]

Perspective warrants continued refinement. As noted by biographer Walter Isaacson, da Vinci honed two traits that aided his scientific pursuits: an omnivorous curiosity, which bordered on the fanatical, and an acute power of observation, which was eerily intense.[25] Da Vinci credited all his scientific and artistic feats to a defining principle denoted as *saper vedere*, or "knowing how to see."[26] In a time of life-altering change, we must calmly refine our vision to go deep and see around corners.

The way innovation legends see and the extraordinary ways they steel themselves to realize their vision changes the world. Even dating back to ancient Greece, the line between genius and insanity has been seen as hazy. Plato referred to it as a "divine mania."[27] Leadership scholar Craig Wright's accounts point to the same conclusion: Geniuses cannot accept the world as described to them. Anything can be improved or reimagined.

Managing this agitation has an unexpected, even counterintuitive, benefit: longevity. Geniuses tend to live a decade longer than the general populace. On average, Wright found that optimistic explorers had 11 to 15 percent longer lifespans. They had 50 to 70 percent greater odds of reaching eighty-five years old than the lesser optimistic groups.[28]

Most of us aren't geniuses. But we can bring creativity to examine and solve new problems with poise. The MIT Leadership Center sees a common characteristic to do so: the ability to ask great questions.

Based on interviews with the world's most innovative leaders, MIT found that articulated curiosity and great questions often brought a catalytic quality to thinking. Their inquiries reframe or open avenues to new perspectives and strategies. Research found that the most successful leaders spent about 30 percent of their workday actively exploring new ideas.[29]

Kevin Kelly, the founding editor of *Wired*, knows a thing or two about what types of questions lead to world-changing ideas. He says a good question is a probe, a what-if scenario. A good question skirts on the edge of what is known and not known, one that is neither silly nor obvious. A good question generates many other good questions. They lead to new depictions of the world, previously out of sight.[30]

These types of questions are presented throughout this book. How do we make sense of a world that doesn't make sense through previous guides? What is the right balance between machine intelligence and human ingenuity? Can we design new frameworks that make us better, more empowered, and more emotionally secure? Uncommon questions are essential to determine the agents we use to manage complexity and find new territories for growth.

There is also practicality to building a questioning instinct. The coming AI boom, driven by large language learning models, is based on human queries. Good questions will become increasingly important to ensure AI systems are used successfully and responsibly.

Prompts, short texts, or spoken words used to train machine learning systems are creating a growing field. The use of prompts will become more widespread and essential in the future.

In this context, questions become table stakes to discern a changing world and embrace new ideas. Adapting with poise takes leadership, character, and an open mindset. The new leadership mindset is increasingly moving toward a more holistic approach that integrates situational awareness, in-depth analysis, a return to humanities, and a natural curiosity.

This perspective, underscored by the MIT Leadership Center's research, emphasizes the importance of calm and curiosity as common denominators. This shift in leadership thinking is not just about fostering business acumen but about cultivating a broader perspective, a deep understanding of human nature, and a questioning instinct.

Albert Einstein is noted for saying, "I have no special talents. I am only passionately curious."[31] The need of the hour is to recognize and nurture it.

CHAPTER 11

MODELS: FRAME A PATH FORWARD

> The key to better understanding the world is to build a latticework of mental models.
>
> —CHARLIE MUNGER[1]

A riddle on paradigm change goes like this: Picture water lilies growing on a pond. On the first day, there is one lily. Each day the number doubles. A month later the lilies cover half the lake. How long before they cover the other half of the lake, so it is full? The lilies that took thirty days to cover half the lake take only one more day to cover the other half. They fill the lake on day thirty-one.

Here's another one. A mythical emperor rewards the inventor of chess with a single grain of rice that doubles for every chessboard square. Up through the board's first half, rewards are measured in spoons and cups. By the end, they grow to a rice pile the size of Mount Everest—from a single unit to eighteen quintillion grains. The analogy visualizing the second half of the board is relevant today. The pattern starts slow and then scales beyond our comprehension.

An unmoored sense results from what author Azeem Azhar calls the "exponential gap." In our inability to perceive rates of change, strange new voids emerge. People and organizations that can't adjust get left behind.[2] Minding the gap is serious business.

The gap affects how accurately we see and frame situations affected by exponential change. Things feel out of whack because the frames we use to make sense of the world, plan, run businesses, and lead people become obsolete. Outmoded or single-view models lose impact and reduce the legibility of new situations.

We need varied ways to see and model scenarios to make sense of the overwhelming inputs. In the case of the chessboard, the calculation for the number of grains on the last (sixty-fourth) square, and the entire board, can be done with the formula for the sum of a geometric series. This exponential compounds to approximately 9.22 quintillion grains. If we imagine this volume as a cube, each side would be roughly 913 miles. This cube would be bigger than many countries, demonstrating the staggering growth that comes from exponential doubling.

New models that help us sense problems can be powerful perspective agents. Without them, we become overwhelmed by sensory inputs and experiences. Mental models provide a frame of reference to decode patterns, anticipate outcomes, and impose order. And yet models misapplied to situations can lead to disorder and failure.[3]

Reframe the Way We See Things

Scott Page is a professor of complex systems, political science, and economics at the University of Michigan. In the fall of 2012, he started an open learning course on Model Thinking with a tablet computer, a $29 camera, and a $90 microphone. The first course attracted sixty thousand students.[4] Less than a decade later, the number was nearly one million.

Students worldwide understood the importance of fusing different models to solve new, complex problems.

Models are essential to speed innovation and decision-making. Consulting firms like BCG and KPMG use them to formulate business strategies. Wall Street firms such as Blackrock and Morgan Stanley rely on them for trading and investment decisions. Technology companies run on them for prediction and personalization of services. In his book, Page identifies at least thirty categories of models to apply to specific scenarios.

The often-referenced archetype of frames is the paradigm. Thomas Kuhn, who introduced the idea, maintained that scientific advancement could be best depicted through frameworks to interpret situations. When those models become well-known and change how a society works, they become paradigms. The most well-known of them become institutions.

The "institutions" covered in this chapter span Harvard Business School, the RAND Corporation, Betaworks, and Y Combinator. Carnegie Mellon's transition framework is newer but may be more consequential than the others in shaping the future.

Matching strategic orientation to the situation informs the models we use. As we'll explore, choice requires a deep study of environments to inform strategic bets placed. Five models for strategic thinking, all relevant today, are framed in exhibit 5.

The Curse of Best Practices

"A business case at Harvard Business School isn't presented as a strategy, financial dilemma, or product situation. It's framed as a detective story. For example, something's gone deeply wrong in a factory. As a chief executive, you must figure out a whodunnit and what you'll ask of whom." This is Jan Rivkin, a Harvard Business School professor, introducing an online audience to the Harvard case study method.[5]

```
Exhibit 5: Leadership Paradigms: Thinking Models
```

	Invent START-UP SCHOOL	Transform TRANSITION DESIGN
REINVENT	Y Combinator	Carnegie Mellon University
ITERATE	Forecast NET ASSESSMENT	Manage CASE METHOD
	RAND	Harvard Business School
	ENTREPRENURIAL	OPERATIONAL

In 1921 the first Harvard Business School case investigated the General Shoe Company to understand management challenges in the retail shoe industry. It was a time of deep unrest. The country struggled with industrialization, urbanization, government corruption, and immigration.

As the CEO, you are tasked with solving a human resources problem. Someone in the company has been agitating the workers, creating unrest and absenteeism. Is this due to increasing prices and stagnating wages? Are supervisors not performing their duties? Are employees overworked and skipping their shifts? The wrong decision could have adverse consequences for workers and the future of the business. To address the problem, you must act like an investigator. You have to get to the root cause of the problem to come up with a solution.

The case method, refined since this first investigation, became a magical artifact at Harvard spanning decades. Harvard's teaching framework is as well-packaged as a Coca-Cola or Nike brand. Its marketing features storytelling, myth-building, and identity-enhancing cues.[6] Its promotional videos are presented like a reality show where the world's best management experts battle the world's toughest situational challenges. Like other high-end brands, the case business is lucrative.

About fifteen million business cases are sold annually to students. Over fifty business schools worldwide now have case collections. Thousands of new cases are written and released every year. They assess management decisions faced by business titans including Amazon, Apple, McDonald's, Microsoft, Toyota Motor Corporation, Walmart, Google, Facebook, and Uber.

The case method remains the pedagogical system of choice for the world's most elite business schools. Before graduating, Harvard Business School students complete five hundred "decision-forcing" exercises for training future managers. The core of the case method takes the student's perspective, not the teacher's, as an all-knowing expert. The student is at the center, surrounded by conflicting scenarios and management inputs. The professor coordinates conversations where the student is the protagonist. The technique is not a one-time event but an ongoing practice that can be applied to everyday life.[7]

Critics say that teaching with case studies sets a limitation for best practices. While valid for incremental improvements, best practices don't apply to new, exponential changes coming into view.

A Model for Invention

The stories of heroic innovation and growth take circuitous routes. The transistors inside computers were initially designed for use in traffic lights and vending machines.[8] The Coca-Cola recipe was marketed as a "brain tonic."[9] Facebook began as a college look book called FaceMash.[10]

Instagram started as Burbn, a location check-in app,[11] and YouTube was originally a dating platform.[12]

To "pivot" is now a catchall phrase used when companies change strategy, markets, or product lines. It's the ethos behind Facebook's mantra to "move fast and break things." To pivot is assumed for early-stage entrepreneurial ventures. Venture capitalists found that what makes entrepreneurs successful is rarely associated with the original idea. Success comes from the founders' willingness to adjust course to changing circumstances. What if you could create a model that institutionalized inventive adaptability?

In the bustling world of start-ups, one name often resonates above others: Y Combinator (YC). In 2005, Paul Graham, a computer scientist and entrepreneur, formed a three-month boot camp with his wife, Jessica Livingston; Trevor Blackwell; and Robert Tappan Morris.[13] They likened it to a summer job. Instead of a salary, they gave seed funding to those starting companies with friends.[14]

YC hit the entrepreneurial jackpot on the first pull. The inaugural wave of YC founders included Alexis Ohanian, founder of Reddit; Emmett Shear, CEO of Twitch; and Sam Altman, CEO of OpenAI.[15] It has since played an instrumental role in launching over two thousand companies, including heavy hitters like Dropbox, Airbnb, Stripe, and DoorDash.

So what exactly is Y Combinator's framework, and how has it achieved such a distinguished track record in the cutthroat world of tech start-ups?

YC provides early-stage companies with the right tools, connections, and guidance to improve their chances of success. The founders of YC believe that a combination of small seed investments, focused training, adaptation, and community-building can make the difference between a start-up's failure and its potential to become a unicorn.

Every year, YC runs two funding cycles, one in winter and one in summer. Thousands of start-ups apply, but only a select few (often less than 10 percent) are chosen to participate in each cycle. Those selected are then invited to move to Silicon Valley for the duration of the three-month program.

Once there, the real work begins. Start-ups are given an initial seed investment in exchange for a 7 percent equity stake. But the true value of the YC experience is far beyond just the money and includes mentorship, assistance with product build, and selling the idea.

Each week, start-ups attend dinners with a range of industry figures, from successful entrepreneurs to venture capitalists. These sessions provide start-ups with firsthand insight into the challenges and strategies of building a successful company.

Outside these dinners, start-ups spend their time building their product, refining their pitch, and seeking product-market fit. YC's environment is designed to reduce distractions, allowing founders to focus entirely on their company.

Each class climaxes with the now famous Demo Day, likened to the NFL Scouting Combine for assessing potential talent. Twice a year, before some of the most influential technology investors, start-up founders present their ideas. They have two-and-a-half minutes to deliver the pitch. Companies launched through their venture are now valued at over $400 billion.

The YC brand, network, and education move founders into a stratosphere of potential, along with the intensity that goes with it. Steven Levy, a Silicon Valley reporter who covered YC in-depth, called its vibe "*American Idol* meets *Wired* magazine."[16]

Hundreds of thousands of students can also participate in free versions of Start-up Schools.[17] Y Combinator has perfected an open-sourced invention and adaptability model for nearly two decades in pursuit of a grand goal: to revolutionize the world using the means of start-up values, encouraging innovation to solve the world's most pressing issues.

A Framework for Category Creation

YC isn't the only start-up game in town. Nestled in the meatpacking district at the heart of lower Manhattan's West Side, 29 Little West 12th Street sits quietly. Surrounded by stylish boutiques, coffee shops, and eateries filled with the city's fashion-forward crowd, a different vibe hums inside its walls.

Betaworks sits as a quiet force in an otherwise modest warehouse. If YC is viewed as a tech accelerator, Betaworks is cast like a movie studio for start-ups. And yet the studio, founded by John Borthwick, can't be constrained by the limitations of a single label. His hub serves as a venture capital firm, a product accelerator, and a technology cooperative. Its unique blend injects the New York tech scene with collaborative, determined energy.

Betaworks is a place for builders. It creates an environment for accelerating ideas with frameworks that enable commercialization. They believe that, as technology changes the world, "building" becomes paramount to future-proofing yourself. "Building" might mean being a coder, but it applies to those building a team at a *Fortune* 500 company or a new nonprofit. At Betaworks, building is just as much a mindset as a skillset.

James Cooper, who helped design the Betaworks space, found a niche between the typical office and WeWork spaces. He said, "As people leave traditional offices, with their water coolers and sense of community and stability—perceived or not—the more they need to find their tribe."[18]

In a space designed for learning and collaboration, people work on frontier technologies with experts, bounce business plans off experienced investors, or hear from titans of technology and policy words.

Pre-pandemic, over 25,000 people went through the Betaworks space to hear from the likes of Andrew Yang, Arianna Huffington, Deepak Chopra, Jaron Lanier, Roger McNamee, Stacey Abrams, and Hillary Clinton.[19] At Betaworks, you never know who you'll run into.

The open and airy space carries hints of influence from digital platforms developed there, like GIPHY, Bitly, Dots, TweetDeck, Instapaper, Digg, and Hugging Face, along with other innovations from their investment portfolio, like Tumblr, Kickstarter, Gimlet, and Stability.AI.

The Betaworks teams study the evolution of technology and bet on a cohort of companies defining new categories. They bring founders together to learn from one another as they embark into uncharted territory.

Betaworks Camp operates through a community-centric framework focused on an emerging technology category, creating an environment encouraging in-depth exploration and development. Camp allows participating start-ups to immerse themselves fully in cutting-edge ideas and research to generate groundbreaking products.

During the twelve-week program, selected start-ups receive seed investment, office space, a program of speaker sessions, and one-on-one mentorship from industry leaders. It also provides founders with financial backing, strategic guidance, and a collaborative workspace conducive to product development. On average, the acceptance rate is around 4 percent across all nine camps, though there's no rigid adherence to a particular number. Betaworks selects as many companies as they are genuinely excited about.[20]

A recent initiative, AI Camp: Augment, focuses on investing in companies that utilize applied machine learning and generative AI to create tools that enhance human cognitive, creative, and collaborative activities. This camp emphasizes products that amplify human behavior, creation, play, work, and thinking abilities. The goal is to foster products that empower and augment human capabilities rather than replace them.[21]

Thinking back to the potential of Web 2.0, Borthwick was early to recognize the promise of a single, connected society to help citizens reach their full potential but believes this has yet to be realized. In his words, as the internet matured, technological promise had "a hole in it."[22]

Borthwick's thesis emphasizes builders thinking "human first and positive-sum." AI presents a once-in-a-generation moment. He believes trying to replicate human action and cognition is a large but finite opportunity; trying to supplement human behavior (or create entirely new ones) is an infinite and unconstrained opportunity.[23]

Jordan Crook, former deputy editor at TechCrunch, is a partner at Betaworks and works on the investments team that manages Betaworks Camps. Instead of reporting on start-ups, she joined Betaworks in November 2022 to be a part of the problem-solving that comes with the territory. She told me that Camp is interesting for two reasons: One is that the development framework is meant to be flexible, given the nature of category creation and the unique mixture of start-ups that inhabit it.[24]

Most accelerator programs concentrate on a specific endgame: Hold a great demo day to attract further investment in new ideas. She said, "We care much less about what happens at Demo Day often because our companies aren't necessarily using the accelerator to raise money. They're using it to be a part of that cohort focused on product development."[25]

As part of the Camp, Betaworks hires a subject-specific researcher alongside a hacker-in-residence. They read and share what's going on in the news. They keep camp companies aware of the latest programming methodologies. New research and methodologies help founders to hack something new together.

Crook notes that Camp is essential to their overall business framework because it helps them vet investment theses. "We invest. We watch it play out and learn about that space, that industry, that competitive landscape.

And we go from there. In Camp, we squeeze much more into a much shorter timeframe. We get a whiff of what's promising, then go hunt."[26]

Betaworks' model embeds accelerated learning to develop new categories. Because they invest in eight to twelve companies at once, what would be serialized learning over the years becomes a highly condensed, accelerated experience. Crook says, "We smash a lot in. We can better learn, adapt, and calibrate our thesis strategy based on collective work."[27]

There is a lot to learn from Betaworks' learning framework. Crook added, "Camp companies come to us with many questions. But we come to them with a lot of questions too. Being together in a single space forces moments of actively trying to learn from one another. Alone or in work bubbles represents only one link of a chain. A lot can be learned that you just don't have access to—things you peripherally cannot perceive without forced communication."[28]

Anticipating Outlier Events

Reflecting on other dimensions of force, few issues rival the stakes of military planning. At the end of World War II, RAND emerged as a bridge between military strategy, research, and development. The policy think tank shaped military, scientific, and educational ideas for the public safety and well-being of the United States.

RAND became an influential institute filled with "intellectual outliers" spanning engineering, physics, mathematics, economics, and statistics. At RAND, complex decision-making could be explored freely. These decisions carried weight for the United States in the 1950s when the Iron Curtain descended, and the Soviet Union detonated its first atomic bomb. The geopolitics of the Cold War made the development of new US security strategies essential.

The intellectual hub was intentionally protected from the daily grind of military and national security affairs. With the necessary space, RAND contributed to system design, economics, and military planning, spanning control, management defense, and budgeting.[29]

Research conducted at RAND paved the way for the formation of the NATO Defense Planning Working Group in the 1960s, which led to NATO contingency studies and the execution of the flexible response defense strategy. Beyond policy influence, technical contributions were equally groundbreaking. RAND was at the forefront of advancements in artificial intelligence, satellite surveillance, tablet computing, and packet-switching technologies.

Since its inception, RAND has emphasized foresight and uncommon strategic acumen. Andy Marshall, a RAND alumnus, codified and deployed a strategic framework called Net Assessment.[30] The phrase originated from nuclear war studies involving potential casualties and damage calculations. In 1973, James R. Schlesinger established the Office of Net Assessment and appointed Mr. Marshall to lead it.

The net assessment methodology Marshall codified investigates the relative capabilities of competitors, cultural influences, and outlier events that alter strategic planning. Unlike other analytical approaches that might assess a country's capabilities in isolation, net assessment is inherently comparative. It seeks to understand the balance of capabilities between two or more entities, often over extended periods.

Net assessments often look decades into the future, trying to understand the current balance and how it might evolve. It requires considering technological developments, economic trends, demographic changes, and other long-term factors.

Assessing strategic factors relies on a range of information sources, from classified intelligence reports to open-source economic data. The goal is to integrate all these diverse threads into a coherent picture of the strategic balance. The strategic depiction involves creating detailed scenarios to understand future conflicts or crises. These include wargaming exercises, where analysts role-play different sides in a simulated conflict to understand potential outcomes and dynamics. The endgame is to provide senior decision-makers with a deep, integrative understanding of the strategic landscape to inform major policy decisions.

Marshall acknowledged, "We tend to look at not very happy futures."[31] Nevertheless, he devoted more than four decades to analyzing emergent complexities shaping strategic warfare.[32] The Department of Defense's internal think tank provided the secretary of defense with assessments of military forces in different regions, emphasizing long-term trends, disparities, and potentials to strengthen the United States military standing. It offered a more complete view of potential threats, helping the military stay one step ahead in its strategic planning.

Known for challenging established ways of thinking, Marshall granted more than $10 million yearly to think tanks, universities, and defense contractors to imagine future conflicts.[33] According to Jeffrey McKitrick, a defense researcher who worked for Marshall in the 1980s, Marshall's approach to working on issues was always to focus on the question. He said, "Too often, people focus on solutions but haven't identified the right questions. He thought it was very important to get the strategic questions right and then start thinking about the answers."[34]

Advocates for net assessment emphasize its difference from frameworks informing systems analysis, operations research, or strategic planning. Instead, it's a way of investigating scenarios from various perspectives to discover shortcomings in knowledge or room for improvement. It requires anticipating environmental changes to help avoid fatal errors in judgment.

Design Thinking for Social Change

A newer framework expands on net assessment, based in design thinking. An accomplished design executive, Terri Irwin landed on this new framework following a moral and philosophical quandary. From 1992 to 2001, she held a creative director post at a prestigious design firm, working with legendary brands including Apple, Nissan, Audi, Sony, and Samsung. After some soul-searching, Irwin eventually left her position, sold everything, and spent two years studying holistic science at Schumacher College in Devon, England.

In 2012, she presented a TED Talk on her journey and an important new vision for design. She said in her speech, "I'd never been as disillusioned with design and felt as rudderless as I did then. Overnight conversations in our industry shifted from design to profit, quality to quantity, and business models predicated upon unbridled growth and acquisition."[35]

A specific client conflict forever changed her view. The client, notorious for its overseas factory operations, desperately needed reputation enhancement. The project would serve as a lifeline, enabling the company to maintain unsustainable business practices, both environmentally and socially. Her team faced an ethical question: Continue the project, cash a check, or resign, choosing not to gloss over exploitative work practices?

Irwin had a long-term choice to make: Design with more care and consideration or move toward a career path that would allow her to make a difference in the world. The moral dilemma posed other questions in design. What role would designers have in the twenty-first century? Could designers create social impact, or were they only used to sell and protect reputations? Was design just rearranging deck chairs on the *Titanic*?

Irwin decided to design differently instead of exacerbating bigger systems issues. She proposed a bold answer: Employ system-level design to address humanity's most challenging issues, such as crime, racial inequity, climate change, terrorism, and ideological divides. She called it Transition Design and created a new framework and department at Carnegie Mellon to explore it.

Her academic collaborations led to a new framework grounded in multilevel perspective. Studies found that transitions happen at a systems level over time. At the top level, collective actions, beliefs, and large movements happen. The middle, what she calls the "regime" level, is where cultural norms, working systems, and protocols exist. Small innovations percolate off the radar at the lower, more niche level to permeate the regime. Irwin adds, "This middle layer is disrupted by both large events from above and innovative events from below. That's where transformations happen."[36]

The framework allowed scholars and scientists to understand the mechanics of how big change happened over time. It's particularly helpful to assess "wicked problems," those difficult to understand and fix and that are constantly in flux. In large organizations wicked problems cross silos of expertise. They're not confined to a single department but pervade multiple domains, making a solution more challenging.

To craft a new path, Irwin and her students at Carnegie Mellon look deep into the anatomy of the situation. They map the entire system's problem and how it affects various stakeholders. The analysis seeks "low-hanging fruit," paths for actionable, mutually beneficial solutions. She asks, "Where do diverse stakeholder groups agree? And where do they disagree? Where can we leverage areas of alignment, to build bridges and get some quick wins to try and get people working together over the mid and longer term?"[37]

Given the need to bridge divisions, wicked problems demand an approach beyond traditional problem-solving methods. We perceive dilemmas through the well-defined and manageable scope of our vision, expertise, or unit. While useful in specific contexts, this structured view limits understanding and ability to tackle complex issues.

According to Irwin, it's like the parable of the blind men and the elephant: Each one perceives something differently despite looking at the same problem. Ensuring everyone is on the same page when defining the problem can be challenging.[38]

As an aid to land a common view, Irwin references Chinese acupuncture. She says acupuncture uses needles to bring a person's system back into balance and health. But unlike knowledge of the body, we don't have maps of complex systems. We need design to illuminate them and their context to develop effective solutions. We must depict the body of elements before we know the treatment.

Carnegie Mellon's transition-design class presentations illustrate how this works in practice.[39] Videos of student work start with defining the complex or "wicked" problems to be investigated. They span healthcare access for low-income families, social isolation of older adults, the declining population of essential pollinators such as bees and butterflies, gentrification, and income inequality in urban areas.

With a system-wide view, student teams dissect these problems methodically. Drawing inspiration from net assessment strategies, their work begins with a comprehensive survey of competitive issues and changes in the social environment.

While investigating affordable healthcare for lower-income communities, the teams construct maps illustrating social, environmental, economic, political, and technological issues. They zoom out and graph the complexity and interconnectedness inherent in healthcare issues. The teams map key stakeholders, their interests, and points of contention. In a healthcare access case, the stakeholders comprised families, insurance providers, and the University of Pittsburgh Medical Center.

In addition to identifying these entities, the team documents shared struggles and aspirations within each group. The stakeholder lens is presented through maps highlighting opposing viewpoints in red, shared interests in green, and complex issues in black. Visualizing the environment helps them see connections and diagnose areas for solutions. The teams also consider the historical trajectory of the problem. In Pittsburgh, for example, this includes industry development and the environmental impact of heavy manufacturing and pollution on residents over time. The final phase involves developing future visions for the problem with proposed solutions at different scales and timeframes.

Reviewing Irwin's team presentations, it becomes clear that addressing problems in isolation prevents us from gaining a holistic view of the more significant, systemic issues that affect us. Unseen or overlooked connections are often territories to solve hard problems.

Transition design recognizes that societies must transition toward more sustainable, equitable, and desirable long-term futures. These transitions need intentional, systems-level change. Visualizing the systems at play is necessary to reshape them.

Carnegie Mellon's design approach recognizes that evolving situations are not static constructs; they are dynamic, evolving, and present new variables to factor in strategic planning.

The *Harvard Business Review* case method, YC and Betaworks innovation models, the Office of the Pentagon's Net Assessment, and Carnegie Mellon's transition design can be thought of as a lattice of leadership frameworks. Together they offer unique problem-solving, decision-making, and strategic-planning approaches. Each strives to provide an actionable perspective to solve even the most wicked problems.

By consciously evolving and mixing models, leaders steer organizations toward more sustainable and equitable paths. Given immense complexities, new models must reflect the revolutionary period ahead, using instruments that give us a new lens into how it takes shape.

CHAPTER 12

INSTRUMENTS: ILLUMINATE THE INVISIBLE

The most important things that will happen in our lives will happen in secret.

—JOSHUA COOPER RAMO[1]

It's Christmas Day, 2021. The Guiana Space Center in Kourou, French Guiana, vibrates with anticipation. The source of excitement is an Ariane 5 rocket about to send a groundbreaking perspective agent into space. Nestled within its payload is an extraordinary expression of ambition, the James Webb Space Telescope (JWST).

Developed by NASA in partnership with the European Space Agency (ESA) and the Canadian Space Agency (CSA), this telescope carries the dreams of astronomers yearning to peer deeper into uncharted depths of the universe. It will allow research teams to revisit the birth of the first galaxies, pierce through interstellar dust clouds, observe divine creations, and search distant exoplanets for signs of potential life.

Based on the Hubble Telescope's ultraviolet and visible light spectrum proficiency, JWST is optimized to capture infrared rays necessary to observe nascent galaxies and see newborn stars. The dust-cloaking interstellar infants scatter visible light, concealing their interiors from our sight. This dust layer is permeable to infrared radiation, providing a window into the early stages of star formation.

Humans cannot see infrared radiation. JWST's infrared capabilities reveal what was previously unseen, the obscured celestial objects hidden behind dust clouds and yet-to-be-imagined views of the universe.

Early observations have led to a range of astronomical breakthroughs. One involved a detailed investigation of the atmospheric cloud belts enveloping the gas and ice giants. The focus shifted to Titan, Saturn's most prominent moon, in the subsequent phase. Here, meticulous tracking of cloud patterns was conducted, presenting a unique view of this celestial body's weather system. The exploration then took a turn toward the complex climate of Pluto, providing a deeper understanding of this distant dwarf planet.

As I write this, astronomy continues to buzz about new discoveries. The JWST unveiled organic molecules in a galaxy over 12 billion light-years away, providing a glimpse into the universe as it existed 1.5 billion years after the big bang. The revelation prompts a reevaluation of theories guiding beliefs and actions behind space exploration.

Exploring the World of Digital Networks

Beyond the natural world, new tools will emerge to examine digital networks as an astronomer, meteorologist, or naturalist would scrutinize the physical world.

The digital world under development is a new universe carrying physical, biological, and social dimensions. Social scientists need new agents resembling telescopes, satellites, and radar systems to understand network dynamics. Such agents will fuse graph models, data, ML algorithms, and simulation software to make sense of virtual worlds.

The scope of the internet today is hard to comprehend. The number of connected mobile devices will rise to 18.22 billion in only a few years.[2] These devices provide access to an expanding universe of web pages, applications, and autonomous agents. By 2025, over 152,200 internet-connected IoT devices will join the network every minute.[3] Additionally, one billion surveillance cameras will track our every move from satellites that sit up to twelve thousand miles in the air and cameras close to the ground.[4]

We will experience points of view previously only available to the gods. With a series of clicks, we will be able to switch from maps to satellites to 3D renderings of land, sea, and transportation networks. We will be able to access a database of communal memories with equal ease. We will listen to anyone who posts their thoughts and worries on social media. We will have an unprecedented view of our collective consciousness and daily actions.

This collective virtual mind will be both fluid and permanent. Every action will move at the speed of light. Our data traces exist in over seven million data centers, the largest spanning over eighteen acres.[5] This far-reaching, comprehensive network of computing devices, servers, undersea cables, wireless connectivity, and software facilitates the continuous transmission of information and resources. We need a better view into the language of networks and the behaviors they facilitate.

While we have immense information powers, Google CEO Eric Schmidt has said that over 99 percent of online content is inaccessible to conventional search engines.[6] A "deep web" of websites, apps, databases, files, and more cannot be accessed through conventional search engines. While we have "the world in our pockets," our knowledge about this hidden digital universe is still in its infancy.

Similar to how JWST discoveries have upended long-held astronomical theory, we will uncover ideas that transcend conventional attitudes and convictions on networked influences. New instruments will empower us to discover the reality of events instead of merely relying on digital hearsay or pre-fed narratives. Kevin Kelly said that the synthesis of all online content and connections—the billions of pages, tweets, movies, games, posts, and streams—is like one vast global book.[7] We are only beginning to learn how to "read" it.

Instruments to Understand Network Connections

Some have a gift of vision that allows them to see the unseen. For instance, biology favors tetrachromats, who see a more vibrant world than the average person. They are born with four cone cells for color vision rather than three. An extra receptor gives them ninety-nine million more hues and shades than the regular eye can register. Artists and futurists emulate tetrachromats. They use technology and imagination to see the present and future accurately. While tetrachromats have a genetic advantage, a deeper and broader vision can be developed through new instruments on the horizon.

Wasim Khaled is working on one. He stands on the front lines of confounding network and narrative conflict leading to online harm and abuse. Khaled is a computer scientist and cofounder of Blackbird.AI, a social intelligence company. An American of Bangladeshi descent, Khaled has experienced the pains and inconveniences of online harassment. Khaled conveyed to me that it wasn't until after 9/11 that he became aware of how fractured society could be. "Being an immigrant who grew up in America, I never truly felt like I belonged. After the attack, I was placed on a no-fly list for seven years because my name resembled one of the hijackers. Checking in for flights was impossible without being subjected to intense interrogation."[8]

In 2012, Khaled saw how easily social media manipulation can influence people's behaviors. People he trusted, including friends and family, embraced narratives they wouldn't entertain in real life. Khaled said, "No matter who you were or where you came from, the masses and individuals were susceptible to information manipulation. As computer scientists and network analysts, we had insight others may not have had."[9]

Terrorist activity informs scientists like Khaled in information warfare tactics. ISIS demonstrated the capacity to wage battles against formidable nations without nuclear arms or conventional armies. They mastered techniques to disrupt communication systems, from influencing media coverage to interfering with air traffic control.

Their stock-in-trade is circulating terror-inducing content and narratives to incite fear. Likewise, al-Qaeda's influence on global affairs since the 9/11 attacks has been profound. Their ability to skew perceptions of world events and upend the general understanding of global affairs exemplifies the extent of a singular, spectacularly devastating event. Khaled invokes vernacular with the world of cybersecurity, likening information tactics to denial-of-service (DoS) attacks on human perception. DoS attacks shut down systems by flooding a target with traffic, a propagation of information that triggers a crash.[10]

Khaled sees the spread of harmful propaganda to build terrorist armies and extremist factions as part of "gray matter warfare." It's an ongoing attack on human thinking, feeling, and acting. Through perception hacks, digital propagandists influence behavior, psychology, and beliefs.[11]

Algorithms, bot propagation, and fake news are all elements of the computational propaganda toolbox. Used to spread false and biased information, they manipulate public opinion to achieve political or ideological goals. Information warfare is standard in internet communication, demonstrated daily in America's culture wars. No physical force is necessary to sow confusion and exert harm. The new war occurs in the public consciousness, involving geopolitical adversaries.

While actual numbers are hard to come by, it's estimated that China spent between $7 billion to $10 billion just a few years ago on a new, state-of-the-art influence operation.[12] It fed narratives favorable to China into movies, television, books, social networks, and the Xinhua News Agency—the voice of the Communist Party of China (CCP).

The range of communications platforms used by the CCP is technologically advanced. In 2019, Xinhua Daily Media Group released the first 5G media lab in Jiangsu. Its control center was a central data hub to spark a propaganda revolution. As part of the operation, Xinhua Zhiyun released its "Media Brain," the first domestically developed AI media platform in China. It has a full suite of intelligent editorial tools to personalize and target messages worldwide. As part of its release, they debuted the world's first 3D standing artificial intelligence news anchor.[13]

Intelligent platforms like Media Brain increase the production and distribution of propaganda at a previously unattainable reach and scale. Systems resembling China's Media Brain will use machine-generated content for fast news production, automatically generating videos in ten seconds or less. As technology improves, customized propaganda will take many forms. It will include personalized newsbots, personalized news feeds, and articles tailored to individual readers.

Sean Gourley, founder and CEO of Primer, a Silicon Valley–based machine intelligence company, puts this capability into context. "Once you start in an automated fashion, all of a sudden, you can scale up very, very quickly." He added, "An AP writer is going to write one article... but what if you could write a hundred? This is a very, very powerful organization powered by increasingly sophisticated technology. I think it is going to imprint the Chinese perspective on the world."[14]

According to Khaled, we need to visualize and study network forces to gauge reach and influence. "We can't put the genie back in the bottle, but we can visualize the 'last mile,' the points before radicalized ideas tip into a kinetic conflict of chaos."[15]

Understanding how to tackle such an issue requires being able to pinpoint it. The best way to think of Blackbird.AI is like a weather map; it predicts the information equivalent of rain, thunderstorms, hurricanes, and tornadoes by assessing the environment and tracking its movements.

Blackbird.AI detects how trending topics and groups of people come together. By looking at intent, the people involved, and the motion of the narrative, it can predict how false stories take root, how they spread, and when they might inflict harm. This flow of online information shapes the analog world. With tools like Blackbird.AI, we can see how, determine the orchestration of information, and be aware of clear and present danger.

Khaled says, "The more informative data, the more strategically you can operate and be less reactionary to threats. It's the ones that actually matter to you now, ones that are of high risk, that allow you to make decisions. You can have a knee-jerk reaction to the volatility of this environment."[16]

Visualizations as News Agents

Flight tracking is another visual perspective agent. Through them you watch a top-secret government flight live, track a drug trafficker's movements as they happen, or calculate the damage celebrity flights do to the atmosphere. For millions of voyeurs worldwide, flight tracking became a new version of must-see TV.

In 2022, Ian Petchenik, an executive from Flightradar24, noticed a dramatic rise in people using the site to track the movements of politicians, celebrities, and criminals. The tracking numbers skyrocketed when Nancy Pelosi took her controversial flight to Taiwan. At its peak, 708,000 people simultaneously viewed a red dot tracking Pelosi's C-40C airplane, SPAR19, flying around the world. Turning in to witness her journey were 2.92 million viewers—three times as many people as watched it on CNN in primetime. Petchenik said, "You get to participate in history in real-time. If the newspaper is the first draft of history, then this is the prewrite."[17]

Petchenik believes it's important that the public directly witness developments and shape outcomes. His platform is a gateway; it helps the public track data in motion and visualize it in a way people can understand. The visibility of network dynamics like flight trackers will be analogous to the physical realm, like van Leeuwenhoek's microscope or Röntgen's X-ray. Such instruments give us new lines of sight.

A case in point is Google Maps, which revolutionized the world of digital mapping. It offered users a seamless combination of aerial photography, satellite imagery, and local street maps. During the pandemic the fusion of these technologies enabled essential services. They tracked infected individuals, visualized caseloads, monitored city conditions, and managed the supply of essential goods. It was central to a new intelligence apparatus outside the government and military.

This brand of intel comes from the Open-Source Intelligence (OSINT) movement, which democratizes access to data previously exclusive to intelligence and law enforcement agencies. The networked intelligence that OSINT communities develop enables people to collaborate, share ideas, and collectively strive toward problem-solving, making the process more inclusive and expansive.[18]

The *open*, *source*, and *intelligence* constructs carry distinct significance within this context. The notion of *open* underscores the necessity for a broad perspective that challenges and reinterprets issues rather than merely substantiating established theories.

The term *source* embodies the imperative of absolute transparency for operational effectiveness in this structure. It calls for an exhaustive revelation of the origin of information, qualifications, and roles within a specific system. Such a process encourages collective decision-making based on critical assessment rather than relying on an individual's projected authority.

Intelligence entails drawing connections among seemingly unrelated data fragments. This facet of intelligence gathering goes beyond conventional compartmentalized thinking, fostering the ability to detect and interpret patterns.

A decade ago, OSINT attracted solitary enthusiasts armed only with an internet connection and shared interests. Today, with an expanse of public data sources, it's becoming an increasingly mainstream practice. No longer a casual hobby, a new generation of network detectives mobilize on demand. They gather, analyze, and disseminate intelligence on significant events.[19]

A notable example is tracking the Russia-Ukraine conflict. As Russian forces started the invasion, through OSINT, people worldwide had an inside look at happenings on the ground. Firsthand reports, videos, and satellite images flooded social media, becoming a fused form of military intelligence and news coverage. The contribution of volunteer networks analyzing and processing data offered a valuable resource for US intelligence services.[20] OSINT was crucial in substantiating the Biden administration's reports of an impending attack in February 2022.

In one instance, the Center for Information Resilience assembled intelligence into a public-facing "Eyes on Russia Map."[21] It collaborated with investigative and geolocating organizations spanning Bellingcat, GeoConfirmed, the Conflict Intelligence Team, and Advance Democracy to present news and intelligence in a few forms. The open-source research community tracked, compiled, stored, and presented on-the-ground events in Ukraine.

The map is visualized intelligence, featuring colorful pins linked to verified video footage, photos, or satellite imagery. When combined, they provide detailed information on the time and place of conflicts, civilian impact, and troop movement. Color-coded markers denote Russian military presence, civilian casualties, infrastructure damage, bombings, and more. The map depicts happenings like no TV broadcast or military briefing previously could.

Ben Strick, director of investigations at the Center for Information Resilience, said, "Originally, open-source was quite a sort of geeky thing to do. Now, we're almost like the people's army."[22]

Assessing Value-to-Information Flows

OSINT intelligence also extends to reimagining newsrooms and field reporting. Over the past two decades, news agencies have seen significant declines in public trust. Sources seeking to capture "all the news that's fit to print" could no longer confine it through prepackaged narratives, general subject areas, or time of day. Singularly authoritative sources can't work in an era of collective intelligence.

Consider the difference a generation makes. *Time* magazine was once the preeminent source of world affairs. While *Time* lives on, its content sits alongside hundreds of other titles on newsreaders like Apple and Google News. When pulled into large language models informing AIs, a *Time* story is one tiny agent in a database with billions of other sources.

New agents rate the type and quality of sources processed. For example, the *Factual* uses algorithms to examine the quality of sources, writer credentials, the language used, and the trustworthiness of a publication. Its AI systems automatically assign scores indicating how factual a story or source is. It analyzes over ten thousand stories daily to help readers find the most informative and least biased articles. These scores rate from a weighted average called Factual Grade, which ranges from 0 to 100 percent. The *Factual* says it assessed ten million articles to determine the grades. Grades above 75 percent are highly likely to be informative, while grades below 50 percent are less likely to be so.[23]

A grading of news brands, as shown in exhibit 6, shows how such ratings work. According to the *Factual*'s algorithms, the *New York Times* scored an average of 70.0 percent; the *Washington Post*, 68.7 percent; the *Guardian*, 64.4 percent; the *Wall Street Journal*, 62.9 percent; the *New York Post*, 51.3 percent; and the *Daily Mail*, 39.5 percent.[24]

Newswires were more credible on average, with Reuters scoring an average of 69.6 percent and the Associated Press, 68.8 percent. Broadcast sources lag considerably. CNBC rated the highest average score of 68.3 percent; BBC, 63.2 percent; ABC News, 67.1 percent; NPR, 62.6 percent; *Al Jazeera*, 59.3 percent; and Fox News, 54.3 percent.[25]

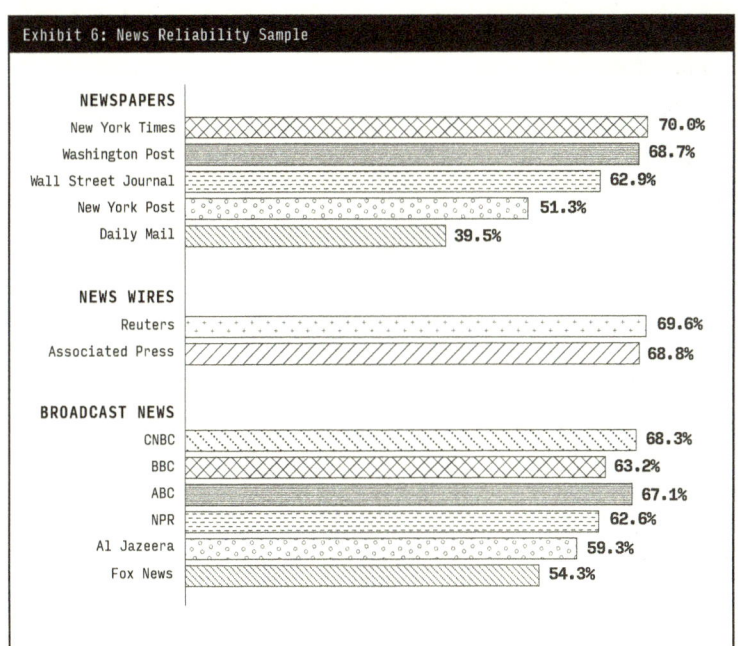

Exhibit 6: News Reliability Sample

The average was 61.9 percent for all 240 news sources analyzed. FactCheck.org rated highest of all sources, at 86.3 percent, followed by *Smithsonian* magazine (85.9 percent) and *FiveThirtyEight* (76.2 percent).[26]

Examples like the *Factual* suggest the type and quality of sources will change based on how they're rated and processed. New gatekeepers will take on radically different constructs than what we see today.

Embedding Perspective into Platforms

Nick D'Aloisio played an instrumental role in shaping what intelligence agents look like. While studying for exams on a spring night back in 2011, he could feel his frustration building. Hours of scouring the web for helpful information boiled down to wasted time. He couldn't understand why the web was inundated with irrelevant, inefficiently presented content. It was then that the idea of Summly struck. He developed an automated application that quickly produced four-hundred- to eight-hundred-character summaries of news articles. It made browsing online faster and more efficient.[27]

After launching, Summly quickly soared to the top of the Apple App Store news section. In just a month, it acquired over five hundred thousand users and was selected by Apple as the "Editor's Choice App of the Week" in forty-eight different countries.[28] In March 2013, Yahoo bought Summly for $30 million.[29]

At the same time, Narrative Science, a Chicago-based AI company, implemented Natural Language Processing (NLP) to accelerate automated production of information. NLP allows computers to comprehend and analyze human language for text analysis, automated translation, and content creation. Many large media corporations, like the Associated Press, Big Ten Network, and Yahoo!, became customers of Narrative Science's NLP platform.

Like Summly, Narrative Science uses systems to automatically create news briefs, sports reports, and fantasy football newsletters. Roger Lee, a general partner of Battery Ventures, who funded the company's $6 million investment, considered it "magic." He commented, "It's like a human wrote it."[30]

In the past ten years, artificial intelligence has advanced to translate languages accurately, master complex video games, and generate realistic images. Exemplified by ChatGPT, generative AI easily creates humanlike thoughts and writes articles, some indistinguishable from the work of seasoned authors and journalists.

NLP laid the groundwork for generative AI set to revolutionize news, networked knowledge production, and how we interact with the content.

Teams of Perspective Agents Become Research Centers

Picture a world where not only are answers to questions returned, but an army of automated entities actively work to find and present the best answers to your queries. Imagine having a team of reporters or virtual PhD candidates researching, uncovering, debating, and giving the optimum responses to your questions. They can comb through research records, OSINT databases, or the entirety of legal precedents. They write scholarly papers, article summaries, or legal briefs. The potential of such bots is so great that it's hard to imagine just how far their capacities can reach.

Open AI's GPT-3 broke open AI's insight potential; it instantly became one of the most prominent AI systems ever produced. It captured the public's imagination, unlike any AI since DeepMind's AlphaGo or IBM's chess-playing DeepBlue. "It galvanized public debate and controversy. It surprises me continuously,"[31] said Arram Sabeti, an inventor with early access to GPT-3. "A witty analogy, a turn of phrase—the repeated experience I have is 'there's no way it just wrote that.' It exhibits things that feel very much like general intelligence."[32]

Generative models like GPT-4 and DALL-E took the possibilities to the next level. GPT-4, the large-scale language model developed by OpenAI, exemplifies the reach of AI systems that generate contextually accurate, coherent, and creative text, enhancing our ability to communicate and generate information. DALL-E, on the other hand, showcases AI's prowess in the art domain by generating unique images from textual descriptions, pushing the boundaries of creative expression.

As we progress along the trajectory of exponential technological growth, these models are expected to become increasingly sophisticated, efficient, and connected. The growth won't be merely linear but exponential, leading to substantial improvements in their performance, capability, and accessibility. This progression indicates a future where AI assists humans and partners alongside them to facilitate novel discoveries and insights.

With their potential to understand and generate humanlike text and images, these generative models will become networked perspective agents for understanding networked worlds. Like JWST, they will enable us to reveal and appreciate wonders previously overlooked or unattainable because of human limitations. By augmenting human capabilities, these AI instruments will open up new dimensions of understanding, creativity, and exploration.

This expedition is likened to the comprehensive studies of physical phenomena undertaken by astronomers, meteorologists, or naturalists. The need for developing and implementing digitally intelligent tools akin to the telescopes, Doppler radars, or taxonomies used by these scientists will grow expansively over the next few decades.

Through these instruments, we will be able to see in ways unlike we've ever been able to before. We land on an important final question to consider: What kinds of worlds will we create with this power?

CHAPTER 13

DESIGN: BUILD NEW WORLDS

When you realize it's your responsibility to be a leader and create the world that you want to see, you have to do it.

—JANELLE MONÁE[1]

The period from the 1920s to the 1940s was the Golden Age of Hollywood, a time of profound technological and creative innovation. The advent of synchronized sound in *The Jazz Singer* in 1927 marked the beginning of "talkies" and the end of the silent film era.[2] Technicolor was first used in the 1935 film *Becky Sharp* and later *The Wizard of Oz* and *Gone with the Wind*.[3] This era revolutionized the film industry and solidified Hollywood's dominance in building emotional worlds.

Revolutionary constructions to come resemble the early days of Hollywood, capturing the spirit of visionaries like Walt Disney. Disney's journey from crafting characters for movie houses to materializing Disneyland on Main Street, USA, exemplifies this shift.

Unlike tightly crafted stories or a single destination, future virtual worlds will be personalized and expansive. David Gelernter, a computer scientist, artist, and writer, predicted decades ago that we would traverse a mirror world of the physical.[4] It would permeate every facet of our existence, creating a mosaic of experiences that fuse the digital and the physical together. Jaron Lanier, the father of VR, framed this new life modality and subsequent cultural revolution that it will create. He says we're at the dawn of a "new everything."[5]

An Arena with Tens of Millions of Fans

In February 2019, EDM star Marshmello took to Twitter to express his gratitude to his fans. He tweeted, "Holy!!! We just made history today. We can all tell our kids one day that we attended the first ever virtual concert @FortniteGame."[6]

Recognizable by a signature white bucket helmet with a painted smile and crossed eyes, Marshmello's real identity was a mystery. The man beneath the plastic cover was revealed as Chris Comstock, a twenty-six-year-old producer and DJ from Philadelphia. As explained by Tim Ingham in *Rolling Stone*, "He's a fictional creation, a blank canvas onto which young music fans can paint whichever personality they wish him to be."[7]

The intrigue surrounding his persona is part of a digital age, world-building feat. Comstock made history in the metaverse. Working with Epic Games, Marshmello's *Fortnite* concert appearance shook the entertainment world. His virtual show drew an astonishing 10.7 million simultaneous users.[8] The show was three times the size of the largest in-person music event ever.

Fortnite was the right place to make history. Its rise to three hundred million users and billions in revenue came from its community-centric design.[9] Its device-agnostic, social-centric model made *Fortnite* a primary gathering spot for hundreds of millions of mostly male teenagers. *Fortnite* became a digital equivalent of the after-school playground—only this one extended across neighborhoods, cities, countries, and continents.

Fortnite's creator, Epic Games, orchestrated Marshmello's act as a real-world, real-life concert, requiring intense technical planning six months in advance. *Fortnite* players naturally joined as avatars. They dressed in virtual swag, danced to Marshmello's hit tracks, and interacted with other players. An estimated 80 percent of those watching didn't consider themselves fans of the artist. Marshmello's weekly YouTube views soared by over one hundred million within a week.[10] His Instagram followers increased by a million within four days.

The *Wall Street Journal* reported digital goods sales in *Fortnite* saw a nearly 300 percent surge on the day of Marshmello's concert. Attendees purchased the limited-edition character skin, distinctive animated dance (an emote), and glider skin for $25. Video-on-demand streams of DJ Marshmello's track "Check This Out" saw an almost 24,000 percent increase within twenty-four hours of his *Fortnite* event.[11]

Epic Games followed with other artist collaborations. The game maker made history again with Travis Scott. Scott's *Fortnite* concert drew a staggering 27 million virtual attendees.[12] Other studios got in on the game. By December 2020, *Roblox*, the virtual world featuring user-generated games and social spaces, joined the party. It hosted a live concert with Lil Nas X, viewed 33 million times in one weekend.[13]

Fortnite and *Roblox* are games at their core. But they expanded into a broader, new virtual canvas for creativity and community gathering. Epic Games CEO Tim Sweeney believes, "Just as every company a few decades ago created a web page, and then at some point every company created a Facebook page, I think we're approaching the point where every company will have a real-time live 3D presence."[14]

The scale of where it can go defies imagination.

Constructing a New World Order

In the late 1920s Walt Disney revolutionized animation, molding it from mere curiosity about motion and flexibility of line into an art form. Like avatar concerts in the metaverse, Disney's *Snow White and the Seven Dwarfs* marked a turning point in animated films. It was the first full-length animated film produced in color. A new type of fantasy world—a story world—was born.

Disney crafted the seven dwarfs with precise detail, each rendered with a delicate, rotund design. Snow White's face was plump and childlike, with appealing features and seductive air. *Cinderella*, *Peter Pan*, *Lady and the Tramp*, *Mary Poppins*, *101 Dalmatians*, *Bambi*, *Pinocchio*, and *Dumbo* followed a similar construction and form.[15]

In the shadow of nuclear threats, families found solace in detailed fantasy creation as an escape. The threat of nuclear Armageddon, new technologies, and social structures created a sense of unease among Americans. In addition to Disney, Americans sought escape in other story worlds like Rod Serling's *Twilight Zone*, *Star Trek*, and *Lost in Space*. Science fiction resonated as cars, highways, and air travel reshaped public life.

Disney's visions, starting with animation and manifesting into real-world parks, rest on presenting the "plausible impossible"—an amalgamation of real and imaginary experiences that fit into a single resonant story. The best ones facilitate and build new sensibilities and beliefs. His biographer, Neal Gabler, noted that in the year of Disney's death, 1966, 240 million people saw a Disney movie, a weekly audience of 100 million watched a Disney television show, 80 million read a Disney book, 50 million listened to Disney records, 80 million bought Disney merchandise, 150 million read a Disney comic strip, 80 million saw a Disney educational film, and nearly 7 million visited Disneyland.[16]

While not as omnipresent as Disney's empire, story worlds are pervasive through various media, including sci-fi novels, fantasy, video games, and brand-building. In the physical world, if you've traversed the Las Vegas strip, Nike store, Rainforest Café, or Harry Potter World, you've experienced a story in spatial form. If you've gone to war in *Call of Duty*, sped around in *Mario Kart*, or built a structure in *Minecraft*, you've shaped virtual zones. And if you're a devoted fan of Taylor Swift, Beyoncé, or BTS, you've joined worlds that have shaped popular culture today.

The virtual build-out will expand as tech giants pour capital and ingenuity into new hardware and software. Beyond feats of technological engineering, the Disneys of the future will make virtual worlds as compelling as reality. They will manifest through new ideas for nation-states, brands, retail, and spiritual forums.

New Realms for Shared Experience

In the 1977 short film *Powers of Ten*, Charles and Ray Eames presented a revolutionary rendering of Earth. It depicted a view from a picnic blanket in a park to the scale of one hundred million light-years away. Exploring reality's boundaries provoked such awe that software engineers re-created Eames's eye from the sky. Instead of film, they rendered it in code using GPS and satellite imagery, presented in vivid detail. Viewers would see an unprecedented bird's-eye view of our place on planet Earth. It encompassed space, movement, time, and location.[17] The vision led to the digital maps we have today.

As our pocket guide to physical locations, they will take on a new complexion as augmented reality and autonomous driving become mainstream. They will offer driving and walking guidance using AR with detailed 8K resolution. It will allow mapmakers and designers to deliver personalized experiences. Think of Zagat restaurant recommendations, virtual bar crawls from *Time Out*, or guided tours embedded by the National Park Foundation.

For decades, computer scientists dreamed of software that could render digital worlds so lifelike that they were indistinguishable from reality.

On June 6, 2023, Tim Cook, the CEO of Apple, suggested how these visions will further take form with Apple Vision. Invoking Steve Jobs's iconic words, "one more thing," Cook introduced a spatial computer, a potential world-building platform without precedent.[18]

Spatial computing combines the user's natural senses within an immersive virtual environment. Users interact through their eyes, hands, and voice, bringing an almost magical physicality to their virtual surroundings.

Imagine you scan a room with a simple flick of your eye, dictate commands with your voice, or manipulate digital objects by waving your hand. Envision experiences surrounding you in your space, turning your living room into interactive galleries, stadiums, and travel destinations. Then consider the cultural impact.

Spatial computers will disrupt TVs and movie theaters, making a standard television screen feel like an enormous hundred-foot-wide display. It may make mobile phones obsolete. A sensory feast, it will make sounds, experiences, and people feel like they are physically present with you.[19]

Soon, augmented reality will become a fully commercialized product, and new, immersive worlds will become commonplace. Networks of innovators are working to create these new immersive environments, with and without a spatial computer at the center.

Fandom through Shared Values

In 2021, our Futures team engaged in a collaborative study with anthropologist Grant McCracken to decode the complex domain of world-building by media entities, brands, and entertainers. The primary motivation for this exploration was to comprehend how to generate value in a time when individuals were progressively fragmenting into specialized groups. These communities gained prominent members jointly united with those mirroring their interests and values. Given new technologies on the horizon, we knew world-building would take on new form. The question was, regardless of platform, what creates sustainable bonds with fans over time? We landed on four absolutes for progressive world builders. To sustain a world, you needed to offer valuable experiences, foster social connectivity, facilitate and strengthen a communal purpose, and cultivate a shared identity.

In essence, world-building in today's fractured social environment requires creating spaces that offer meaningful experiences, foster genuine connections, and facilitate participation in the experience. Exhibit 7 shows that creating compelling, emotionally engaging worlds requires that we think through the experiences, social connectivity, purpose, and identity-building that they facilitate.

Exhibit 7: World-Building Framework

OFFERING COMMUNITIES A VALUABLE EXPERIENCE	ENABLING SOCIAL CONNECTIVITY
Form factor: physical or digital	**Reach:** enable social connection
Type: app, web, AR, VR, product-driven	**Identity:** make people look good to their cohorts
Access: designed to be private or public	**Share:** make the private public
Awareness: designed to be promoted or discovered	

EMPOWERING THEM TO CRAFT THEIR IDENTITY	ALIGNING BRAND PURPOSE WITH COMMUNITY PURPOSE
Feel more: emotionally inspired	Educational
Be more: identity-enhancing	Activist
Learn more: knowledge-enhancing	Performative
Do more: action-oriented	Entertainment
Make more: creative-oriented	Wellness
	Safety and security
	Functional
	Informative

Later, during my book research on world-building, I ventured to one of the best representations of it: Harry Styles's Love on Tour residency in New York. There I ventured into an ocean of shimmering body glitter, rainbow-hued hair, and a flurry of feathered adornments. Someone joked I was one of thirty-four individuals spotted as a "golf dad" in Madison Square Garden. The atmosphere was electrifying.

From the opening act's first notes to the last song's final strains, fans felt genuine collective exuberance. Values that Styles advocates—love, acceptance, freedom of expression, and individuality—were on full display. For fifteen nights in New York city—and across hundreds of thousands of social media accounts—Harry's House could aptly be described as a joy parade. It lived IRL at MSG and far beyond with images and video traversing through social media networks. The parade of love was a big score for promoters. Styles's residency sold 277,000 tickets, generating $63 million.[20]

For Taylor Swift fans, every night on the 2023 Eras tour was like being at the Super Bowl, featuring sky-high ticket prices, tailgating, and dressing for the event. Ticket holders and tailgaters took over streets and parking lots near the venues. "Taylor-gating" became so pervasive that cities banned them. But for fans who were allowed to pre-party, "the Swifties with no tickets having the #TaylorGating parties in the parking lots is a beautiful thing."[21]

The average price to get into the show was $920.[22] Swift boosted hotel occupancy rates in cities more than major sporting events like the NCAA Final Four. The same went for other cities where rooms were booked months in advance. Restaurants and bars filled up, and many extended their stays to visit local attractions and amusement parks. In some cities, planners built makeshift exhibits for fans. By the end of the tour, Swift could net anywhere between $500 million and $1.5 billion. Swift's huge economic impact became so vast, economists coined it "Swiftonomics."[23]

How does fandom reach such heights? For her devoted followers, Taylor Swift is the center of their world. It's one not tied down to any virtual platform or location. "Swifties" will go where she goes, physically and emotionally.

Scholars note the genius in how Swift brings fans into her emotional ups and downs. Intrigue is designed into her songs. Her writing is deep in figurative language. She uses simile, metaphor, paradox, irony, and personification. Themes of reputation, revenge, and romance showed recompositions of her identity and journey as a celebrity.[24] By memorializing her life through music, her work is a well of behind-the-scenes intrigue Swifties crave.

Taylor's ascent is also a master class in care as a business strategy. Her reputation is the result of thoughtful fan outreach and connection. New language emerged around digital connection (#TayLurking),[25] in-person events (Rep Rooms),[26] and gifting events (Swiftmas).[27] She appears with her fans live streaming Instagram videos and reposts fan content on her social channels. Followers say the difference between being a fan of Taylor Swift and being one of another celebrity is that Taylor always goes the extra mile. One said, "She spends hours stalking us online, invites us into her home, and sends us packages."[28]

It's these careful acts that translate fandom into a field force. Swifties have created a massive digital footprint on websites, wikis, blogs, and social media posts of recordings, photos, and backstories. They amount to a living, breathing "Taylornet."[29]

Digital fandom made it possible for Taylor Swift to accomplish a feat no other recording artist had ever achieved, taking over all ten spots on *Billboard*'s top singles chart simultaneously.[30] In her way, she has built a virtual world, a fan-supported metaverse that informs her creative direction, musical production, and marketing. Unlike any other artist, she's created a fandom world in constant motion.

Swift's superstardom suggests intentional design is the essential starting point for world-building. Another artist, Janelle Monáe, expertly crafts worlds that push the contours of identity through another genre likened to "identity worlds."

Monáe creates distinct fantasy worlds in her image, presented as powerful rebukes to the predominance of white, male-centric precedent. Monáe is pansexual, polyamorous, and an Afrofuturist. In her music and fashion style, she mixes her Cuban, African American, Native American, and European influences into a unique form. Her show business resume reflects her polymorphous identity. She is a best-selling music artist, has appeared in Oscar-nominated films, and is an activist for LGBTQIA+, women, and Black communities. She wants to give a different perspective and way of thinking.

Monáe's music genre is "future soul," expressed through personas living in her self-constructed future.[31] Monáe's alter-ego, Cindi Mayweather, was the protagonist of her concept album *Metropolis: Suite I (The Chase)*. She portrayed Cindi as a heroic freedom fighter. She's on a mission to right the wrongs of the past.

Her WondaLand is another imaginary world, a metaphorical realm for characters reconsidering their identities and history.[32] It carries an attitude and message that challenges any form of labels or categorization. As a symbolic space, WondaLand is conceived of as a place for questioning identity, where people can try on new perspectives and attitudes and bring new insights back into the "real" world.

Constructing Institutions in the Cloud

World-building is not limited to entertaining and celebrity culture. Some of the most extensive, influential world-building efforts will occur in government and territory expansion in virtual worlds.

The Network State, a book by Balaji Srinivasan, is a step-by-step manual for creating new digital governments.[33] Srinivasan believes technology will fundamentally overhaul how we think about governments and territories under state control.

He says that just as the printing press, musket, and industrialization led to the birth of nation-states, the internet and cryptocurrency will create new governing models. As Srinivasan puts it, we are moving into the era of "great protocol politics."[34] It will be an era dominated by the next internet and decentralized technologies like blockchain. He suggests that we are transitioning from an age of geopolitics toward one of techno-politics.

Technology alters how people govern themselves, yet nation-states and borders remain unchanged. In the future, lines will undoubtedly shift. If we think of the metaverse as a mirror world of the physical, the concept of land-based, enclosed borders applies to emerging worlds, too.

New forms of government, "land capture," and conflict among nation-states and digital barons will arise. While *The Network State* is a conceptual idea, real-world examples are taking shape. For guidance on how world-building and public policy comes together, look to Taiwan.

Audrey Tang, a technologist and convener, realizes new possibility. Her vision contrasts Balaji's. Tang deploys digital tools that make her government better. As Taiwan's first digital minister, she implements principles of the Web 2.0 era to foster transparency, citizen involvement, and consensus.[35]

Her political career began as an activist, part of the 2014 Sunflower Movement protesting against the Taiwanese government. Tang made her voice heard through the tech collective, Gov-Zero (g0v).[36] It enabled citizens to form a "shadow government" and design a path for better relations between the Taiwanese people and the state. Tang is now in charge, a hacker within this system. Her remit spans policy innovation, open government projects, and youth involvement. She is the youngest and first transgender cabinet member in Taiwan.[37]

With input from citizens and hundreds of engineers, Tang's government creates a digital version of the public square. People engage in the democratic process through presidential hackathons, e-petition sites, and participatory budgeting.

To develop this democratic world, Tang collaborated with civic technologists, circumventing the traditional bureaucratic process. True to form, she functions as a remote-working minister. Anyone can converse with her every Wednesday from 10 a.m. to 10 p.m. The only rule is that the discussion must be publicly posted online.[38]

She codified elements through vTaiwan, which utilizes open-source tools to submit ideas, give out data, and participate in voting.[39] A critical component was Pol.is, a public discussion board focused on policy development.[40] It lets users communicate their opinions on a topic or theme through public statements and voting. It applies machine learning to analyze the feedback and detect patterns in the replies. It discovers where people share similar opinions or hold different views. Analysis of responses helps it locate common ground and stimulate more meaningful conversations.

Tang's programs were central to Taiwan's response to the spread of the COVID-19 virus. She viewed it as a double crisis: a health pandemic and an infodemic.[41] Tang spearheaded the implementation of Taiwan's digital contact tracing system to track and suppress the virus. She also helped the government to combat false and misleading information. A public dashboard tracked the proliferation rate of fake news that could clarify the accuracy of the information in less than two hours.

This effort required a biological mindset tuned to virality. Tang's dashboard monitored how different versions of information spread. She found an average transmission rate of ten (each person shares with ten more persons). Daily press conferences focused on variants with the highest R-values—the metric tracking information flow of false narratives.[42]

Tang's citizens' brigade also worked tirelessly to distribute masks.[43] Using over a hundred tools from g0v and civic partners, they connected six thousand pharmacies to the national healthcare network. This infrastructure featured an interactive map of locations with access to masks. Chatbots were deployed for those less familiar with maps. Voice assistants enabled those with impaired vision to get the same information.

In a few months, Taiwan managed to get 75 percent of the population to wear face masks. The country, with 24 million citizens, had only 451 cases and 7 deaths six months into the pandemic. By comparison, the United States saw more than 3.4 million cases and 136,000 deaths.[44]

As these examples illustrate, we stand on the verge of a revolutionary epoch in new world-building. They will encompass the domains of fantasy, environments, entertainment, identity, and advocacy. Enabled by the artistic talent and intellect of our generation's greatest minds, emerging worlds possess the potential to unlock the gateway to future states in which we aspire to live.

It's a big leap to envision and act on the potential. To quote Walt Disney, "First, think. Second, dream. Third, believe. And finally, dare."[45] Indeed, we must dare to dream beyond the horizons of our current reality, think boldly about the possibilities that lie ahead, and believe in our collective ability to shape these visions into tangible experiences.

As expert potters shape clay into an exquisite artifact, we will sculpt an unformed mass of ideas into meticulously designed worlds. This world-building process and inhabiting them will emerge as the pivotal agent of perspective and transformation.

Ultimately, world-building will serve as a powerful conduit for realizing our most ambitious dreams and passions, embodying a shared aspiration: Build new institutions we believe in again.

CONCLUSION

AGENTS OF WELL-BEING

Technology can be a tool or a weapon. It can also be a trap. As we navigate transitions ahead, it's evident that technology alters what we think and how we think. It alters our psyche. It changes what we do. We must better anticipate what new technological conveniences and experiences do to us. The cases throughout the book emphasize that we consider how technology, and the new perspectives it fosters, affects the soul.

Generative AI and virtual cohabitation force big questions: Will we gravitate to a digital world tailored to every desire over a real-life (IRL) existence? Will our increasing reliance on machines lead to deep ambivalence and diminished agency? Can we harness great technologies to lead extraordinary lives versus getting destroyed by them? These are existential questions we need to ask.

In the Pixar classic *WALL-E*, a scene satirizes the conveniences of technology. Plump, lazy, and brain-deads float through a hermetically sealed entertainment world. Their hoverchairs feature screens affixed inches from their faces. They sip on oversized meals ready to eat in cups while changing channels and fashions at the touch of a button. In this Axiom bubble, they are pets of a greater being—technology.[1]

The humans on the spaceship Axiom have become so disconnected from their environment, each other, and even their bodies that they are entirely dependent on screens and machines for their existence.

The film is a warning about the dangers of consumerism and technology. It's also a critique of the values and priorities of a technologically fascinated society.

In confronting the future, productivity and economic potential will improve our standard of living. However, as we progress through the second quarter of the twenty-first century, we must reevaluate what constitutes a high-quality life.

Beneath the surface of technological progress and increased wealth, growing unease fuels mental health, personal relationships, and spiritual fulfillment.

As information access and social media usage have grown, markers of happiness, contentment, and connection have declined over the past two decades. We now face the challenge of preserving the soul of society.

* * *

A way to approach such an existential challenge can be found in one of academia's longest-running studies of human happiness and well-being.

The Harvard Study of Adult Development, one of the longest-running studies on human happiness and well-being, has been in progress for over eight decades. Initiated in 1938, this longitudinal study aims to identify the psychosocial predictors of healthy aging.[2] It focuses on various factors, from physical and mental health to marital success and career satisfaction. The collected data includes medical records, blood samples, brain scans, self-reported surveys and questionnaires, and face-to-face interviews.

The study, supported by other research from psychologists and academic partnerships, finds four paths to well-being. Hedonistic happiness elicited by entertainment, fashions, and indulgences is most apparent. While pleasurable, it's not a durable means of contentment. The second, informed by Aristotle, is eudemonic, the feeling that one's life has meaning. It carries more weight and is less dependent on the ups and downs of escapism and pleasure-seeking. A third flavor studied at Columbia University finds a psychologically rich life a significant factor. It's realized through traveling to new places, meeting new people, and exploring new ideas. If nothing more, cultivating perspective agents can greatly enhance exposure to the new and novel.

The most significant discovery from the Harvard study is the profound impact of relationships on happiness and health. Meaningful relationships with family, friends, and community are identified as vital not just for happiness but also for overall health and longevity.

People who are more socially connected to family, friends, and community are happier, healthier, and live longer than people who are less well connected. Dr. Robert Waldinger, professor of psychiatry at Harvard Medical School, who oversees the study, said, "The people who were the most satisfied in their relationships at age fifty were the healthiest at age eighty." He added that it's not just the number of friends you have or whether you're in a committed relationship, but the quality of your close relationships that matters.[3]

Contemporary research validates ancient philosophical teachings of Greek sagas, most notably Epicurus. Epicurus identified three cardinal elements for a fulfilling life. As Waldinger noted, genuine friends' presence and companionship were paramount, dating back to ancient times. Epicurious also advocated freedom and autonomy in one's professional pursuits, indicating that meaningful work brings intrinsic satisfaction. Finally, he stressed the importance of an "examined life," emphasizing the need for individuals to have a guiding philosophy or faith, offering purpose and direction.[4]

The enduring concept of well-being, confirmed by the most comprehensive academic studies on happiness to date, prompts reflection on whether technology facilitates, overrides, or skews these principles. While technological marvels are incredible enablers, we cannot forget (or overlook) what makes us human, how we construct a future that elevates us, and how we don't get blinded by the light.

Without a clear intention, technologies can lead to drift and a decline in personal agency. Forms of drift come in the form of time lost doomscrolling, rabbit holing on TikToks, or arguing on social media. Being adrift elevates chances to be influenced and controlled by circumstances outside of your own mind. To drift is to be intellectually lazy. To drift is to be controlled by fear, conspiracy, conflict, vanity, and apathy. In this state, it becomes impossible to think accurately and constructively.

In contrast, those who think for themselves don't drift on things that matter. They seek perspectives and sources that enhance depictions of reality and how to benefit from it. They're vigilant in using agents and tools for thought and action. And, reflecting philosophical truisms, they stay principled regardless of external influences, and notably, technological influences.

Using perspective agents that lead to betterment is this book's central theme. Improving and supporting each other through the great transition ahead, in a principled way, is the most important perspective to strive for.

ACKNOWLEDGMENTS

Writing this book has been a collaborative effort, and while many hands have touched its pages, the friendships I've made and strengthened throughout the process stand out the most. For me, the process was as much about the friendly collaboration as content shared on the pages.

I must extend heartfelt gratitude to my wife, Missy, and my kids, Isabelle, Audrey, and Nick. Without their unwavering faith and perspective, this book surely would not have happened.

I thank my longtime friends—those I've reconnected with and the new ones I've made along the way. A debt of gratitude goes to Douglas Rushkoff, who supported and coached me throughout the development process. Also, I am grateful to Sudhir Venkatesh for his sound counsel, editing suggestions, and encouragement to expand lines of thinking for maximum benefit.

I am grateful for my work colleagues and clients at Weber Shandwick, who offered invaluable insight, feedback, and energy to push me to see things expansively. Thanks go to Gail Heimann for her inspired leadership and our Futures team for keeping a pulse on changes reflected throughout the book. A specific shout-out goes to Kelly

Sullivan, Patrick Chaupham, Julia Dixon, Mike Connery, Jess Adelson, and Daria Dubois for doing what they do every day. And my thanks go to Cindy Sato. I'm indebted to her wisdom, friendship, and patience in keeping things, and me, on track.

The ideas and cases in this book were informed by a group of highly intelligent, visionary, and ethically minded individuals who, together, helped paint the picture of opportunity and challenge found throughout the text. Thanks go to Andrew McLuhan, Tracey Follows, Aaron Z. Lewis, Andy Berndt, Jamie Cohen, Marcha Johnson, Claire Wardle, Rik Willard, Brett Robinson, Chris Carmichael, Matt Kein, Marina Gorbis, and Grant McCracken. Special recognition also goes to Mark Stahlman and the cohort behind the Center for the Study of Digital Life for keeping the focus locked in on human potential.

I also thank my publishing partners at Greenleaf Book Group for their guidance throughout this process. Deep appreciation goes to Rebecca Logan, my editor, who made the writing throughout worth reading. In addition, I thank Gili Karev and the team at Klaris for their advice and counsel.

Finally, thanks go to my early readers: Rich Janow, the Ervin family, Avery Garland, and the Weber Shandwick Futures fellows, class of summer '23 (Alli Keeler, Denise Ramos, Lilly Callahan, Christine Madden, Idira Marzbani, Annika McTamaney, and Parker Piccolo Hill), who pointed out areas that needed more depth and perspective. Their input and contribution to important territories was invaluable.

NOTES

Foreword

1. *Explorations: Studies and Culture and Communication* 1 (1953): iii.

Author's Note

1. Nick Ripatrazone, "How Marshall McLuhan Was the Patron Saint of *Wired* Magazine," *Literary Hub*, March 30, 2022, https://lithub.com/how-marshall-mcluhan-was-the-patron-saint-of-wired-magazine.
2. Marshall McLuhan, Kathryn Hutchinson, and Eric McLuhan, *City as Classroom: Understanding Language and Media* (Agincourt, ON: Book Society of Canada, 1977), 1.

Part I

1. Gillian Tett, "The Problem with CEOs and Second-Hand Pessimism," *Financial Times*, January 12, 2023, https://www.ft.com/content/558e8a3b-bbac-4696-80e8-2ccb56c97bdb.
2. Tett, "The Problem with CEOs."
3. Elon Musk, Twitter post, January 16, 2023, https://twitter.com/elonmusk/status/1615195812388274177.

4. Hamilton Nolan, "The Worst Thing about Davos? The Masters of the Universe Think They Are Do-Gooders," *The Guardian*, January 19, 2023, https://www.theguardian.com/commentisfree/2023/jan/19/davos-masters-of-the-universe.
5. "Why the Davos Consensus 'Is Always Wrong': Pro," CNBC, January 24, 2014, https://www.cnbc.com/video/2014/01/24/why-the-davos-consensus-is-always-wrong-pro.html.
6. Izabella Kaminska, "Hear Me Out: Klaus Schwab Used to Be Cool," *UnHerd*, January 19, 2023, https://unherd.com/thepost/hear-me-out-klaus-schwab-used-to-be-cool/.

Chapter 1

1. Arthur C. Clarke, *Profiles of the Future: An Inquiry into the Limits of the Possible* (New York: Harper and Row, 1973), 21.
2. Dan Milmo, "ChatGPT Reaches 100 Million Users Two Months after Launch," *The Guardian*, February 2, 2023, https://www.theguardian.com/technology/2023/feb/02/chatgpt-100-million-users-open-ai-fastest-growing-app.
3. Sam Altman, Twitter post, February 26, 2023, https://twitter.com/sama/status/1629880171921563649?lang=en.
4. Jeremy Laird, "Nvidia Predicts AI Models One Million Times More Powerful than ChatGPT within 10 Years," *PC Gamer*, February 23, 2023, https://www.pcgamer.com/nvidia-predicts-ai-models-one-million-times-more-powerful-than-chatgpt-within-10-years/.
5. MIT Media Lab, "Marvin Minsky, 'Father of Artificial Intelligence,' Dies at 88," *MIT News*, January 25, 2016, https://news.mit.edu/2016/marvin-minsky-obituary-0125.
6. "Society of Mind," *Wikipedia*, May 23, 2023, https://en.wikipedia.org/wiki/Society_of_Mind.
7. Jordyn Greenberg, "Top AI Tools That Improve the Employee Experience," *TLNT*, Jul 27, 2023, https://www.tlnt.com/articles/top-ai-tools-that-improve-the-employee-experience-and-make-your-job-easier.
8. Eray Eliaçık, "Consensus AI Makes Accessing Scientific Information Easier than Ever," *Dataconomy*, March 27, 2023, https://dataconomy.com/2023/03/27/what-is-consensus-ai-search-engine-how-to/.

9. Andy Park, "ChatPDF: Use This AI Tool to Chat with Any PDF Documents," YouTube, May 16, 2023, https://www.youtube.com/watch?v=DZrmDCMDWVE.
10. Joshua Benton, "What If ChatGPT Was Trained on Decades of Financial News and Data? BloombergGPT Aims to Be a Domain-Specific AI for Business News," Nieman Lab, April 3, 2023, https://www.niemanlab.org/2023/04/what-if-chatgpt-was-trained-on-decades-of-financial-news-and-data-bloomberggpt-aims-to-be-a-domain-specific-ai-for-business-news/.
11. Benj Edwards, "Surprising Things Happen When You Put 25 AI Agents Together in an RPG Town," *Ars Technica*, April 11, 2023, https://arstechnica.com/information-technology/2023/04/surprising-things-happen-when-you-put-25-ai-agents-together-in-an-rpg-town/.
12. Edwards, "Surprising Things Happen."
13. Lauren Clark, "Learn from Others' Experiences with More Perspectives on Search," *Keyword* (blog), May 10, 2023, https://blog.google/products/search/google-search-perspectives/.
14. David Chalmers, *Reality+* (New York: W. W. Norton, 2022), xiv.
15. Neil Postman, *Amusing Ourselves to Death* (New York: Penguin Books, 1984).
16. American Psychological Association (APA), "No Spoilers! Most People Don't Want to Know Their Future," 2017, https://www.apa.org/news/press/releases/2017/02/know-future.
17. Institute for the Future, "A Majority of Americans Report That They Rarely or Never Think about the Far Future," April 13, 2017, https://legacy.iftf.org/americanfuturegap/.
18. Institute for the Future, "Toward Future Readiness: A Playbook for Building Foresight Capacity," April 2022, https://www.iftf.org/projects/a-playbook-for-building-foresight-capacity/.
19. Jane McGonigal, *Imaginable: How to See the Future Coming and Feel Ready for Anything—Even Things That Seem Impossible Today* (New York: Spiegel and Grau, 2022).
20. Mark Murphy, "Leadership Styles Are Often Why CEOS Get Fired," *Forbes*, June 16, 2015, https://www.forbes.com/sites/markmurphy/2015/07/16/leadership-styles-are-often-why-ceos-get-fired/?sh=3c5c90e84988.

21. Carlota Perez, *Technological Revolutions and Financial Capital: The Dynamics of Bubbles and Golden Ages* (Cheltenham, UK: Edward Elgar, 2002).
22. Thomas Kuhn, *The Structure of Scientific Revolutions* (Chicago: University of Chicago Press, 1962).
23. David Adler, "Schumpeter's Theory of Creative Destruction," *IRLE* (blog), September 30, 2019, https://www.cmu.edu/epp/irle/irle-blog-pages/schumpeters-theory-of-creative-destruction.html.
24. David Foster Wallace, "This Is Water," commencement speech at Kenyon College, Gambier, OH, May 21, 2005, https://fs.blog/david-foster-wallace-this-is-water/.
25. Activate Consulting, "Activate Technology and Media Outlook, 2024," accessed October 20, 2023, https://www.activate.com/insights-archive/Activate-Technology-and-Media-Outlook-2024.pdf.
26. Celestine Chua, "Great Minds Discuss Ideas. Average Minds Discuss Events. Small Minds Discuss People," *Personal Excellence* (blog), accessed October 20, 2023, https://personalexcellence.co/blog/great-minds/.

Chapter 2

1. Winston Churchill, speech delivered in March 1944.
2. See the Liminal Spaces Twitter account, at https://twitter.com/SpaceLiminalBot.
3. See the r/LiminalSpace Reddit account, at https://www.reddit.com/r/LiminalSpace/.
4. See the #liminalspaces TikTok account, at https://www.tiktok.com/tag/liminalspaces?lang=en.
5. National Intelligence Council, "Global Trends, 2040," March 2021, https://www.dni.gov/index.php/gt2040-home.
6. ARK Invest, "Big Ideas, 2023," 2023, https://ark-invest.com/big-ideas-2023/.
7. Victor Turner, *The Ritual Process: Structure and Anti-structure* (London: Aldine, 1969).
8. Timothy Carson, "A Liminality Primer," Liminality Project, accessed October 20, 2023, https://www.theliminalityproject.org/the-liminality-primer/.

9. Marc Andreessen, "Marc Andreessen: Interview with an Icon," *Knowledge Project Podcast*, January 25, 2022, https://fs.blog/knowledge-project-podcast/marc-andreessen/.
10. "The Weirdness Is Coming," *New York Magazine*, November 13, 2019, https://nymag.com/intelligencer/2019/11/2029-predictions-based-on-2019.html.
11. Allison P. Davis, "A Vibe Shift Is Coming," *New York Magazine*, February 16, 2022, https://www.thecut.com/2022/02/a-vibe-shift-is-coming.html.
12. Old Spice, "Old Spice and Arby's Create Epic Collab to Defeat the Meat Sweats," *Hypebeast*, June 30, 2022, https://hypebeast.com/2022/6/old-spice-arbys-meat-sweats-defense-collaboration.
13. KFC, "Make This Mother's Day Finger Lickin' Good with a Sides Lovers Meal from KFC and the Kentucky Fried Buckquet from Proflowers," April 27, 2022, https://global.kfc.com/press-releases/make-this-mothers-day-finger-lickin-good-with-a-sides-lovers-meal/.
14. Megan Schaltegger, "Oscar Mayer Is Selling a Sheet Mask That Looks Like Bologna Sausage," *Thrillist*, January 19, 2022, https://www.thrillist.com/news/nation/oscar-mayer-bologna-sausage-sheet-mask-skincare.
15. "How to Think about the Future," *Fortune*, January 1967, https://www.amazon.com/FORTUNE-MAGAZINE-JANUARY-Think-Future/dp/B005NXGCQA.
16. "How to Think about the Future."
17. "Future Shock," *Wikipedia*, May 27, 2019, https://en.wikipedia.org/wiki/Future_Shock.
18. Arthur Symons, *The Symbolist Movement in Literature* (London: Archibald Constable, 1908), 4.
19. Russell Reynolds, "Global CEO Turnover Index," 2023, https://www.russellreynolds.com/en/insights/reports-surveys/global-ceo-turnover-index.
20. Molly Innes, "CMO Tenure Falls to Lowest Level in More than a Decade," *Marketing Week*, May 5, 2023, https://www.marketingweek.com/cmo-tenure-falls/.
21. PwC, "PwC's 26th Annual Global CEO Survey: Winning Today's Race While Running Tomorrow's," January 16, 2023, https://www.pwc.com/gx/en/issues/c-suite-insights/ceo-survey-2023.html.

22. Douglas A. Ready, Carol Cohen, David Kiron, and Benjamin Pring, "The New Leadership Playbook for the Digital Age," *MIT Sloan Management Review*, January 21, 2020, https://sloanreview.mit.edu/projects/the-new-leadership-playbook-for-the-digital-age/#chapter-2.
23. Arundhati Roy, *War Talk* (Cambridge, MA: South End Press, 2003), 75.

Chapter 3

1. Quoted in Andrew Doe and John Tobler, *In Their Own Words: The Doors* (London: Omnibus Press, 1988), 85.
2. Auren Hoffman, "Why the Famous Peter Thiel Interview Question Is So Predictive," *Safe Graph*, January 2, 2020, https://www.safegraph.com/blog/why-the-famous-peter-thiel-interview-question-is-so-predictive.
3. Nicholas Thompson, "Our Minds Have Been Hijacked by Our Phones: Tristan Harris Wants to Rescue Them," *Wired*, July 26, 2017, https://www.wired.com/story/our-minds-have-been-hijacked-by-our-phones-tristan-harris-wants-to-rescue-them/.
4. Melissa Bauman and Valerie Nelson, "Social Media's Role in the Erosion of Truth," RAND Corporation, November 12, 2016, https://www.rand.org/blog/2016/11/social-medias-role-in-the-erosion-of-truth.html.
5. Bruce Goldman, "Addictive Potential of Social Media Explained," *Scope* (blog), October 29, 2021, https://scopeblog.stanford.edu/2021/10/29/addictive-potential-of-social-media-explained/.
6. Siona Singletary, "Is Social Media Destroying Humankind?," TEDx Sydney, September 14, 2018, https://tedxsydney.com/idea/is-social-media-destroying-humankind/.
7. Peter Dizikes, "Study: On Twitter, False News Travels Faster than True Stories," *MIT News*, March 8, 2016, https://news.mit.edu/2018/study-twitter-false-news-travels-faster-true-stories-0308.
8. Peter Schwartz and Peter Leyden, "The Long Boom: A History of the Future, 1980–2020," *Wired*, July 1, 1997, https://www.wired.com/1997/07/longboom/.
9. Paul Keegan, "The Digerati!," *New York Times*, May 21, 1995, https://www.nytimes.com/1995/05/21/magazine/the-digerati.html.

10. John Perry Barlow, "A Declaration of the Independence of Cyberspace," Electronic Frontier Foundation, February 8, 1996, https://www.eff.org/cyberspace-independence.

11. Steven Heller and John Plunkett, "Reputations: John Plunkett," *Eye Magazine* 7, no. 28 (Summer 1998), https://www.eyemagazine.com/feature/article/reputations-john-plunkett.

12. "Everything You Need to Know about TIME's Person of the Year," *Time*, December 13, 2021, https://time.com/4586372/time-person-of-the-year-facts/.

13. Eugene Wei, "Status Update, and How Everyone IPO'd in the 21st Century," *Remains of the Day* (blog), November 13, 2019, https://www.eugenewei.com/blog/2019/11/4/status-update.

14. Amanda Fortini, "Break the Internet: Kim Kardashian," *Paper*, November 12, 2014, https://www.papermag.com/break-the-internet-kim-kardashian-cover-1427450475.html#rebelltitem1.

15. Emma Spedding, "The Man behind Kim Kardashian's Paper Magazine Cover on How to Break the Internet," *Telegraph*, April 18, 2016, https://www.telegraph.co.uk/fashion/people/the-man-behind-kim-kardashians-paper-magazine-cover-on-how-to-br/.

16. Fortini, "Break the Internet."

17. Janice Turner, "Don't Mess with Arianna Huffington," *The Times*, March 22, 2014, https://www.thetimes.co.uk/article/dont-mess-with-arianna-huffington-k5tt6q9s0w2.

18. Michael Shapiro, "Six Degrees of Aggregation," *Columbia Journalism Review*, May–June 2012, https://archives.cjr.org/cover_story/six_degrees_of_aggregation.php.

19. Shapiro, "Six Degrees."

20. David Sarno, "A Brief History of the Huffington Post," *Los Angeles Times*, February 7, 2011, https://www.latimes.com/archives/la-xpm-2011-feb-07-la-fi-huffington-post-timeline-20110207-story.html.

21. Shapiro, "Six Degrees."

22. Joshua Benton, "The Leaked New York Times Innovation Report Is One of the Key Documents of This Media Age," Nieman Lab, May 15, 2014, https://www.niemanlab.org/2014/05/the-leaked-new-york-times-innovation-report-is-one-of-the-key-documents-of-this-media-age/.

23. Belinda Luscombe, "Arianna Huffington: Media Mogul," *Time*, April 21, 2011, https://content.time.com/time/specials/packages/article/0,28804,2066367_2066369_2066496,00.html.
24. Benton, "The Leaked New York Times."
25. Jonathan Mahler, "Gawker's Moment of Truth," *New York Times*, June 12, 2015, https://www.nytimes.com/2015/06/14/business/media/gawker-nick-denton-moment-of-truth.html.
26. Carlson Nicholas, "This Gawker.com Style Guide from 2008 Proves Nick Denton's Blog Invented Web Writing," *Business Insider*, August 19, 2016, https://www.businessinsider.com/gawkercom-style-guide-from-2008-2016-8.
27. Mahler, "Gawker's Moment of Truth."
28. Caitlin Petre, "'Traffic Whoring' or Simply Optimizing? Finding the Boundaries between Clean and Dirty Metrics," Nieman Lab, January 6, 2022, https://www.niemanlab.org/2022/01/traffic-whoring-or-simply-optimizing-finding-the-boundaries-between-clean-and-dirty-metrics.
29. Weber Shandwick, "Civility in America: An Annual Nationwide Survey," January 1, 2012, https://webershandwick.com/news/civility-in-america-an-annual-nationwide-survey.
30. Nick Denton, "How Things Work," *Gawker*, August 22, 2016, https://www.gawker.com/how-things-work-1785604699.
31. Owen Thomas, "Peter Thiel Is Totally Gay, People," *Gawker*, December 19, 2007, https://www.gawker.com/335894/peter-thiel-is-totally-gay-people.
32. Eriq Gardner, "Gawker to Pay Hulk Hogan $31 Million to Settle Sex Tape Lawsuit," *Hollywood Reporter*, November 2, 2016, https://www.hollywoodreporter.com/business/business-news/nick-denton-announces-gawker-settlement-hulk-hogan-943414/.
33. Jonah Peretti, "Capitalism and Schizophrenia," *Genius*, January 1, 1996, https://genius.com/Jonah-peretti-capitalism-and-schizophrenia-annotated.
34. Jonah Peretti, "Nike Emails," *Shey.net*, accessed July 26, 2023, http://shey.net/niked.html.
35. Jill Abramson, *Merchants of Truth: The Business of News and the Fight for Facts* (New York: Simon and Schuster, 2019), 17.

36. Jonah Peretti, "Culture Jamming, Memes, Social Networks and the Emerging Media Ecology," University of Washington, accessed October 20, 2023, https://depts.washington.edu/ccce/polcommcampaigns/peretti.html.
37. Jonah Peretti, "Notes on Contagious Media," DocPlayer, accessed July 26, 2023, https://docplayer.net/198519266-Notes-on-contagious-media-jonah-peretti.html.
38. Abramson, *Merchants of Truth*, 17.
39. Noah Robischon, "How BuzzFeed's Jonah Peretti Is Building a 100-Year Media Company," *Fast Company*, February 16, 2016, https://www.fastcompany.com/3056057/how-buzzfeeds-jonah-peretti-is-building-a-100-year-media-company.
40. Cates Holderness, "What Colors Are This Dress?," *BuzzFeed*, February 26, 2015, https://www.buzzfeed.com/catesish/help-am-i-going-insane-its-definitely-blue.
41. Ben Smith, "The Dress," *BuzzFeed*, February 27, 2015, https://www.buzzfeed.com/bensmith/culture-web-culture.
42. Tasneem Nashrulla, "We Blew Up a Watermelon and Everyone Lost Their Freaking Minds," *BuzzFeed*, April 8, 2016, https://www.buzzfeednews.com/article/tasneemnashrulla/we-blew-up-a-z-watermelon-and-everyone-lost-their-freaking-min.
43. Paul Farhi and Elahe Izadi, "BuzzFeed News, a Digital Media Pioneer, to Shut Down," *Washington Post*, April 20, 2023, https://www.washingtonpost.com/media/2023/04/20/buzzfeed-news-closing/.
44. Gay Talese, "Tom Wolfe's Seventies," *Esquire*, December 1979, https://classic.esquire.com/article/1979/12/01/tom-wolfes-seventies.
45. Claire E. Robertson, Nicolas Prollochs, Kaoru Schwarzenegger, Philip Parnamets, Jay J. Van Bavel, and Stefan Feuerriegel, "Negativity Drives Online News Consumption," *Nature Human Behaviour* 7 (March 2023): 812–822.
46. William J. Brady, Julian A. Wills, John T. Jost, Joshua A. Tucker, and Jay J. Van Bavel, "Emotion Shapes the Diffusion of Moralized Content in Social Networks," *PNAS* 114, no. 28 (2017), https://doi.org/10.1073/pnas.1618923114.
47. Brady et al., "Emotion Shapes."
48. Lisa DePaulo, "Breitbart in Full: The GQA," *GQ*, March 1, 2012, https://www.gq.com/story/andrew-breitbart-interview-lisa-depaulo.

49. Joan Coaston, "Breitbart Is Dead: But Breitbart Will Live On," *Vox*, January 14, 2018, https://www.vox.com/2018/1/14/16875288/bannon-breitbart-conservative-media.
50. Christopher Beam, "Media Is Everything. It's Everything," *Slate*, March 15, 2010, https://slate.com/news-and-politics/2010/03/andrew-breitbart-slate-s-2010-profile-of-the-late-conservative-commentator.html.
51. Glynnis MacNicol, "Breitbart Says He Has a Picture of Weiner's 'Weiner' (NSFW)," *Business Insider*, June 8, 2011, https://www.businessinsider.com/breitbart-weiner-photo-penis-2011-6; UPI, "Man Fires Gun in D.C. Restaurant While Investigating 'Pizzagate' Conspiracy," *Breitbart*, December 5, 2016, https://www.breitbart.com/news/man-fires-gun-in-d-c-restaurant-while-investigating-pizzagate-conspiracy/.
52. Jeremy W. Peters, "Andrew Breitbart, Conservative Blogger, Dies at 43," *New York Times*, March 12, 2012, https://www.nytimes.com/2012/03/02/us/andrew-breitbart-conservative-blogger-dies-at-43.html.
53. William Strauss and Neil Howe, *The Fourth Turning* (New York: Broadway Books), 1997.
54. Hoover Institution, "Andrew Breitbart—Media War," YouTube, June 14, 2011, https://www.youtube.com/watch?v=b8CpON8VrRU.
55. Elaine Godfrey, "The Honey Badger Don't Care—but I Do," *The Atlantic*, September 21, 2022, https://www.theatlantic.com/politics/archive/2022/09/honey-badger-steve-bannon-political-mascot/671484/.
56. Yochai Benkler, Robert Faris, and Hal Roberts, *Network Propaganda: Manipulation, Disinformation, and Radicalization in American Politics* (Oxford: Oxford University Press, 2018), 33.
57. Benkler, Faris, and Roberts, *Network Propaganda*, 14.
58. Carolyn E. Schmidt, "'Network Propaganda' Explored," *Harvard Gazette*, October 25, 2018, https://news.harvard.edu/gazette/story/2018/10/network-propaganda-takes-a-closer-look-at-media-and-american-politics/.
59. Serena Giusti and Elisa Piras, eds., *Democracy and Fake News: Information Manipulation and Post-truth Politics* (New York: Routledge, 2021), https://www.researchgate.net/publication/342946132_Democracy_and_Fake_News_Information_Manipulation_and_Post-Truth_Politics.
60. Daniel Victor and Liam Stack, "Stephen Bannon and Breitbart News, in Their Words," *New York Times*, November 14, 2016, https://www.nytimes.com/2016/11/15/us/politics/stephen-bannon-breitbart-words.html.

61. Stephen Daw, "A Complete Timeline of Kevin Hart's Oscar-Hosting Controversy, from Tweets to Apologies," *Billboard*, January 13, 2020, https://www.billboard.com/music/awards/kevin-hart-oscar-hosting-controversy-timeline-8492982/.
62. Murtaza Hussain, "The New Information Warfare," *The Intercept*, November 25, 2017, https://theintercept.com/2017/11/25/information-warfare-social-media-book-review-gaza/.
63. Sean Illing, "'Flood the Zone with Shit': How Misinformation Overwhelmed Our Democracy," *Vox*, January 16, 2020, https://www.vox.com/policy-and-politics/2020/1/16/20991816/impeachment-trial-trump-bannon-misinformation.

Chapter 4

1. Marshall McLuhan, *Counter Blast* (New York: Harcourt, Brace, 1969), 41.
2. Securities and Exchange Commission, "United States of America before the Securities and Exchange Commission," release no. 88477, March 25, 2020, https://www.sec.gov/litigation/suspensions/2020/34-88477.pdf.
3. Samantha Subramanian, "The Deep Conspiracy Roots of Europe's Strange Wave of Cell-Tower Fires," *Politico*, May 18, 2020, https://www.politico.com/news/magazine/2020/05/18/deep-conspiracy-roots-europe-wave-cell-tower-fires-264997.
4. Isobel Cockerelle, "Meet the Celebrities Pushing 5G Coronavirus Conspiracies to Millions of Fans," *Coda Story*, April 14, 2020, https://www.codastory.com/waronscience/celebrities-5g-conspiracies/.
5. Kevin McSpadden, "Bill Gates Thinks This Is the Deadliest Threat to Humankind," *Time*, May 28, 2015, https://time.com/3899414/bill-gates-disease-epidemic-ebola-threat-to-humanity-disaster/.
6. Daisuke Wakabayashi, Davey Alba, and Marc Tracy, "Bill Gates, at Odds with Trump on Virus, Becomes a Right-Wing Target," *New York Times*, April 17, 2020, https://www.nytimes.com/2020/04/17/technology/bill-gates-virus-conspiracy-theories.html.
7. Katherine Schaeffer, "A Look at the Americans Who Believe There Is Some Truth to the Conspiracy Theory That COVID-19 Was Planned," Pew Research Center, July 24, 2020, https://www.pewresearch.org/short-reads/2020/07/24/a-look-at-the-americans-who-believe-there-is-some-truth-to-the-conspiracy-theory-that-covid-19-was-planned/.

8. Justin Chan, "People Are Praising This Steak Brand for Its 'Random as Hell' Tweets," *Yahoo! News*, April 21, 2020, https://www.yahoo.com/now/2020-04-21-people-are-praising-this-steak-brand-for-its-random-as-hell-tweets-24061774.html.
9. Steak-umm, Twitter post, April 6, 2020, https://twitter.com/steak_umm/status/1336349251442454531?s=20.
10. Travis M. Andrews, "Meet the Minds behind the Bizarre, Truth-Bombing Steak-Umm Twitter Account," *Washington Post*, April 21, 2020, https://www.washingtonpost.com/technology/2020/04/21/steak-umm-twitter-account-feed/.
11. Jeff Beer, "How Steak-Umm—Yes, That Steak-Umm—Became a Voice of Reason in the Pandemic," *Fast Company*, April 7, 2020, https://www.fastcompany.com/90487288/how-steak-umm-yes-that-steak-umm-became-a-voice-of-reason-in-the-pandemic.
12. World Health Organization, "Naming the Coronavirus Disease (COVID-19) and the Virus That Causes It," 2020, https://www.who.int/emergencies/diseases/novel-coronavirus-2019/technical-guidance/naming-the-coronavirus-disease-(covid-2019)-and-the-virus-that-causes-it.
13. David J. Sencer CDC Museum, "COVID-19 Timeline," March 15, 2023, https://www.cdc.gov/museum/timeline/covid19.html.
14. Centers for Disease Control and Prevention, "Transcript for the CDC Telebriefing Update on COVID-19," February 26, 2020, https://www.cdc.gov/media/releases/2020/t0225-cdc-telebriefing-covid-19.html.
15. Jake Coyle, "Tom Hanks, Rita Wilson Test Positive for Coronavirus," *Associated Press*, March 12, 2020, https://apnews.com/article/health-us-news-ap-top-news-virus-outbreak-public-health-8418cfae82b1a86b95cbbca96d7c1826.
16. Joe Mussatto, "'Don't Let Them Tip the Ball': Oral History of How COVID Dashed March 11 Thunder-Jazz Game," *Oklahoman*, March 11, 2021, https://www.oklahoman.com/story/sports/nba/thunder/2021/03/11/thunder-jazz-march-11-covid-nba-postponed-game-shutdown-coronavirus-rudy-gobert-utah-oklahoma-city/6930268002/.
17. Mark Murray, "Sixty Percent Believe Worst Is Yet to Come for the US in Coronavirus Pandemic," *NBC News*, March 15, 2020, https://www.nbcnews.com/politics/meet-the-press/sixty-percent-believe-worst-yet-come-u-s-coronavirus-pandemic-n1159106.

18. John Fritze and David Jackson, "Trump Calls to 'Liberate' States Where Protesters Have Demanded Easing Coronavirus Lockdowns," *USA Today*, April 17, 2020, https://www.usatoday.com/story/news/politics/2020/04/17/coronavirus-trump-calls-liberate-virginia-michigan-minnesota/5152120002/.

19. National Institutes of Health, "COVID-19 Was Third Leading Cause of Death in the United States in Both 2020 and 2021," July 5, 2022, https://www.nih.gov/news-events/news-releases/covid-19-was-third-leading-cause-death-united-states-both-2020-2021.

20. Alan Silberberg, *Bots against Us: The Ongoing Information War against the United States* (Self-published, 2019), Kindle loc. 90.

21. "How Do Fake News Sites Make Money?," *BBC News*, February 9, 2017, https://www.bbc.com/news/av/business-38919403.

22. Edgar Alvarez, "Why Are People Pretending to Be Dead on Instagram?," *Engadget* (blog), September 19, 2018, https://www.engadget.com/2018-09-19-instagram-rip-comments-prank.html.

23. Taylor Lorenz, "The Teens Who Rack Up Thousands of Followers by Posting the Same Photo Every Day," *The Atlantic*, October 4, 2018, https://www.theatlantic.com/technology/archive/2018/10/teens-who-post-same-thing-every-day-instagram/572155/.

24. Amanda Mull, "I Joined a Stationary-Biker Gang," *The Atlantic*, November 4, 2019, https://www.theatlantic.com/magazine/archive/2019/12/the-tribe-of-peloton/600748/.

25. Chris Perry, "What Comes after the Coherence Crash?," *Medium*, August 9, 2022, https://medium.com/media-genius/what-comes-after-the-coherence-crash-ecbe0f8005b5.

26. Douglas Rushkoff, *Present Shock* (New York: Current, 2014).

27. James Suber and Jacob Ware, "Examining Extremism: QAnon," Center for Strategic and International Studies, June 10, 2021, https://www.csis.org/blogs/examining-extremism/examining-extremism-qanon.

28. Emma Grey Ellis, "Trump's Presidency Has Spawned a New Generation of Witches," *Wired*, October 30, 2019, https://www.wired.com/story/trump-witches/.

29. "Witchtok," TikTok, accessed July 26, 2023, https://www.tiktok.com/discover/witchtok-tiktok?lang=en.

30. See the r/UnethicalLifeProTips Reddit account, at https://www.reddit.com/r/UnethicalLifeProTips/.
31. Gatebox, "Living with Characters," November 13, 2021, https://www.gatebox.ai.
32. "Special Effects and Virtual Guests: China Weddings Go Online," *News International*, May 11, 2020, https://www.thenews.com.pk/amp/657055.
33. Pearse Anderson, "Campus Is Closed, So College Students Are Rebuilding Their Schools in Minecraft," *The Verge*, March 31, 2020, https://www.theverge.com/2020/3/31/21200972/college-students-graduation-minecraft-coronavirus-school-closures.
34. Perry, "What Comes after the Coherence Crash?"
35. Donald D. Hoffman, "The Interface Theory of Perception," *Psychonomic Bulletin and Review* 22 (2015): 1480–1506.
36. Donald D. Hoffman, *The Case against Reality: How Evolution Hid the Truth from Our Eyes* (New York: Penguin, 2020), Kindle loc. 103–104.
37. Michael Shermer, "Did Humans Evolve to See Things as They Really Are?," *Scientific American*, November 1, 2015, https://www.scientificamerican.com/article/did-humans-evolve-to-see-things-as-they-really-are/.
38. Closer to Truth, "Donald Hoffman—Why Did Consciousness Emerge?," YouTube, December 10, 2022, https://www.youtube.com/watch?v=L4Y1kvpjO9Q.
39. Amanda Gefter, "The Evolutionary Argument against Reality," *Quanta Magazine*, April 21, 2016, https://www.quantamagazine.org/the-evolutionary-argument-against-reality-20160421/.
40. Hoffman, *The Case against Reality*, Kindle loc. 14.
41. Hoffman, *The Case against Reality*, Kindle loc. 3301.

Chapter 5

1. "William Hogarth's Satire on False Perspective (1754)," *Public Domain Review*, accessed July 26, 2023, https://publicdomainreview.org/collection/william-hogarth-satire-on-false-perspective/.
2. "William Hogarth's Satire."

3. Nate Silver, "Why FiveThirtyEight Gave Trump a Better Chance than Almost Anyone Else," *FiveThirtyEight*, November 11, 2016, https://fivethirtyeight.com/features/why-fivethirtyeight-gave-trump-a-better-chance-than-almost-anyone-else/.
4. "Hillary Clinton Has an 80 Percent Chance of Winning the Presidency," *New York Times*, September 12, 2016, https://www.nytimes.com/newsgraphics/2016/09/12/presidential-forecast-updates/newsletter.html.
5. Lauren Gambino, "Hillary Clinton Clear Debate Winner among Group of Undecided Voters," *The Guardian*, September 27, 2016, https://www.theguardian.com/us-news/2016/sep/27/presidential-debate-focus-group-frank-luntz-hillary-clinton-winner.
6. Gilad Lotan, "#TrumpWon? Trend vs. Reality," *Medium*, September 29, 2016, https://medium.com/i-data/trumpwon-trend-vs-reality-16cec3badd60.
7. Lotan, "#TrumpWon?"
8. Willy Stanley, "All the President's Memes," *New York Times*, January 14, 2019, https://www.nytimes.com/2019/01/14/magazine/all-the-presidents-memes.html.
9. Claire Wardle, Zoom interview by the author, April 4, 2022.
10. Jeffrey Jones, "Confidence in US Institutions Down; Average at New Low," Gallup, July 5, 2022, https://news.gallup.com/poll/394283/confidence-institutions-down-average-new-low.asp.
11. Gian M. Volpicelli, "This Was the Year When Finance Jumped the Doge," *Wired UK*, December 21, 2021, https://www.wired.co.uk/article/defi-gamestop-memes-doge-musk.
12. Tom Foster, "What Everyone Got Wrong about GameStop, Reddit, and Robinhood," *Texas Monthly*, May 5, 2022, https://www.texasmonthly.com/arts-entertainment/what-everyone-got-wrong-about-gamestop-reddit-robinhood/.
13. Zack Abrams, "A Year after the Epic GameStop Rally, Here Is How Much Reddit Still Influences Meme Stocks," *Business of Business*, February 22, 2022, https://www.businessofbusiness.com/articles/reddit-vs-wall-street-by-the-numbers-one-year-later-wallstreetbets-gamestop-amc-cloverhealth-tesla-blackberry/.

14. Thyagaraju Adinarayan, "JPMorgan Offers Hedge Funds a Way to Dodge Meme-Stock Shocks," *Bloomberg*, December 9, 2021, https://www.bloomberg.com/news/articles/2021-12-09/jpmorgan-offers-hedge-funds-a-way-to-dodge-meme-stock-shocks?in_source=embedded-checkout-banner.
15. Allison Morrow, "The Year Reddit Changed Wall Street Forever," CNN, December 19, 2021, https://www.cnn.com/2021/12/19/investing/stocks-week-ahead-reddit-wallstreetbets-gamestop/index.html.
16. Jennifer Hughes and Andrew Edgecliffe-Johnson, "Meme-Stock Groups Have Raised $5bn in 2 Years since Trading Frenzy," *Financial Times*, January 27, 2023, https://www.ft.com/content/adc1de86-a09d-4dcf-a54f-2e52ab68cffd.
17. Jeff O'Brien, "A Growing Army of Online Trolls Is Using Dangerous Lies to Take Down Executives and Companies: Now They're Coming for You," *Fortune*, June 22, 2022, https://fortune.com/2022/06/02/online-trolls-using-dangerous-lies-to-take-down-executives-and-companies/.
18. O'Brien, "A Growing Army of Online Trolls."
19. See the US Ministry of Truth Twitter account, at https://twitter.com/USMiniTru.
20. "Tucker Carlson Makes Bizarre Claim That Joe Biden Is Going to Use 'Men with Guns' to Force People to Believe What He Says," Media Matters for America, April 28, 2022, https://www.mediamatters.org/tucker-carlson/tucker-carlson-makes-bizarre-claim-joe-biden-going-use-men-guns-force-people-believe.
21. Homeland Security, Twitter post, May 18, 2022, https://twitter.com/DHSgov/status/1526988380155924481.
22. Nomaan Merchant and Amanda Seitz, "New 'Disinformation' Board Paused amid Free Speech Questions," *Associated Press*, May 18, 2022, https://apnews.com/article/government-and-politics-national-security-83c67505703c02b0de154b21abd5c569.
23. Taylor Lorenz, "How the Biden Administration Let Right-Wing Attacks Derail Its Disinformation Efforts," *Washington Post*, May 18, 2022, https://www.washingtonpost.com/technology/2022/05/18/disinformation-board-dhs-nina-jankowicz/.

24. Shakil Hamid, "They Don't Trust Us; We Don't Trust Them," *American Conservative*, July 9, 2022, https://www.theamericanconservative.com/they-dont-trust-us-we-dont-trust-them/.

25. Peter Dizikes, "Study: On Twitter, False News Travels Faster than True Stories," *MIT News*, Massachusetts Institute of Technology, March 8, 2018, https://news.mit.edu/2018/study-twitter-false-news-travels-faster-true-stories-0308.

26. Bharat N. Anand, *The Content Trap: A Strategist's Guide to Digital Change* (New York: Random House, 2016), xxv.

27. Joshua Cooper Ramo, *The Seventh Sense* (New York: Little, Brown, 2016), 37.

Chapter 6

1. Barbara W. Tuchman, *A Distant Mirror: The Calamitous 14th Century* (New York: Random House, 2014), xxvi.

2. *Severance*, season 1, episode 1, "Good News about Hell," created by Dan Erickson, directed by Ben Stiller, aired February 18, 2022, on Apple TV.

3. Howard Gardner, "From the Cradle to the Mainframe," *New York Times*, July 22, 1984, https://www.nytimes.com/1984/07/22/books/from-the-cradle-to-the-mainframe.html.

4. Sherry Turkle, *The Second Self: Computers and the Human Spirit* (Cambridge, MA: MIT Press, 2005).

5. Sherry Turkle, *Life on the Screen: Identity in the Age of the Internet* (New York: Simon and Schuster, 1995), 11–13.

6. Turkle, *Life on the Screen*, 192.

7. Tracey Follows, Zoom interview by the author, December 22, 2022.

8. Tracey Follows, *The Future of You: Can Your Identity Survive 21st-Century Technology?* (London: Elliott and Thompson, 2022).

9. Follows, interview by the author.

10. Tracey Follows, "The Human Effect," group conversation hosted by Weber Shandwick, May 23, 2023.

11. Follows, interview by the author.

12. PopTech, "Nick Felton: Tracing Our Lives," YouTube, February 23, 2010, https://www.youtube.com/watch?v=JwoLfg6xR8o.

13. Margaret Rhodes, "This Guy Obsessively Recorded His Private Data for 10 Years," *Wired*, October 19, 2015, https://www.wired.com/2015/10/nicholas-felton-obsessively-recorded-his-private-data-for-10-years/.
14. Nick Yee and Jeremy Bailenson, "The Proteus Effect: The Effect of Transformed Self-Representation on Behavior," *Human Communication Research* 33, no. 3 (2007): 271–290.
15. Market Research, "Quantified Self in Healthcare Market Outlook and Forecasts, 2021–2028," April 2021, https://www.marketresearch.com/Mind-Commerce-Publishing-v3122/Quantified-Self-Healthcare-Outlook-Forecasts-14459820/.
16. Steve Calechman, "10,000 Steps a Day—or Fewer?," *Harvard Health Publishing* (blog), July 11, 2019, https://www.health.harvard.edu/blog/10000-steps-a-day-or-fewer-2019071117305.
17. Elaine St. Peter, "For Older Women, Just 7,500 Steps a Day Lowers Mortality," *Harvard Gazette*, June 4, 2019, https://news.harvard.edu/gazette/story/2019/06/for-older-women-just-7500-steps-a-day-lowers-mortality/.
18. Pedro F. Saint-Maurice, Richard P. Troiano, David R. Bassett Jr., Barry I. Graubard, Susan A. Carlson, Eric J. Shiroma, Janet E. Fulton, and Charles E. Matthews, "Association of Daily Step Count and Step Intensity with Mortality among US Adults," *JAMA* 323, no. 12 (2020): 1151–1160.
19. Summer Jasinski, "Pour Decisions: How Alcohol Negatively Impacts Your Biometric Data," WHOOP, August 22, 2022, https://www.whoop.com/thelocker/how-alcohol-negatively-impacts-your-biometic-data/.
20. WHOOP, "Impact of Marijuana (THC) on Sleep, Heart Rate & HRV," April 20, 2022, https://www.whoop.com/thelocker/impact-of-marijuana-sleep-resting-heart-rate-hrv/.
21. John D. McKinnon, "FTC Reaches Settlement with Flo Health over Fertility-Tracking App," *Wall Street Journal*, January 13, 2021, https://www.wsj.com/articles/ftc-reaches-settlement-with-flo-health-over-fertility-tracking-app-11610568915.
22. Natasha Lomas, "Flo Gets FTC Slap for Sharing User Data When It Promised Privacy," *TechCrunch*, January 13, 2021, https://techcrunch.com/2021/01/13/flo-gets-ftc-slap-for-sharing-user-data-when-it-promised-privacy/.

23. Drew Donnelly, "China Social Credit System Explained—What Is It and How Does It Work?," *Horizons*, September 28, 2023, https://joinhorizons.com/china-social-credit-system-explained/.
24. Nicole Kobie, "The Complicated Truth about China's Social Credit System," *Wired UK*, June 7, 2019, https://www.wired.co.uk/article/china-social-credit-system-explained.
25. Nathan VanderKlippe, "Chinese Blacklist an Early Glimpse of Sweeping New Social-Credit Control," *Globe and Mail*, January 4, 2018, https://www.theglobeandmail.com/news/world/chinese-blacklist-an-early-glimpse-of-sweeping-new-social-credit-control/article37493300/.
26. Donnelly, "China Social Credit System."
27. Matt Klein, *Audience Capture* (Self-published, 2023), https://kleinkleinklein.com/audience-capture.
28. Erving Goffman, *The Presentation of Self in Everyday Life* (Albany, NY: Anchor Books, 1959).
29. Matt Klein, Zoom interview by the author, May 5, 2023.
30. "Hot or Not," *Wikipedia*, September 6, 2023, https://en.wikipedia.org/wiki/Hot_or_Not.
31. "History of Facebook," *Wikipedia*, September 19, 2023, https://en.wikipedia.org/wiki/History_of_Facebook.
32. "BecauseImHot—Crunchbase Company Profile & Funding," *Crunchbase*, accessed July 27, 2023, https://www.crunchbase.com/organization/becauseimhot.
33. "Beauty Is between Eyes, Mouth of the Beholden: Study," *Independent*, December 18, 2009, https://www.independent.co.uk/life-style/fashion/news/beauty-is-between-eyes-mouth-of-the-beholden-study-5513275.html.
34. Rosalind Gill, "90% of Young Women Report Using a Filter or Editing Their Photos before Posting," *ScienceDaily*, March 8, 2021, https://www.sciencedaily.com/releases/2021/03/210308111852.htm.
35. Tate Ryan-Mosley, "Beauty Filters Are Changing the Way Young Girls See Themselves," *MIT Technology Review*, April 2, 2021, https://www.technologyreview.com/2021/04/02/1021635/beauty-filters-young-girls-augmented-reality-social-media/.

36. Claire Kathryn Pescott, "'I Wish I Was Wearing a Filter Right Now': An Exploration of Identity Formation and Subjectivity of 10- and 11-Year Olds' Social Media Use," *Social Media + Society* 6, no. 4 (2020), https://doi.org/10.1177/2056305120965155.

37. Catherine Page Jeffery, "Is 13 Too Young to Have a TikTok or Instagram Account?" *The Guardian*, February 9, 2023, https://www.theguardian.com/lifeandstyle/2023/feb/10/is-13-too-young-to-have-a-tiktok-or-instagram-account.

38. Dove Canada, "It's Time to Have the Selfie Talk—New Dove Self-Esteem Project Research Finds 80% of Canadian Girls Are Using Photo Editing Apps by the Age of 13," April 20, 2021, https://www.newswire.ca/news-releases/it-s-time-to-have-the-selfie-talk-new-dove-self-esteem-project-research-finds-80-of-canadian-girls-are-using-photo-editing-apps-by-the-age-of-13-866468860.html.

39. Caroline Rocha, "AR Talks: Caroline Rocha," *Lenslist* (blog), May 6, 2019, https://blog.lenslist.co/2019/05/06/ar-talks-caroline-rocha/.

40. Ryan-Mosley, "Beauty Filters Are Changing."

41. Jia Tolentino, "The Age of Instagram Face," *New Yorker*, December 12, 2019, https://www.newyorker.com/culture/decade-in-review/the-age-of-instagram-face.

42. Tolentino, "The Age of Instagram Face."

43. Susruthi Rajanala, Mayra B. C. Maymone, and Neelam A. Vashi, "Selfies—Living in the Era of Filtered Photographs," *JAMA Facial Plastic Surgery* 20, no. 6 (2018): 443.

44. Elizabeth Cassidy, "Doctors Say Apps like Snapchat and Facetune Can Trigger Body Dysmorphia," *Yahoo! Life*, August 3, 2018, https://www.yahoo.com/lifestyle/doctors-apps-snapchat-facetune-trigger-224539132.htm.

45. Emily Rella, "The Pandemic Created a Perfect Storm for the Plastic Surgery Industry amid the 'Zoom Boom' Phenomenon: Doctors Are Expecting Another Boom This Holiday Season," *Entrepreneur*, December 21, 2021, https://www.entrepreneur.com/living/the-pandemic-created-a-perfect-storm-for-the-plastic/403703.

46. Lecia Bushak, "TikTok's Most Popular Plastic Surgeon Influencers," *MM+M*, November 11, 2022, https://www.mmm-online.com/home/channel/tiktoks-most-popular-plastic-surgeon-influencers/.

47. Refinery 29, "The Truth behind Instagram-Famous Plastic Surgeons," YouTube, June 23, 2018, https://www.youtube.com/watch?v=zyKjMVyDJx8.

48. American Society of Plastic Surgeons, "Survey Finds Demand for Cosmetic Surgery, Driven by Women under 45, Surged after the Pandemic," August 24, 2022, https://www.plasticsurgery.org/news/press-releases/survey-finds-demand-for-cosmetic-surgery-driven-by-women-under-45-surged-after-the-pandemic.

49. Tolentino, "The Age of Instagram Face."

50. Assemblée nationale, "Texte de La Commission N°1006—Proposition de Loi," March 22, 2023, https://www.assemblee-nationale.fr/dyn/16/textes/l16b1006_texte-adopte-commission.

51. Jennifer Weil, "Labeling Influencers' Filtered, Retouched Images May Become Mandatory in France," *Women's Wear Daily*, March 24, 2023, https://wwd.com/business-news/media/labeling-influencers-filtered-retouched-images-may-become-mandatory-france-1235594442/.

52. Laura Pitcher, "The Beauty Filter Rebellion Has Begun with TikTok's Latest Trend," *Nylon*, April 5, 2022, https://www.nylon.com/beauty/removing-beauty-filter-tiktok-trend-tear-in-my-heart.

53. Chris Perry, "The Information Disorder Inside of Us," *Medium*, April 29, 2021, https://medium.com/mlearning-ai/the-information-disorder-inside-of-us-15ea8052aabf.

Chapter 7

1. Darren Murph, Zoom interview by the author, August 22, 2023.

2. Zaidleppelin, "On Quiet Quitting," TikTok, July 25, 2022, https://www.tiktok.com/@zaidleppelin/video/7124414185282391342?lang=en.

3. Sarah Jackson, "Top 10 Workplace Trends on TikTok This Year: Quiet Quitting, Bare Minimum Mondays, and More," *Business Insider*, June 23, 2023, https://www.businessinsider.com/top-work-trends-tiktok-quiet-quitting-hiring-act-your-wage-2023-5.

4. Cal Newport, "The Year in Quiet Quitting," *New Yorker*, December 29, 2022, https://www.newyorker.com/culture/2022-in-review/the-year-in-quiet-quitting.

5. Erin L. Kelly, Lisa F. Berkman, Laura D. Kubzansky, and Meg Lovejoy, "7 Strategies to Improve Your Employees' Health and Well-Being," *Harvard Business Review*, October 12, 2021, https://hbr.org/2021/10/7-strategies-to-improve-your-employees-health-and-well-being.
6. Rani Molla, "Burnout Was Supposed to Get Better: It Hasn't," *Vox*, October 20, 2022, https://www.vox.com/recode/2022/10/20/23413380/burnout-remote-work-economy-quits-slack-future-forum.
7. Jon Clifton, "The Power of Work Friends," *Harvard Business Review*, October 7, 2022, https://hbr.org/2022/10/the-power-of-work-friends.
8. Jon Clifton, "The World's Workplace Is Broken—Here's How to Fix It," Gallup, June 14, 2022, https://www.gallup.com/workplace/393395/world-workplace-broken-fix.aspx.
9. Greg Iacurci, "2022 Was the 'Real Year of the Great Resignation,' Says Economist," CNBC, February 1, 2023, https://www.cnbc.com/2023/02/01/why-2022-was-the-real-year-of-the-great-resignation.html; US Bureau of Labor Statistics, "Job Openings and Labor Turnover Summary," Economic News Release no. USDL-23-1890, February 1, 2023, https://www.bls.gov/news.release/jolts.nr0.htm.
10. Josef Pieper, *Leisure: The Basis of Culture* (New York: Pantheon Books, 1952).
11. William Arruda, "How Hustle Culture May Hurt Your Career," *Forbes*, August 22, 2022, https://www.forbes.com/sites/williamarruda/2022/08/07/how-hustle-culture-may-hurt-your-career/?sh=79c9c61c3ee8.
12. Eddy Martinez, "Norwalk Author Explores Artisan Resurgence in New Book," *Norwalk Hour*, September 4, 2022, https://www.thehour.com/news/article/Norwalk-author-explores-artisan-resurgence-in-new-17417451.php.
13. Jared Polites, "Why Artisans Will Be Powerful in the New Economy," *Entrepreneur*, August 26, 2020, https://www.entrepreneur.com/leadership/why-artisans-will-be-powerful-in-the-new-economy/354514.
14. "Vitalik Buterin," *Wikipedia*, September 18, 2023, https://en.wikipedia.org/wiki/Vitalik_Buterin.
15. Vitalik Buterin, "My 40-Liter Backpack Travel Guide," June 20, 2022, https://vitalik.ca/general/2022/06/20/backpack.html.

16. Tsugio Makimoto, "The Age of the Digital Nomad," *IEEE Journal of Solid-State Circuits* 5, no. 1 (Winter 2013): 40–47, https://www.shmj.or.jp/makimoto/pdf/makimoto_05_01.pdf.

17. Nicholas Cocks, "Work-Life Harmony: Thriving in a New Normal Where Boundaries Are Blurred," *TechNode Global*, January 26, 2023, https://technode.global/2023/01/26/work-life-harmony-thriving-in-a-new-normal-where-boundaries-are-blurred/.

18. Joel Balsam, "The Dream of an 'Internet Country' That Would Let You Work from Anywhere," *Time*, September 8, 2022, https://time.com/6211405/internet-country-plumia-remote-work/.

19. Joseph Hernandez, "Roam If You Want To: Live and Work Internationally Thanks to This Start-Up," *Chicago Tribune*, May 6, 2016, https://www.chicagotribune.com/lifestyles/ct-roam-if-you-want-to-live-and-work-internationally-thanks-to-this-start-up-20160506-story.html.

20. See Natalie Sisson's the Suitcase Entrepreneur, at https://suitcaseentrepreneur.com.

21. See Matthew Karstan's *Expert Vagabond* blog, at https://expertvagabond.com.

22. See Rob Lloyd's *Stop Having a Boring Life* blog, at https://stophavingaboringlife.com.

23. Pieter Levels, "Growing a Community for Digital Nomads to $33,000/Mo," *Indie Hackers*, accessed July 27, 2023, https://www.indiehackers.com/interview/growing-a-community-for-digital-nomads-to-33-000-mo-126df0fc5e.

24. Jonathan Beckman, "Don't Settle: The Rise of Digital Nomads," *The Economist*, March 21, 2018, https://www.economist.com/1843/2018/03/21/dont-settle-the-rise-of-digital-nomads.

25. "Embracing Remote Work: Meet the Oracles," *CNBC Workforce Wire*, November 13, 2020, https://www.cnbc.com/video/2020/11/13/embracing-remote-work-meet-the-oracles.html.

26. Murph, interview by the author.

27. Murph, interview by the author.

28. Murph, interview by the author.

29. Chris Anderson, "The Long Tail," *Wired*, October 1, 2004, https://www.wired.com/2004/10/tail/.
30. Goldman Sachs, "The Creator Economy Could Approach Half-a-Trillion Dollars by 2027," April 19, 2023, https://www.goldmansachs.com/intelligence/pages/the-creator-economy-could-approach-half-a-trillion-dollars-by-2027.html.
31. Adobe, "Adobe 'Future of Creativity' Study: 165M+ Creators Joined Creator Economy since 2020," August 25, 2022, https://news.adobe.com/news/news-details/2022/Adobe-Future-of-Creativity-Study-165M-Creators-Joined-Creator-Economy-Since-2020/.
32. Morning Consult Pro, "Influencer Engagement Report," October 2019, https://pro.morningconsult.com/analyst-reports/influencer-report.
33. See Ryan Kaji's *Ryan's World* YouTube channel, at https://www.youtube.com/channel/UChGJGhZ9SOOHvBB0Y4DOO_w.
34. See Jennifer Lopez's *Jennifer Lopez* YouTube channel, at https://www.youtube.com/channel/UCr8RjWUQ_9KYcIPmWiqBroQ.
35. See Snoop Dogg's *SnoopDoggTV* YouTube channel, at https://www.youtube.com/channel/UC-OO324clObi3H-U0bP77dw.
36. See Dwayne Johnson's *The Rock* YouTube channel, at https://www.youtube.com/user/therock.
37. Jay Caspian Kang, "The Boy King of YouTube," *New York Times*, January 5, 2022, https://www.nytimes.com/2022/01/05/magazine/ryan-kaji-youtube.html.
38. J. Clara Chan, "The Bucket List Family's Crowdfunding Success Is Creating a Blueprint for Creators," *Hollywood Reporter*, October 25, 2022, https://www.hollywoodreporter.com/business/digital/the-bucket-list-family-crowdfunding-success-blueprint-creators-1235243956/.
39. Chan, "The Bucket List."
40. Mark Rober, "MrBeast: The 100 Most Influential People of 2023," *Time*, April 13, 2023, https://time.com/collection/100-most-influential-people-2023/6270005/mrbeast-jimmy-donaldson/.
41. Josh Richards, Zoom interview by the author, May 5, 2023.
42. Josh Richards, "I've Learned. I'm Learning. I Want to Use My Platform to Work Hard for Good," *Medium*, June 9, 2020, https://medium.com/

@josh_76229/ive-learned-i-m-learning-i-want-to-use-my-platform-to-work-hard-for-good-440f9da2afdf.

43. Richards, interview by the author.
44. Richards, interview by the author.
45. Richards, interview by the author.
46. Richards, interview by the author.
47. Richard Florida, "The Rise of the Creator Economy," Creative Class Group, November 2022, https://creativeclass.com/reports/The_Rise_of_the_Creator_Economy.pdf.
48. Upwork, "Upwork Study Finds 22% of American Workforce Will Be Remote by 2025," December 15, 2020, https://www.upwork.com/press/releases/upwork-study-finds-22-of-american-workforce-will-be-remote-by-2025.
49. Pieter Levels, "There Will Be 1 Billion Digital Nomads by 2035," *levels.io* (blog), October 25, 2015, https://levels.io/future-of-digital-nomads/.
50. Juliet B. Schor, William Attwood-Charles, Mehmet Cansoy, Isak Ladegaard, and Robert Wengronowitz, "Dependence and Precarity in the Platform Economy," *Theory and Society* 49 (2020): 833–861.
51. Gianpiero Petriglieri, Susan Ashford, and Amy Wrzesniewski, "The 4 Things You Need to Thrive in the Gig Economy," *Harvard Business Review*, April 11, 2018, https://hbr.org/2018/03/thriving-in-the-gig-economy.
52. Jan Hatzius, Joseph Briggs, Devesh Kodnani, and Giovanni Pierdomenico, "The Potentially Large Effects of Artificial Intelligence on Economic Growth," Goldman Sachs Economic Research, March 26, 2023, https://www.key4biz.it/wp-content/uploads/2023/03/Global-Economics-Analyst_-The-Potentially-Large-Effects-of-Artificial-Intelligence-on-Economic-Growth-Briggs_Kodnani.pdf.
53. Hatzius et al., "The Potentially Large Effects."
54. Reem Nadeem, "AI in Hiring and Evaluating Workers: What Americans Think," Pew Research Center, April 20, 2023, https://www.pewresearch.org/internet/2023/04/20/ai-in-hiring-and-evaluating-workers-what-americans-think/.

55. David Autor, David A. Mindell, and Elisabeth B. Reynolds, "The Work of the Future," *MIT Technology Review*, December 17, 2021, https://www.technologyreview.com/2021/12/17/1040693/the-work-of-the-future-2/.

56. Dell Technologies, "Realizing 2030: A Divided Vision of the Future," accessed October 20, 2023, https://www.delltechnologies.com/content/dam/delltechnologies/assets/perspectives/2030/pdf/Realizing-2030-A-Divided-Vision-of-the-Future-Summary.pdf.

57. "Your Job Is (Probably) Safe from Artificial Intelligence," *The Economist*, May 7, 2023, https://www.economist.com/finance-and-economics/2023/05/07/your-job-is-probably-safe-from-artificial-intelligence.

58. Alec Ross, *The Industries of the Future* (New York: Simon and Schuster, 2016).

59. PwC, "Workforce of the Future—the Competing Forces Shaping 2030," April 4, 2017, https://www.pwc.com/gx/en/services/people-organisation/publications/workforce-of-the-future.html.

Chapter 8

1. Sophia the Robot, Twitter post, August 7, 2018, https://twitter.com/RealSophiaRobot/status/1026895268908687360?ref_src=twsrc%5Etfw.

2. Ned Zeman, "Manti Te'o on the Hoax and Life After: 'Honestly, I'm Never Going to Be Completely Normal,'" *Vanity Fair*, April 25, 2013, https://www.vanityfair.com/culture/2013/06/manti-teo-girlfriend-nfl-draft.

3. Matt Fortuna, "Te'o Leads Irish after Tragic Week," ESPN, September 16, 2012, https://www.espn.com/blog/notre-dame-football/post/_/id/9136/teo-leads-irish-after-tragic-week.

4. Zeman, "Manti Te'o on the Hoax."

5. Jack Dickey and Timothy Burke, "Manti Te'o's Dead Girlfriend, the Most Heartbreaking and Inspirational Story of the College Football Season, Is a Hoax," *Deadspin*, January 16, 2013, https://deadspin.com/manti-teos-dead-girlfriend-the-most-heartbreaking-an-5976517.

6. Laura Martin, "The Complicated True Story of 'The Girlfriend Who Didn't Exist' and Manti Te'o's Catfish," *Esquire*, August 16,

2022, https://www.esquire.com/uk/culture/film/a40904885/the-girlfriend-who-didnt-exist-manti-teo-catfish-true-story/.

7. Federal Trade Commission, "FTC Data Show Romance Scams Hit Record High; $547 Million Reported Lost in 2021," February 10, 2022, https://www.ftc.gov/news-events/news/press-releases/2022/02/ftc-data-show-romance-scams-hit-record-high-547-million-reported-lost-2021.

8. Il Bong Mun and Hun Kim, "Influence of False Self-Presentation on Mental Health and Deleting Behavior on Instagram: The Mediating Role of Perceived Popularity," *Frontiers in Psychology* 12 (April 2021), https://doi.org/10.3389/fpsyg.2021.660484.

9. Jason Fagone, "He Couldn't Get Over His Fiancee's Death: So He Brought Her Back as an A.I. Chatbot," *San Francisco Chronicle*, July 23, 2021, https://www.sfchronicle.com/projects/2021/jessica-simulation-artificial-intelligence/.

10. Elyakim Kislev, "The Uncanny Future of Romance with Robots Is Already Here," *Daily Beast*, April 17, 2022, https://www.thedailybeast.com/the-future-of-human-machine-relationships-is-already-upon-us.

11. Parmy Olson, "My Girlfriend Is a Chatbot," *Wall Street Journal*, April 10, 2020, https://www.wsj.com/articles/my-girlfriend-is-a-chatbot-11586523208.

12. Ben Thompson, "An Interview with Replika Founder and CEO Eugenia Kuyda," *Stratechery Plus*, April 20, 2023, https://stratechery.com/2023/an-interview-with-replika-founder-and-ceo-eugenia-kuyda/.

13. Thompson, "An Interview with Replika Founder."

14. Thompson, "An Interview with Replika Founder."

15. Matt Fuchs, "Meet the New Robot Companions Helping to Fight Depression and Loneliness in Aging Adults," *Fortune*, July 12, 2022, https://fortune.com/well/2022/07/12/robots-help-solve-depression-and-loneliness-epidemic-in-aging-adults/.

16. Ariel Grossman, "Meet Anita's New Best Friend—a Table-Top Robot," *NoCamels*, May 3, 2023, https://nocamels.com/2023/05/meet-anitas-new-best-friend-a-table-top-robot/.

17. Guo Meiping, "What Is 'Society 5.0' at the G20 Summit?" China Global Television Network, June 28, 2019, https://news.cgtn.com/news/2019-06-28/What-is-Society-5-0-at-the-G20-summit--HT4YQ8BXlC/index.html.

18. Claire Parker, "Japan Records Its Largest Natural Population Decline as Births Fall," *Washington Post*, June 3, 2022, https://www.washingtonpost.com/world/2022/06/03/japan-low-births-population-decline-2021/.

19. Ryan Browne, "World's First Robot 'Citizen' Sophia Is Calling for Women's Rights in Saudi Arabia," CNBC, December 5, 2017, https://www.cnbc.com/2017/12/05/hanson-robotics-ceo-sophia-the-robot-an-advocate-for-womens-rights.html.

20. Tomas Hauer, "Importance and Limitations of AI Ethics in Contemporary Society," *Humanities and Social Sciences Communication* 9, no. 272 (August 2022), https://doi.org/10.1057/s41599-022-01300-7.

21. Kendra Cherry, "The Uncanny Valley: Why Realistic Robots Are Creepy," *Verywell Mind*, October 10, 2020, https://www.verywellmind.com/what-is-the-uncanny-valley-4846247.

22. Browne, "World's First Robot."

23. "Sophia (Robot)," *Wikipedia*, September 20, 2023, https://en.wikipedia.org/wiki/Sophia_(robot).

24. "Sophia the Robot Joins Borderless Capital through the Sotheby's Artwork Auction, Won for $5M HKD," *PR Newswire*, October 18, 2021, https://www.prnewswire.com/in/news-releases/sophia-the-robot-joins-borderless-capital-through-the-sotheby-s-artwork-auction-won-for-5m-hkd-814355913.html.

25. Adam Conner-Simons and Rachel Gordon, "Detecting Emotions with Wireless Signals," *MIT News*, September 20, 2016, https://news.mit.edu/2016/detecting-emotions-with-wireless-signals-0920.

26. Craig Smith, "50 Impressive Tinder Statistics," *DMR*, April 7, 2015, https://expandedramblings.com/index.php/tinder-statistics/.

27. Liam Barnett, "Tinder Statistics 2022 & Fun Facts That You Didn't Know Before," *DatingZest*, February 5, 2021, https://datingzest.com/tinder-statistics/.

28. Jenna Owsianik and Ross Dawson, "Future of Sex Report: Detailed Predictions on the Impact of Technology on Human Sexuality," *Future of Sex*, accessed July 27, 2023, https://futureofsex.net/future-of-sex-report/.

29. Helena Horton, "By 2050, Human-on-Robot Sex Will Be More Common than Human-on-Human Sex, Says Report," *Daily Telegraph*, September 29, 2015, https://www.telegraph.co.uk/technology/

news/11898241/By-2050-human-on-robot-sex-will-be-more-common-than-human-on-human-sex-says-report.html.

30. See the RealGirl App site, at https://www.realgirlapp.com/.

31. Jessica Buchleitner, "Valley of the Uncanny Dolls: Sex Tech and the Evolution of Intimacy," L'Atelier, January 27, 2022, https://atelier.net/insights/valley-uncanny-dolls-sex-tech-evolution.

32. Margaret Gibson and Clarissa Carden, *Living and Dying in a Virtual World: Digital Kinships, Nostalgia, and Mourning in Second Life* (Cham, Switzerland: Palgrave Macmillan, 2018), https://www.academia.edu/44376628/Living_and_Dying_in_a_Virtual_World_Digital_Kinships_Nostalgia_and_Mourning_in_Second_Life.

33. Daniel Cox, "The State of American Friendship: Change, Challenges, and Loss," Survey Center on American Life, June 8, 2021, https://www.americansurveycenter.org/research/the-state-of-american-friendship-change-challenges-and-loss/.

34. Jon Clifton, "The Power of Work Friends," *Harvard Business Review*, October 7, 2022, https://hbr.org/2022/10/the-power-of-work-friends.

35. American Psychological Association, "Health Advisory on Social Media Use in Adolescence," May 2023, https://www.apa.org/topics/social-media-internet/health-advisory-adolescent-social-media-use.

36. Sarah Holder, "'Where to Meet People' Internet Searches Spike amid Loneliness Epidemic," *Bloomberg*, May 10, 2023, https://www.bloomberg.com/news/articles/2023-05-10/-how-to-meet-people-google-searches-reach-new-highs.

37. Tiffany Lo, "Chinese Single Women Spend £178 a Day to Bring a Fake Boyfriend Home," *Daily Mail*, January 18, 2017, https://www.dailymail.co.uk/news/peoplesdaily/article-4131430/Desperate-women-rent-boyfriends-Chinese-New-Year.html.

38. See the RentAFriend website, at https://rentafriend.com/.

39. Stuart McGurk, "Meet the Podcaster Helping a Worried World Fall Asleep," *GQ*, April 12, 2020, https://www.gq-magazine.co.uk/lifestyle/article/sleep-with-me-drew-ackerman.

40. Morty, "About Us," accessed July 27, 2023, https://morty.app/about.

41. Andy Fitch, "Will Only the Rich Not Be Lonely: Talking to Noreena Hertz," *BLARB* (blog), February 6, 2021, https://blog.lareviewofbooks.org/interviews/will-rich-lonely-talking-noreena-hertz/.

42. US Department of Health and Human Services, "New Surgeon General Advisory Raises Alarm about the Devastating Impact of the Epidemic of Loneliness and Isolation in the United States," May 3, 2023, https://www.hhs.gov/about/news/2023/05/03/new-surgeon-general-advisory-raises-alarm-about-devastating-impact-epidemic-loneliness-isolation-united-states.html.

43. US Department of Health and Human Services, "Our Epidemic of Loneliness," 2023, https://www.hhs.gov/sites/default/files/surgeon-general-social-connection-advisory.pdf.

44. Sherry Turkle, "There Will Never Be an Age of Artificial Intimacy," *New York Times*, August 11, 2018, https://www.nytimes.com/2018/08/11/opinion/there-will-never-be-an-age-of-artificial-intimacy.html.

Chapter 9

1. Carl Sagan, *The Demon-Haunted World: Science as a Candle in the Dark* (New York: Ballantine Books, 1996), 29.

2. Gregory Smith, "About Three-in-Ten US Adults Are Now Religiously Unaffiliated," Pew Research Center, December 14, 2021, https://www.pewresearch.org/religion/2021/12/14/about-three-in-ten-u-s-adults-are-now-religiously-unaffiliated/.

3. "The World's Religions Face a Post-pandemic Reckoning," *The Economist*, January 8, 2022, https://www.economist.com/international/2022/01/08/the-worlds-religions-face-a-post-pandemic-reckoning.

4. "The World's Religions."

5. Jeffery Jones, "US Church Membership Falls Below Majority for First Time," Gallup, March 29, 2021, https://news.gallup.com/poll/341963/church-membership-falls-below-majority-first-time.aspx.

6. Pew Research Center, "Modeling the Future of Religion in America," September 13, 2022, https://www.pewresearch.org/religion/2022/09/13/modeling-the-future-of-religion-in-america/.

7. Elizabeth King and W. David Todd, "About the Book," accessed July 27, 2023, https://automatonmonk.com/about-the-book/.

8. Thuy Ong, "Pepper the Robot Is Now a Buddhist Priest Programmed to Chant at Funerals," *The Verge*, August 24, 2017, https://www.theverge.com/2017/8/24/16196752/robot-buddhist-priest-funeral-softbank.

9. "BlessU-2! 'Robot Priest' Offers Auto-Blessings in German Church," *Economic Times*, May 30, 2017, https://economictimes.indiatimes.com/magazines/panache/blessu-2-robot-priest-offers-auto-blessings-in-german-church/articleshow/58908597.cms?from=mdr.

10. David Crary, "ChatGPT Is Coming for Religion and Lazy Pastors Might Use It to Write Their Sermons—but It 'Has No Soul,'" *Fortune*, February 15, 2023, https://fortune.com/2023/02/15/chatgpt-religion-writing-sermons-has-no-soul/.

11. Sarah Perez, "Meditation and Mindfulness Apps Continue Their Surge amid the Pandemic," *TechCrunch*, May 28, 2020, https://techcrunch.com/2020/05/28/meditation-and-mindfulness-apps-continue-their-surge-amid-pandemic/.

12. Jenna Wortham, "The Rise of the Wellness App," *New York Times*, February 17, 2021, https://www.nytimes.com/2021/02/17/magazine/wellness-apps.html.

13. "'The Holy City' Review—Take a Virtual Trip to Jerusalem," *VR Voyaging*, May 21, 2022, https://www.vrvoyaging.com/the-holy-city-review/.

14. Alexander Bard and Jan Söderqvist, *Syntheism: Creating God in the Internet Age* (Stockholm: Stockholm Text, 2014), 75.

15. Mark Piesing, "Is the Internet God? Alexander Bard's Syntheism Paves the Way for a New Elite," *The Guardian*, October 7, 2014, https://www.theguardian.com/technology/2014/oct/07/god-internet-alexander-bard-syntheism-new-elite.

16. Alexander Bard, "What If the Internet Is God? Alexander Bard at TEDxStockholm," YouTube, November 4, 2013, https://www.youtube.com/watch?v=tXA7TewF53w.

17. Jim Rutt, "Alexander Bard on God in the Internet Age," *Jim Rutt Show*, November 23, 2020, https://jimruttshow.blubrry.net/the-jim-rutt-show-transcripts/transcript-of-episode-95-alexander-bard-on-god-in-the-internet-age/.

18. Global Future 2045, "22 Leading Scientists, Technologists, Entrepreneurs and Spiritual Leaders Issue Open Letter to UN Secretary-General Ban Ki-moon," March 12, 2013, https://news.cision.com/

global-future-2045/r/22-leading-scientists--technologists--entrepreneurs-and-spiritual-leaders-issue-open-letter-to-un-se,c9384329.

19. Meghan O'Gieblyn, "God in the Machine: My Strange Journey into Transhumanism," *The Guardian*, April 18, 2017, https://www.theguardian.com/technology/2017/apr/18/god-in-the-machine-my-strange-journey-into-transhumanism.

20. Meghan O'Gieblyn, "Ghost in the Cloud," *N+1* 28 (Spring 2017), https://www.nplusonemag.com/issue-28/essays/ghost-in-the-cloud/.

21. David Pierce, "Julian Huxley and Transhumanism," *BLTC*, accessed July 27, 2023, https://www.huxley.net/transhumanism/index.html.

22. Donna Haraway, "A Cyborg Manifesto," in *Simians, Cyborgs and Women: The Reinvention of Nature* (New York: Routledge, 1991), 149–181, https://theanarchistlibrary.org/library/donna-haraway-a-cyborg-manifesto.

23. Wesley J Wildman and Kate J. Stockly, *Spirit Tech: The Brave New World of Consciousness Hacking and Enlightenment Engineering* (New York: St. Martin's, 2021), 80.

24. Wildman and Stockly, *Spirit Tech*, 80.

25. Wildman and Stockly, *Spirit Tech*, 80.

26. Brett Robinson, Zoom interview by the author, October 22, 2023.

27. Robinson, interview by the author.

28. Cathy Lynn Grossman, "Don't Fence Me In: Religion & Spirituality Books for 2021," *Publishers Weekly*, March 19, 2021, https://www.publishersweekly.com/pw/by-topic/industry-news/religion/article/85846-don-t-fence-me-in.html.

29. Kursat Ozenc, "The 3 Most Unconventional Designers of 21st Century—Starting with Design Shaman," *Medium*, April 4, 2016, https://medium.com/ritual-design/a-new-breed-of-21st-century-designers-b73712963b4.

30. Jorge Arango, "Arvind Venkataramani on Rituals," *Informed Life* (podcast), August 2, 2020, https://theinformed.life/2020/08/02/episode-41-arvind-venkataramani/.

31. See the Ritual Design Toolkit website, at https://www.ritualdesign.net/.

32. Arvind Venkataramani and Adam Menter, "Integrating Selves and Systems through Ritual," *Proceedings of Relating Systems Thinking and*

Design RSD9 Symposium, 2020, https://openresearch.ocadu.ca/id/eprint/3598/1/Venkataramani_Integrating_RSD9-2020.pdf.

33. Arango, "Arvind Venkataramani on Rituals."
34. Derek Beres, "The Rise of Spiritual Capitalism," *Big Think*, April 11, 2016, https://bigthink.com/personal-growth/the-selling-of-spirituality/.

Part III

1. Marc Andreessen, "Why Software Is Eating the World," Andreessen Horowitz, August 20, 2011, https://a16z.com/2011/08/20/why-software-is-eating-the-world/.
2. Marc Andreessen, "It's Time to Build," Andreessen Horowitz, April 18, 2020, https://a16z.com/2020/04/18/its-time-to-build/.

Chapter 10

1. Adam Grant, *Think Again: The Power of Knowing What You Don't Know* (New York: Viking, 2021), Kindle loc. 104.
2. Jacqueline Brassey, Aaron De Smet, and Michiel Kruyt, *Deliberate Calm: How to Learn and Lead in a Volatile World* (New York: Harper Collins, 2022).
3. Brassey, De Smet, and Kruyt, *Deliberate Calm*.
4. Brassey, De Smet, and Kruyt, *Deliberate Calm*, 21.
5. Mark Stahlman, Zoom interview by the author, March 22, 2022.
6. Mark Stahlman, Zoom interview by the author, September 1, 2021.
7. Mark Stahlman, Zoom interview by the author, January 26, 2022.
8. Stahlman, interview by the author, March 22, 2022.
9. Mark Stahlman, "Digital Catholic Social Teaching by Mark Stahlman, Session 4: Human Dignity—Artificial Humanity," YouTube, March 20, 2022, https://www.youtube.com/watch?v=F-9CAS0aW2A.
10. Megan Leonhardt, "Crisis on Campus: 60% of College Kids Are Living with Mental Health Disorders, and Schools Are Woefully Unprepared," *Fortune*, July 12, 2022, https://fortune.com/well/2022/07/12/mental-health-crisis-college-schools-unprepared/.

11. Stahlman, interview by the author, January 26, 2022.
12. Flo Conway and Jim Siegelman, *Dark Hero of the Information Age* (New York: Basic Books, 2005), 10.
13. Conway and Siegelman, *Dark Hero*, 123.
14. Conway and Siegelman, *Dark Hero*, 123.
15. Louis Anslow, "The Original AI Doomer: Dr. Norbert Wiener," *Pessimists Archive*, June 2, 2023, https://newsletter.pessimistsarchive.org/p/the-original-ai-doomer-dr-norbert.
16. Norbert Weiner, *The Human Use of Human Beings* (Boston: Houghton Mifflin, 1954), 46.
17. Christian Madsbjerg, *Sensemaking: The Power of the Humanities in the Age of the Algorithm* (New York: Hatchette, 2017), Kindle loc. 153.
18. Tim Askew, "Why the Liberal Arts Are Necessary for Long-Term Success," *Inc.*, March 14, 2018, https://www.inc.com/tim-askew/why-liberal-arts-are-necessary-for-long-term-success.html.
19. Dan Elias Bliss, "11 Remarkably Successful CEOs with Liberal Arts Degrees," *Global Experiences* (blog), accessed October 20, 2023, https://www.globalexperiences.com/blog/ceos-liberal-arts-degrees.
20. Fred Beuttler, Zoom interview by the author, August 31, 2022.
21. Great Books Foundation, "History of the Great Books Foundation," accessed October 20, 2023, https://www.greatbooks.org/nonprofit-organization/history/.
22. Beuttler, interview by the author.
23. Malcolm Gladwell, *Blink: The Power of Thinking without Thinking* (New York: Penguin, 2005).
24. Isaac Asimov, *Science Past, Science Future* (Garden City, NY: Doubleday, 1975), 208.
25. Walter Isaacson, *Leonardo da Vinci* (New York: Simon and Schuster, 2017), 178.
26. Amy Herman, *Visual Intelligence: Sharpen Your Perception, Change Your Life* (New York: Harper Collins, 2016), 6.
27. Yulia Ustinova, *Divine Mania: Alteration of Consciousness in Ancient Greece* (Oxfordshire, UK: Routledge and CRC Press, 2020).

28. Craig Wright, *The Hidden Habits of Genius* (New York: HarperCollins, 2020), Kindle loc. 2026–2035.
29. Eric Brown, "Asking the Questions That Unlock Innovation," *MIT News*, April 6, 2018, https://news.mit.edu/2018/mit-leadership-center-hal-gregersen-asking-questions-that-unlock-innovation-0406.
30. Kevin Kelly, *The Inevitable: Understanding the 12 Technological Forces That Will Shape Our Future* (New York: Penguin Books, 2016), 289.
31. Marcel Schwantes, "This Famous Albert Einstein Quote Nails It: The Smartest People Today Display This 1 Trait," *Inc.*, February 15, 2018, https://www.inc.com/marcel-schwantes/this-1-simple-way-of-thinking-separates-smartest-people-from-everyone-else.html.

Chapter 11

1. Quoted in Sam Instone, "What Does It Mean to Live a Good Life?," *The National*, December 29, 2022, https://www.thenationalnews.com/business/money/2022/12/30/what-does-it-mean-to-live-a-good-life.
2. Azeem Azhar, *The Exponential Age* (New York: Diversion Books, 2021).
3. Kenneth Cukier, Viktor Mayer-Schonberger, and Francis de Vericourt, *Framers: Human Advantage in an Age of Technology and Turmoil* (New York: Dutton, 2021).
4. Scott Page, *The Model Thinker* (New York: Basic Books, 2018), xii.
5. Jan Rivkin, "Celebrating General Shoe Company, the Inaugural HBS Case," *Harvard Business School Newsroom*, April 12, 2019, https://www.hbs.edu/news/articles/Pages/first-hbs-case-study-general-shoe-company.aspx.
6. "Exploring the Relevance and Efficacy of the Case Method 100 Years Later," *Harvard Business Publishing*, April 12, 2019, https://hbsp.harvard.edu/inspiring-minds/the-centennial-of-the-business-case-part-1.
7. "Exploring the Relevance."
8. "History of the Transistor," *Wikipedia*, October 18, 2019, https://en.wikipedia.org/wiki/History_of_the_transistor.
9. Kat Eschner, "Coca-Cola's Creator Said the Drink Would Make You Smarter," *Smithsonian*, March 29, 2017, https://www.smithsonianmag.com/smart-news/coca-colas-creator-said-drink-would-make-you-smarter-180962665/.

10. Lucas Downey, "Mark Zuckerberg: Founder and CEO of Meta (formerly Facebook)," *Investopedia*, September 16, 2021, https://www.investopedia.com/terms/m/mark-zuckerberg.asp.
11. Megan Garber, "Instagram Was First Called 'Burbn,'" *The Atlantic*, July 2, 2014, https://www.theatlantic.com/technology/archive/2014/07/instagram-used-to-be-called-brbn/373815/.
12. Stuart Dredge, "YouTube Was Meant to Be a Video-Dating Website," *The Guardian*, March 16, 2016, https://www.theguardian.com/technology/2016/mar/16/youtube-past-video-dating-website.
13. Steven Levy, "How Y Combinator Changed the World," *Wired*, December 21, 2021, https://www.wired.com/story/how-y-combinator-changed-the-world/.
14. Paul Graham, "Summer Founders Program," March 2005, http://www.paulgraham.com/summerfounder.html.
15. Ivan De Luce, "Y Combinator's First Batch: Where Are They Now?" *Business of Business*, January 14, 2021, https://www.businessofbusiness.com/articles/y-combinator-where-are-they-now-first-batch-reddit-twitch/.
16. Steven Levy, "A Boot Camp for the Next Tech Billionaires," *Newsweek*, May 20, 2007, https://www.newsweek.com/boot-camp-next-tech-billionaires-100977.
17. Levy, "How Y Combinator Changed the World."
18. James Cooper, "Creating a New Product: Betaworks Studios," *Medium*, March 8, 2018, https://medium.com/zooperheiss/creating-a-new-product-betaworks-studios-99ab53bd67fc.
19. Analisa Svehaug, interview by the author, August 3, 2023, New York City.
20. Jordan Crook, Roam interview by the author, July 12, 2023.
21. John Borthwick, "AI Camp: Augment," *Medium*, April 13, 2023, https://medium.com/@Borthwick/ai-camp-augment-2b98ee222e5.
22. John Borthwick, "Building Bicycles for Our Minds," *Medium*, September 12, 2018, https://medium.com/render-from-betaworks/building-bicycles-for-our-minds-c79a2dd0b958.
23. Borthwick, "AI Camp."
24. Crook, interview by the author.
25. Crook, interview by the author.

26. Crook, interview by the author.
27. Crook, interview by the author.
28. Crook, interview by the author.
29. James R. Schlesinger, *Defense Planning and Budgeting: The Issue of Centralized Control* (Santa Monica, CA: RAND, 1968), https://www.rand.org/pubs/papers/P3813.html.
30. RAND, "Andrew Marshall, RAND Researcher Who Founded Department of Defense's 'Internal Think-Tank,' Dies at 97," March 26, 2019, https://www.rand.org/news/press/2019/03/26.html.
31. Matt Schudel, "Andrew Marshall, Pentagon's Gnomic 'Yoda' of Long-Range Planning, Dies at 97," *Washington Post*, March 27, 2019, https://www.washingtonpost.com/local/obituaries/andrew-marshall-pentagons-gnomic-yoda-of-long-range-planning-dies-at-97/2019/03/27/cde33692-509a-11e9-88a1-ed346f0ec94f_story.html.
32. "Andrew Marshall (Foreign Policy Strategist)," *Wikipedia*, June 29, 2023, https://en.wikipedia.org/wiki/Andrew_Marshall_(foreign_policy_strategist).
33. Schudel, "Andrew Marshall."
34. Schudel, "Andrew Marshall."
35. Terry Irwin, "Design a Worldview for Social Impact: Terry Irwin at TEDxArtCenterCollegeOfDesign," YouTube, July 23, 2012, https://www.youtube.com/watch?v=-te2OsCFWlc.
36. Terry Irwin, Teams interview by the author, June 26, 2023.
37. Irwin, interview by the author.
38. Terry Irwin, "Transition Design: Design for Systems-Level Change," YouTube, June 17, 2022, https://www.youtube.com/watch?v=WzRGFiFZwq0.
39. Carnegie Mellon, "Transition Design Seminar 2023," YouTube, April 28, 2023, https://www.youtube.com/watch?v=5OEyerhMw1I&t=6s.

Chapter 12

1. Joshua Cooper Ramo, *The Seventh Sense: Power, Fortune, and Survival in the Age of Networks* (New York: Back Bay Books, 2016), 183.

2. Federica Laricchia, "Number of Mobile Devices Worldwide, 2019–2023," *Statista*, October 18, 2022, https://www.statista.com/statistics/245501/multiple-mobile-device-ownership-worldwide/.
3. Bojan Jovanović, "Internet of Things Statistics for 2020—Taking Things Apart," *DataProt*, May 13, 2022, https://dataprot.net/statistics/iot-statistics/.
4. Paul Bischoff, "Surveillance Camera Statistics: Which City Has the Most CCTV Cameras?" *Comparitech*, May 17, 2021, https://www.comparitech.com/vpn-privacy/the-worlds-most-surveilled-cities/.
5. "12 Largest Data Centers in the World in 2021 [by Size]," *RankRed*, February 17, 2021, https://www.rankred.com/largest-data-centers-in-the-world/.
6. Trace Dominguez, "How Much of the Internet Is Hidden?," *Seeker*, September 2, 2015, https://www.seeker.com/how-much-of-the-internet-is-hidden-1792697912.html.
7. Kevin Kelly, "We Are the Web," *Wired*, August 1, 2005, https://www.wired.com/2005/08/tech/.
8. Wasim Khaled, Teams interview by the author, November 16, 2022.
9. Khaled, interview by the author, November 16, 2022.
10. Wasim Khaled, Zoom interview by the author, June 7, 2023.
11. Khaled, interview by the author, June 7, 2023.
12. Ben Dubow, "The Rise of China's International Propaganda Empire," CEPA, March 15, 2021, https://cepa.org/article/the-rise-of-chinas-international-propaganda-empire/.
13. Xiaocui Wang, Chuanlin Liu, and Yue Qi, "Research on New Media Content Production Based on Artificial Intelligence Technology," *Journal of Physics: Conference Series* 1757 (2021), https://iopscience.iop.org/article/10.1088/1742-6596/1757/1/012062/pdf.
14. Kelsey Ables, "What Happens When China's State-Run Media Embraces AI?," *Columbia Journalism Review*, July 21, 2018, https://www.cjr.org/analysis/china-xinhua-news-ai.php.
15. Khaled, interview by the author, November 16, 2022.
16. Khaled, interview by the author, November 16, 2022.

17. Wilfred Chan, "From Celebrity Jets to Pelosi's Taiwan Trip, Flight Trackers Are the Sleeper Hit of the Summer," *The Guardian*, August 4, 2022, https://www.theguardian.com/world/2022/aug/03/flight-trackers-flightradar24-ads-b-exchange.
18. Michael Glassman and Min Ju Kang, "Intelligence in the Internet Age: The Emergence and Evolution of Open Source Intelligence (OSINT)," *Computers in Human Behavior* 28 (2012): 673–682.
19. Justin Doubleday, "New OSINT Foundation Aims to 'Professionalize' Open Source Discipline across Spy Agencies," *Federal News Network*, July 27, 2022, https://federalnewsnetwork.com/inside-ic/2022/07/new-osint-foundation-aims-to-professionalize-open-source-discipline-across-spy-agencies/.
20. Jamie Wild, "The Double Lives of Open-Source Intelligence Hobbyists," *Morning Brew*, March 11, 2022, https://www.morningbrew.com/daily/stories/2022/03/11/the-double-lives-of-open-source-intelligence-hobbyists.
21. Center for Information Resilience, "Eyes on Russia Map," accessed October 20, 2023, https://maphub.net/Cen4infoRes/russian-ukraine-monitor.
22. Jeff Wise, "The DIY Intelligence Analysts Feasting on Ukraine," *Intelligencer*, March 4, 2022, https://nymag.com/intelligencer/2022/03/the-osint-analysts-feasting-on-ukraine.html.
23. "How It Works," *The Factual* (blog), accessed October 20, 2023, https://www.thefactual.com/how-it-works/.
24. Phillip Meylan, "The Factual's Media Ecosystem, 2022," *The Factual* (blog), February 17, 2022, https://web.archive.org/web/20230331005814/https://www.thefactual.com/blog/biased-factual-reliable-new-sources/.
25. Meylan, "The Factual's Media Ecosystem."
26. Meylan, "The Factual's Media Ecosystem."
27. Devindra Hardawar, "Yahoo Acquires News Summarization App Summly—Will Be Integrated in Yahoo's Mobile Side," *VentureBeat*, March 25, 2013, https://venturebeat.com/entrepreneur/yahoo-acquires-news-summarization-app-summly-will-be-integrated-in-yahoos-mobile-side/.
28. "Case Study: The Development of the Summly Mobile News App," *The Drum*, February 14, 2004, https://www.thedrum.com/news/2014/02/14/case-study-development-summly-mobile-news-app.

29. Hardawar, "Yahoo Acquires News."
30. Steve Lohr, "In Case You Wondered, a Real Human Wrote This Column," *New York Times*, September 10, 2011, https://www.nytimes.com/2011/09/11/business/computer-generated-articles-are-gaining-traction.html.
31. Will Douglas Heaven, "Why GPT-3 Is the Best and Worst of AI Right Now," *MIT Technology Review*, February 24, 2021, https://www.technologyreview.com/2021/02/24/1017797/gpt3-best-worst-ai-openai-natural-language/.
32. Kelsey Piper, "GPT-3, Explained: This New Language AI Is Uncanny, Funny—and a Big Deal," *Vox*, August 13, 2020, https://www.vox.com/future-perfect/21355768/gpt-3-ai-openai-turing-test-language.

Chapter 13

1. Quoted in Deena Campbell, "My Fair Lady," *Vibe Vixen*, August 21, 2013, https://www.vibe.com/features/vixen/vixen-cover-story-janelle-monae-my-fair-lady-285037/.
2. Lee Pfeiffer, "The Jazz Singer," *Britannica*, October 5, 2023, https://www.britannica.com/topic/The-Jazz-Singer-film-1927.
3. "Technicolor," *Wikipedia*, September 24, 2023, https://en.wikipedia.org/wiki/Technicolor.
4. David Gelernter, *Mirror Worlds; Or, the Day Software Puts the Universe in a Shoebox . . . How It Will Happen and What It Will Mean* (Oxford: Oxford University Press, 1991).
5. Jaron Lanier, *Dawn of the New Everything* (New York: Picador, 2017).
6. Marshmello, Twitter post, February 2, 2019, https://twitter.com/marshmello/status/1091777060194836480.
7. Tim Ingham, "Why Marshmello's Fortnite Show Will Prove 'Revolutionary' for the Music Industry," *Rolling Stone*, February 22, 2019, https://www.rollingstone.com/music/music-features/marshmello-fortnite-show-will-prove-revolutionary-for-the-music-industry-797399/.
8. Ingham, "Why Marshmello's Fortnite."
9. Mansoor Iqbal, "Fortnite Usage and Revenue Statistics (2018)," *Business of Apps*, November 28, 2018, https://www.businessofapps.com/data/fortnite-statistics/.

10. Ingham, "Why Marshmello's Fortnite."
11. Sarah Needleman and Anne Steele, "Fortnite-Marshmello Mashup Showcases New Avenues for Games, Music," *Wall Street Journal*, February 9, 2019, https://www.wsj.com/articles/a-glimpse-of-fortnites-future-music-and-dancing-without-the-guns-11549720800.
12. Austen Goslin, "Fortnite's Travis Scott Event Drew over 27 Million Players," *Polygon*, April 24, 2020, https://www.polygon.com/fortnite/2020/4/24/21235017/fortnite-travis-scott-event-concert-astronomical-12-3-million-concurrent-players-record.
13. Malindy Hetfeld, "Lil Nas X's Roblox Concert Has Been Viewed 33 Million Times," *PC Gamer*, November 17, 2020, https://www.pcgamer.com/lil-nas-xs-roblox-concert-has-been-viewed-33-million-times/.
14. Todd Martens, "Epic's Tim Sweeney Reveals a More Connected, 'Fortnite'-Driven, Game-Unified World," *Los Angeles Times*, May 13, 2020, https://www.latimes.com/entertainment-arts/story/2020-05-13/epic-games-outlines-a-fortnite-driven-more-connected-future.
15. Neal Gabler, *The Triumph of the American Imagination* (New York: Knopf, 2008).
16. Gabler, *The Triumph*.
17. Eames Office, "Powers of Ten and the Relative Size of Things in the Universe," March 13, 2018, https://www.eamesoffice.com/the-work/powers-of-ten/.
18. Apple, "WWDC 2023—June 5," YouTube, June 5, 2023, https://www.youtube.com/watch?v=GYkq9Rgoj8E.
19. Apple, "Introducing Apple Vision Pro," YouTube, June 5, 2023, https://www.youtube.com/watch?v=TX9qSaGXFyg.
20. Eric Frankenberg, "Harry Styles' 15 Madison Square Garden Shows Break a Major Billboard Boxscore Record," *Billboard*, December 2, 2022, https://www.billboard.com/pro/harry-styles-madison-square-garden-shows-break-boxscore-record/.
21. Jane Daly, Twitter post, May 19, 2023, https://twitter.com/dalybeauty/status/1659574167715414018.
22. Nicolas Vega, "Taylor Swift Is This Summer's Most In-Demand Artist—Eras Tour Tickets Sell for an Average of $920," CNBC, May 26, 2023, https://www.cnbc.com/2023/05/26/taylor-swift-beyonc-metallica-summer-2023s-top-10-hottest-artist-.html.

23. Saraiva Bloomberg, "Welcome to 'Swiftonomics': What Taylor Swift Reveals about the U.S. Economy," *Los Angeles Times*, November 23, 2022, https://www.latimes.com/business/story/2022-11-23/what-taylor-swift-reveals-about-us-economy.

24. Brendan Canavan and Claire McCamley, "The Passing of the Postmodern in Pop? Epochal Consumption and Marketing from Madonna, through Gaga, to Taylor," *Journal of Business Research* 107 (February 2020): 222–230.

25. See #TayLurking, Instagram, https://www.instagram.com/explore/tags/taylurking/top/.

26. Kara Johnson, "A Look inside Taylor Swift's 'Rep Room,'" *Culturess*, May 12, 2018, https://culturess.com/2018/05/12/a-look-inside-taylor-swifts-rep-room/.

27. Alex West, "Taylor Swift Files Trademark for 'Swiftmas' ahead of the Holiday Season," *Daily Mirror*, September 21, 2023, https://www.mirror.co.uk/3am/us-celebrity-news/taylor-swift-files-trademark-swiftmas-30999349.

28. Katie Collins, "How Taylor Swift Flipped Online Fandom on Its Head for the Better," *CNET*, June 8, 2018, https://www.cnet.com/culture/internet/how-taylor-swift-flipped-online-fandom-on-its-head-for-the-better/.

29. Caroline Mimbs Nyce, "Weirdly, Taylor Swift Is Extremely Close to Creating a True Metaverse," *The Atlantic*, October 21, 2022, https://www.theatlantic.com/ideas/archive/2022/10/taylor-swift-fandom-true-metaverse/671814/.

30. Gary Trust, "Taylor Swift Makes History as First Artist with Entire Top 10 on Billboard Hot 100, Led by 'Anti-Hero' at No. 1," *Billboard*, October 31, 2022, https://www.billboard.com/music/chart-beat/taylor-swift-all-hot-100-top-10-anti-hero-1235163664/.

31. Justin Curto, "Janelle Monáe Solves the Mystery of When She'll Drop New Music," *Vulture*, February 16, 2023, https://www.vulture.com/2023/02/janelle-mone-new-single-float.html.

32. Brittany Spanos, "Janelle Monáe Frees Herself," *Rolling Stone*, April 26, 2018, https://www.rollingstone.com/music/music-features/janelle-monae-frees-herself-629204/.

33. Balaji Srinivasan, *The Network State: How to Start a New Country* (Amazon Digital Services, 2022).

34. Benedict Macon-Cooney, "From Nation-States to Network States," *Discourse*, February 9, 2022, https://www.discoursemagazine.com/ideas/2022/02/09/from-nation-states-to-network-states/.
35. "Audrey Tang," *Wikipedia*, September 2, 2023, https://en.wikipedia.org/wiki/Audrey_Tang.
36. See the g0v website, at https://g0v.tw/intl/en/.
37. "Audrey Tang."
38. Medha Basu, "Audrey Tang, Digital Minister, Taiwan," *GovInsider*, December 15, 2017, https://govinsider.asia/intl-en/article/audrey-tang-digital-minister-taiwan.
39. Chris Horton, "The Simple but Ingenious System Taiwan Uses to Crowdsource Its Laws," *MIT Technology Review*, August 21, 2018, https://www.technologyreview.com/2018/08/21/240284/the-simple-but-ingenious-system-taiwan-uses-to-crowdsource-its-laws/.
40. See the Polis website, at https://pol.is/home.
41. Asia Society, "Executive Roundtable with Audrey Tang," YouTube, February 8, 2022, https://www.youtube.com/watch?v=lCA4YG1NYEM.
42. New Local, "Audrey Tang on Using Tech to Make Democracy Better and Trust Communities," YouTube, April 6, 2022, https://www.youtube.com/watch?v=NCet0d-_8o4.
43. Nicole Jao, "'Mask Diplomacy' a Boost for Taiwan," *Foreign Policy*, April 13, 2020, https://foreignpolicy.com/2020/04/13/taiwan-coronavirus-pandemic-mask-soft-power-diplomacy/.
44. Christina Farr and Michelle Gao, "How Taiwan Beat the Coronavirus," CNBC, July 15, 2020, https://www.cnbc.com/2020/07/15/how-taiwan-beat-the-coronavirus.html.
45. January Nelson, "145+ Inspirational Walt Disney Quotes on Dreams," *Thought Catalog*, September 16, 2020, https://thoughtcatalog.com/january-nelson/2020/09/walt-disney-quotes/.

Conclusion

1. *WALL-E*, directed by Andrew Stanton (Pixar Animation Studios, 2008).
2. Colby Itkowitz, "For 79 Years, This Groundbreaking Harvard Study Has Searched for the Key to Happiness: Should It Keep Going?," *Washington*

Post, April 17, 2017, https://www.washingtonpost.com/news/inspired-life/wp/2017/04/17/this-harvard-study-found-the-one-thing-we-need-for-happier-healthier-lives-but-researchers-say-theres-more-to-learn/.
3. Robert Waldinger, Zoom interview by the author, June 29, 2023.
4. Waldinger, interview by the author.

SELECTED BIBLIOGRAPHY

Anand, Bharat Narendra. *The Content Trap: A Strategist's Guide to Digital Change.* New York: Random House, 2016.

Andersen, Janna Quitney. *Imagining the Internet: Personalities, Predictions, Perspectives.* Lanham, MD: Rowman and Littlefield, 2005.

Azhar, Azeem. *The Exponential Age: How Accelerating Technology Is Transforming Business, Politics, and Society.* New York: Diversion Books, 2021.

Bard, Alexander, and Jan Söderqvist. *Syntheism: Creating God in the Internet Age.* Stockholm: Stockholm Text, 2014.

Benkler, Yochai, Robert Faris, and Hal Roberts. *Network Propaganda: Manipulation, Disinformation, and Radicalization in American Politics.* Oxford: Oxford University Press, 2018.

Brassey, Jacqueline, Aaron De Smet, and Michiel Kruyt. *Deliberate Calm: How to Learn and Lead in a Volatile World.* New York: Harper Business, 2022.

Breitbart, Andrew. *Righteous Indignation: Excuse Me While I Save the World!* New York: Grand Central, 2011.

Brockman, John, ed. *Possible Minds: Twenty-Five Ways of Looking at AI.* New York: Penguin Press, 2019.

Conway, Flo, and Jim Siegelman. *Dark Hero of the Information Age*. New York: Basic Books, 2005.

Cowen, Tyler. *Average Is Over: Powering America beyond the Age of the Great Stagnation*. New York: Dutton, 2013.

Cukier, Kenneth, Viktor Mayer-Schönberger, and Francis de Vericourt. *Framers: Human Advantage in an Age of Technology and Turmoil*. New York: Dutton, 2021.

Follows, Tracey. *The Future of You: Can Your Identity Survive 21st-Century Technology?* London: Elliott and Thompson, 2022.

Gabler, Neal. *Life: The Movie; How Entertainment Conquered Reality*. New York: Vintage Books, 2000.

Gelernter, David Hillel. *Mirror Worlds; Or, the Day Software Puts the Universe in a Shoebox . . . How It Will Happen and What It Will Mean*. Oxford: Oxford University Press, 1991.

Gladwell, Malcolm. *Blink: The Power of Thinking without Thinking*. New York: Penguin, 2005.

Goffman, Erving. *The Presentation of Self in Everyday Life*. Albany, NY: Anchor Books, 1959.

Harari, Yuval N. *21 Lessons for the 21st Century*. New York: Random House, 2018.

Hoffman, Donald. *The Case against Reality: How Evolution Hid the Truth from Our Eyes*. New York: Penguin, 2020.

Jarvis, Jeff. *The Gutenberg Parenthesis*. London: Bloomsbury Academic, 2023.

Kislev, Elyakim. *Relationships 5.0: How AI, VR, and Robots Will Reshape Our Emotional Lives*. New York: Oxford University Press, 2022.

Kissinger, Henry, Eric Schmidt, and Daniel P. Huttenlocher. *The Age of A.I.: And Our Human Future*. New York: Little, Brown, 2021.

Kuhn, Thomas S. *The Structure of Scientific Revolutions*. Chicago: University of Chicago Press, 1962.

Madsbjerg, Christian. *Sensemaking: The Power of the Humanities in the Age of the Algorithm*. New York: Hatchette, 2017.

McCracken, Grant. *Dark Value: How to Find Hidden Value in the Digital Economy*. N.p., 2016.

———. *Return of the Artisan: How America Went from Industrial to Handmade*. New York: Simon and Schuster, 2022.

McGonigal, Jane. *Imaginable: How to See the Future Coming and Feel Ready for Anything—Even Things That Seem Impossible Today*. New York: Random House, 2022.

McLuhan, Marshall, and Lewis H. Lapham. *Understanding Media: The Extensions of Man*. New York: McGraw-Hill, 1964.

McLuhan, Marshall, and Eric McLuhan. *Laws of Media: The New Science*. Toronto: University of Toronto Press, 2007.

Nichols, Tom. *The Death of Expertise: The Campaign against Established Knowledge and Why It Matters*. Oxford: Oxford University Press, 2017.

Page, Scott E. *The Model Thinker: What You Need to Know to Make Data Work for You*. New York: Basic Books, 2018.

Pentland, Alex. *Social Physics: How Social Networks Can Make Us Smarter*. New York: Penguin Books, 2015.

Perez, Carlota. *Technology Revolutions and Financial Capital: The Dynamics of Bubbles and Golden Ages*. Cheltenham, UK: Edward Elgar, 2003.

Pieper, Josef. *Leisure, the Basis of Culture*. New York: Pantheon Books, 1952.

Ramo, Joshua Cooper. *The Seventh Sense*. New York: Little, Brown, 2016.

Ross, Alec. *The Industries of the Future*. New York: Simon and Schuster, 2016.

Rushkoff, Douglas. *Present Shock: When Everything Happens Now*. New York: Current, 2014.

———. *Team Human*. New York: W. W. Norton, 2019.

Schwartz, Peter, Peter Leyden, and Joel Hyatt. *The Long Boom: A Vision for the Coming Age of Prosperity*. New York: Basic Books, 2000.

Sorgner, Stefan Lorenz. *On Transhumanism*. University Park: Penn State University Press, 2022.

Strauss, William, and Neil Howe. *The Fourth Turning*. New York: Broadway Books, 1997.

Sull, Donald. *The Upside of Turbulence: Seizing Opportunity in an Uncertain World*. New York: HarperCollins, 2009.

Tett, Gillian. *Anthro-Vision: A New Way to See in Business and Life*. New York: Avid Reader Press, 2021.

Thiel, Peter, and Blake Masters. *Zero to One: Notes on Startups, or How to Build the Future*. London: Virgin Books, 2001.

Toffler, Alvin. *Future Shock*. New York: Bantam Books, 1970.

Turkle, Sherry. *The Second Self*. New York: Simon and Schuster, 1984.

Waldinger, Robert, and Marc Schulz. *The Good Life: Lessons from the World's Longest Scientific Study of Happiness*. New York: Simon and Schuster, 2023.

Wiener, Norbert. *Cybernetics; Or, the Control and Communication in the Animal and the Machine*. 2nd ed. Cambridge, MA: MIT Press, 2019.

———. *The Human Use of Human Beings*. London: Sphere Books, 1968.

Wihbey, John P. *The Social Fact: News and Knowledge in a Networked World*. Cambridge, MA: MIT Press, 2019.

Wildman, Wesley J., and Kate J. Stockly. *Spirit Tech: The Brave New World of Consciousness Hacking and Enlightenment Engineering*. New York: St. Martin's, 2021.

Wright, Craig. *The Hidden Habits of Genius*. New York: HarperCollins, 2020.

ABOUT THE AUTHOR

Photo by Damian Rintelman

CHRIS PERRY is the chairman of Futures at Weber Shandwick, a leading global communications consultancy. Drawing on more than thirty years of digital and media experience, Perry helps global business leaders decode technology, communications, and culture, translating trends into commercial opportunities. His writing and work have been featured in *Forbes*, *Fortune*, the *New York Times*, the *Washington Post*, *Ad Age*, and *Strategy + Business*. He is the creator of *Perspective Agents*, a platform that investigates the effects of technological change on human affairs.

www.ingramcontent.com/pod-product-compliance
Lightning Source LLC
Chambersburg PA
CBHW031144020426
42333CB00013B/503